Our Life with Mr Gurdjieff

Thomas de Hartmann (1885–1956) was born in the Ukraine and was already an acclaimed composer in St Petersburg before he met Gurdjieff in December 1916. In 1906 he had married Olga Arkadievna de Shumacher, who became Gurdjieff's secretary during the crucial years when the Gurdjieff / de Hartmann music was composed and Gurdjieff began his own major writings. De Hartmann had nearly finished the Russian draft of his book about the years spent with Gurdjieff when he died unexpectedly. Olga prepared an abridged translation of it and completed his work with an epilogue of her own. She herself died in 1979. The present edition has been fully revised and expanded by Thomas C. Daly from unpublished parts of the Russian text and from memoirs of Olga de Hartmann.

Thomas C. Daly has had over forty years of experience in the production of documentary films for the National Film Board of Canada, where he was an Executive Producer during the Board's most celebrated and creative years. Already familiar with the books of Ouspensky from the age of ten, he then became drawn to Gurdjieff's writings. He met the de Hartmanns in 1951 and it was in his parents' apartment in Toronto that the first Canadian group took shape. When Thomas de Hartmann died, Olga de Hartmann developed the Gurdjieff Foundation of Canada in Montreal, and on her death, left Thomas C. Daly to continue her work there.

Georgi Ivanovich Gurdjieff, 1917

Our Life with Mr Gurdjieff

THOMAS AND OLGA DE HARTMANN

Definitive Edition

Substantially enlarged from unpublished material
in the original Russian manuscripts of Thomas de Hartmann
and further expanded from memoirs of Olga de Hartmann

Edited by T. C. Daly and T. A. G. Daly

ARKANA
PENGUIN BOOKS

ARKANA

Published by the Penguin Group
Penguin Books Ltd, 27 Wrights Lane, London w8 5TZ, England
Penguin Books USA Inc., 375 Hudson Street, New York, New York 10014, USA
Penguin Books Australia Ltd, Ringwood, Victoria Australia
Penguin Books Canada Ltd, 10 Alcorn Avenue, Toronto, Ontario, Canada M4V 3B2
Penguin Books (NZ) Ltd, 182–190 Wairau Road, Auckland 10, New Zealand

Penguin Books Ltd, Registered Offices: Harmondsworth, Middlesex, England

First published by Cooper Square Publishers, Inc. 1964
Published in Penguin Books 1972
Copyright © Olga de Hartmann, 1964

New edition, revised and enlarged from memoirs of Olga de Hartmann,
published by Harper & Row, Publishers 1983
Copyright © Thomas C. Daly, 1983

This definitive edition first published by Penguin Books 1992
1 3 5 7 9 10 8 6 4 2

Printed in England by Clays Ltd, St Ives plc

Contents

Foreword

Of the many forms in which G. I. Gurdjieff embodied his teaching, three stand out as unique: his system of ideas, his 'Movements' and his music. In each case Gurdjieff worked with one particular pupil who had a special capacity to receive, absorb and transmit to others the material given. In relation to the ideas it was P. D. Ouspensky; for the Movements, Jeanne de Salzmann; and for the music, Thomas de Hartmann. All three of them and their spouses have been major transmitters of Gurdjieff's teaching, and they figure closely in this book, which spans twelve years beginning in 1917.

Thomas and Olga de Hartmann joined Gurdjieff in St Petersburg just as the revolution was starting, and followed him without a break through the growth of his Institute, which began in Essentuki and Tiflis in the Caucasus, moved on to Constantinople and Berlin, and finally settled in the Prieuré d'Avon at Fontainebleau near Paris.

There Gurdjieff chose Olga de Hartmann to be his secretary, assistant and manager of the household. She arranged much of the Prieuré's business and translated for Gurdjieff at meetings with outsiders. It was also there that Gurdjieff began to work with Thomas de Hartmann on the composition of the remarkable collection of piano pieces that has come to be known as 'the Gurdjieff/ de Hartmann music'.

The de Hartmanns left Gurdjieff in 1929 to live on their own, and finally settled in Garches, where they stayed throughout World

War II. They did not go back to Gurdjieff again, but they never wavered in their devotion to his teaching. And when Gurdjieff died in 1949, they joined forces with Jeanne de Salzmann, who inherited responsibility for all Gurdjieff's Work.

In 1951 the de Hartmanns moved to New York to give guidance to Gurdjieff's groups in America and to support Madame Ouspensky and her pupils at her farm in New Jersey. In the same year I myself met them for the first time and they became my teachers.

Thomas de Hartmann was already writing his book about the years he and Olga had spent with Gurdjieff, and I used to hear tantalizing fragments of the parts being worked on when I visited them in their New York apartment or at Madame Ouspensky's farm, or when they came to Toronto, where they started the first Canadian group in 1953.

In 1956 Thomas de Hartmann died unexpectedly, leaving the book unfinished. His widow, undaunted, continued to devote her first energies to the Gurdjieff Work, among other things founding the group in Montreal that was to grow into the Gurdjieff Foundation of Canada. But as soon as she could, she turned again towards finishing her husband's book, and finally was able, through Cooper Square, a New York publisher, to commission its English release in 1964, with an epilogue of her own to complete the story. The same edition was republished in the Penguin Metaphysical Library in 1972.

When Olga de Hartmann died in 1979, at the age of 94, she left the copyright of the Gurdjieff/de Hartmann music to her Montreal foundation, and the rest of her belongings to me personally. Among her voluminous archives two compelling items stood out, needing immediate attention: her husband's music notebooks of the Prieuré period, all handwritten in Russian, and her own memoirs, written in English. To work with the music we had to learn Russian, a slow but rewarding process, in which my elder son, Tom, joined me, fascinated. Olga's memoirs, however, were immediately accessible to our curiosity. These proved insufficient for a separate publication, but they complemented her husband's words most fittingly. And since, at that time, the original book was virtually unobtainable, this was an ideal opportunity to combine their two accounts in a new edition, alternating their voices as they themselves did in real life when they spoke to us all on special occasions. I edited the manuscript – a fairly simple interweaving of pages from the original book with the appropriate sections of the memoirs, typed by my wife, Ruth. The result was fine-tuned at a session with author/editor Jacob Needleman, and family friend R. G. 'Pete' Colgrove, who had looked after Olga de Hartmann during her last years. That 'expanded' edition was published by Harper & Row in 1983.

By then Tom and I had learned enough Russian to explore de Hartmann's original handwritten manuscript for his book – 300 closely packed pages of Old Style lettering and spelling. We had always assumed that the published English text was a direct translation of what de Hartmann had written, but even a preliminary exploration showed some notable differences. It became increasingly evident that, having to commission and pay the full cost of the first edition out of her limited resources, Olga de Hartmann had had to abridge the text, omitting many smaller items and condensing many others.

Retranslation – with the generous help of Svetlana Arnoldovna Rajewsky, Russian teacher and singer, who knew the de Hartmanns well – revealed a considerable body of valuable new material. It also showed that Thomas de Hartmann had a greater flair for character description, sense of storytelling, and clarity of time and place than had been apparent before. It was clear that a new and further expanded edition was called for, this time a much more ambitious and all-absorbing work. Tom now fully shared the editorial jobs and responsibilities, while Ruth, with equal devotion, began the long task of typing the many stages of, and corrections to, the text. Penguin Books were interested in publishing it, and invited us to include as much new material as possible in this definitive edition. In complying with that request we have introduced all the material that we feel is worthwhile, either in itself or as enhancing what was already there. These selected additions have increased the book by about one-third.

As we assembled the new material with the old, we began to glimpse de Hartmann's grand, but simple, design – to follow and portray the evolution of Gurdjieff's Work as it changed its outer form and 'dress', so to speak, depending on the conditions surrounding it and the nature of the people attracted by it and available to it. As we tried to fit each new piece into its place in accordance with this vision, the material began to arrange itself into natural groupings, mainly in chronological order, with occasional references backwards or forwards in time.

This led us to adopt a new format of twenty-six short chapters, one for each 'natural grouping', in place of the former seven rather formless chapters and Olga de Hartmann's epilogue, which had no indicators to help one find one's bearings. To make up for this lack, we have introduced titles to let the reader know where each chapter is taking place or what the general content is, without (we hope) 'giving away' any discoveries that are better arrived at in the course of reading.

We have retained the practice of the previous edition, in which, in the main text, Thomas de Hartmann's words appear in roman type, while portions by Olga de Hartmann are set in italic. The new sections have been integrated in the same manner, with only minor editorial changes to smooth out links and eliminate duplication.

We have updated the introductory material on Gurdjieff and Thomas de Hartmann, and added a new section on Olga de Hartmann. All three sections are designed mainly to give some impression of the background and character of each person.

For reference and study we have provided new maps, a chronology and an index, as well as editors' notes about changes and corrections that have been made in the text itself. For those who like to experience the *sound* of their reading, it would be well to consult the note on pronunciation of Russian names on page xii before starting the book.

If there is anything I regret about de Hartmann's text, it is that he died just at the point where he was beginning to write about his musical collaboration with Gurdjieff. We can never know what more he intended to write about that, but, happily, the world will now be able to know, experience and work with the music itself. B. Schott's Söhne, the venerable German publishing house that printed first editions of such composers as Mozart, Beethoven and Wagner in their own day, is currently publishing the definitive edition of the Gurdjieff/de Hartmann music for piano. The last of the four volumes is due for release by 1993. Those who wish to hear how de Hartmann himself played some of this music and, in one case, to hear the sound of his voice speaking about it, can obtain cassettes or compact discs through Triangle Editions Inc., P.O. Box 452, Lenox Hill Station, New York, NY 10021.

Meanwhile, in this book, one is privileged to hear the inner thoughts and feelings of both the de Hartmanns, more extensively and completely than ever before, concerning their life-expanding experiences with Gurdjieff and their fellow pupils. It is their heart-felt tribute to their teacher, thanking him in the best way they could, by sharing with others the fruits of what they had come to understand through his Work.

Thomas C. Daly
December 1991

Editors' Notes

Revised translation from the Russian

The modern international practice of transcribing Russian into Latin letters has generally been adopted here. Certain Russian terms – *burka*, *lineika*, verst – have been retained and explained as they appear.

Corrections in translation have been made as required. For example, the word *Gruzenian*, incorrectly translated 'Circassian' in former editions, has been corrected to 'Georgian'. 'Circassian' (from the Russian *Cherkess*) now occurs only once.

Pronunciation of Russian names

Words transliterated from the Russian have approximately the same sounds as in English, with the following notable exceptions:

'Kh' is used for the Russian letter that has the same sound as 'ch' in German or in the Scottish word 'loch'. 'Zakharov' (formerly spelled 'Zaharoff') has that sound, which is closer to 'h' than to 'k'. The accent falls on the second syllable: 'Za-*kha*-rov'.

The equivalent of 'th' is pronounced 'f'. So, in Russian, de Hartmann's personal name, Thoma, is pronounced 'Foma', *not* 'Toma'.

'Zh' is pronounced as 'z' in 'azure': '*Zhu*-kov'.

Names formerly ending in -off or -eff are now spelled -ov and -ev (with the same sound as before), except where the spelling was established differently by the person concerned, as in the case of Gurdjieff.

Gurdjieff's name, as spelled in Russian, would be pronounced 'Gyurd-*zhee*-ev', with the accent on the second syllable. Perhaps that is why the de Hartmanns always pronounced his name in English as 'Gurd-*jeeff*'.

Petrov has the accent on the last syllable: 'Pe-*trov*'.

Stjernvall was always pronounced by the de Hartmanns as '*Shern*-vall'.

Maps and place-names

Maps of Russia as it was at the end of the tsarist era, showing the places where the events in this book occurred, will be found on pages 4 and 18. Much research has gone into their preparation, requiring a study in depth of Russian maps from the late nineteenth century to the present day. Several of the places mentioned by de Hartmann were hard to identify and locate in the kaleidoscopic differences of names for the same places in different languages and eras. Most helpful of all were the Baedeker guidebooks of Russia preceding the Revolution, which have helped to pin down almost exactly the route of the expedition across the Caucasus mountain range.

Place-names are given as de Hartmann wrote them according to Russian usage at the onset of World War I. Since then, many of these names have changed and cannot be found on more recent maps. Some simply have different spellings, but others were replaced by the name belonging to the language of the local populace. Both types of change are listed on the next page in parentheses beside the name used in this book. In some cases the names were changed for political reasons; these names are listed, with the official dates of change.

For simplicity's sake, we have retained the name St Petersburg throughout this book, except twice, when Olga refers to her parents in Leningrad in 1924. St Petersburg becomes shortened in certain uses, as for example, 'my Petersburg acquaintances' or

'Muscovites and Petersburghers'. Any attempt to alter the name to fit each historical context became ludicrous and confusing. It is ironic and fitting that the name has officially reverted to St Petersburg in time to be included here.

Name in this book	Changed to
Alexandropol	Leninakan (1924)
	Kumayri (1991)
Batum (Batumi)	
Constantinople (Istanbul)	
Ekaterinodar (Yekaterinodar)	Krasnodar (1920)
Erivan (Yerevan)	
Essentuki (Yessentuki)	
Pera (Beyolgu)	
St Petersburg	Petrograd (1914)
	Leningrad (1924)
	St Petersburg (1991)
Tiflis (Tbilisi)	
Trebizond (Trabzon)	
Tsarskoye Selo	Detskoye Selo (1917)
	Pushkin (1937)

On Gurdjieff

My father was widely known as an ashokh, *the name given every-where in Asia and the Balkan peninsula to the local bards who composed, recited or sang poems, songs, legends, folk tales and all sorts of stories. He was often invited to evening gatherings to which many people who knew him came in order to hear his stories and songs. At these gatherings he would recite one of the many legends or poems he knew, according to the choice of those present, or he would render in song the dialogues between the different characters. The whole night would sometimes not be long enough for finishing a story and the audience would meet again on the following evening.*

G. I. Gurdjieff*

Georgi Ivanovich Gurdjieff was born of a Greek father and an Armenian mother in a region of Asia Minor that was a melting-pot of nationalities and religions. He was the eldest of six children, with a brother and four sisters, one of whom died while still in her youth. During his childhood the family lived in Alexandropol and Kars, both then in Armenia, but the date and even the place of his birth remain uncertain. His own writings are vague, ambiguous and sometimes contradictory about this and other matters, as

* Condensed from G. I. Gurdjieff, *Meetings with Remarkable Men*, Harmonds-worth, Arkana, 1990, pp. 32–4.

if he wished to turn attention away from himself as a person and towards the transmission of the knowledge he had collected.

His introduction to the world of traditional wisdom, poetry and music through his father's talent was rich and deeply impressive. Not only was this a constant influence absorbed at home, but during his childhood his father took him to several contests among *ashokhs* who came together from Persia, Turkey, the Caucasus and even Turkestan. At such events, lasting weeks or even months, the contestants would improvise questions and answers in verse and song on religious and philosophical themes or on the meaning and origin of some well-known legend.

In this most natural way Gurdjieff was early experienced in the world of music, poetry and philosophy, and inherited in great measure his father's alertness of mind, retentive memory and love of the collected lore of ancient peoples.

Wishing him to grow up free from squeamishness, repulsion, timidity and fear, Gurdjieff's father took every opportunity during his childhood to inculcate in him an attitude of indifference to them.

He would sometimes slip a frog, a worm, a mouse, or some other animal likely to evoke such impulses, into my bed, and would make me take non-poisonous snakes in my hands and even play with them ... He always forced me to get up early in the morning and go to the fountain and splash myself all over with cold spring water, and afterwards to run about naked; and if I tried to resist he would never yield, and although he was very kind and loved me, he would punish me without mercy.

I often remembered him for this in later years and in these moments thanked him with all my being. If it had not been for this I would never have been able to overcome all the obstacles and difficulties that I had to encounter later during my travels.*

* ibid., pp. 44–5.

The family moved to nearby Kars after Russia took it from Turkey in 1878. There Gurdjieff was chosen to sing in the choir of the Russian Orthodox cathedral. His strong clear voice and exceptional mind came to the notice of Father Borsh, the cathedral dean, who assumed responsibility for Gurdjieff's further education and opened to him the world of science, including medicine, astronomy and chemistry. Father Borsh wished to enable him to become 'a physician for the body and a confessor for the soul'.*

With a far-ranging taste and thirst for knowledge, Gurdjieff set out at an early age on a search to understand for himself 'the sense and aim of man's existence'. In company with several other like-minded men and women, who called themselves 'Seekers of the Truth', he sought to gather knowledge, wherever the trail might lead, of ways whereby the 'highest' could be developed in oneself.

For this he had to find and gain access to many, sometimes secret, schools of ancient wisdom throughout the Near East and beyond, as far as India and Tibet. Among the most notable of these was an Essene school reputed to have existed in the days of Jesus Christ. In the Islamic world he studied the methods of many orders of dervishes and penetrated to Mecca itself.

To gain access to one monastery in Kafiristan, a country where recognizable foreigners were in danger of immediate death, he and his friend Skridlov, a professor of archaeology and fellow 'Seeker of the Truth', decided to find their way disguised as a 'Sayyid' and a 'Persian dervish' respectively. To perfect their roles, they spent a whole year letting their hair grow long and learning the necessary sacred chants, practices and instructive sayings of former times.

Little by little, through the teachings and practices of different schools, Gurdjieff found living answers to the questions that so deeply concerned him. In many of these schools Gurdjieff also found sacred 'gymnastics', dances, rituals and other forms of movement practised as a means of self-knowledge and self-development,

* ibid., p. 53.

the science of which was to become one of the chief pillars of his own teaching. Likewise, he studied the sacred music that emanated from such schools, and that sometimes had a power to touch and awaken the inner being and assist it to reach for contact with 'Higher Being'.

After some twenty years of search and the collecting of ancient wisdom from living sources, Gurdjieff began to shape a teaching of his own, designed to make such understanding more accessible to peoples of the West. In 1913 he appeared in Moscow and organized his own school there, later establishing it also in St Petersburg and dividing his time between the two. He began to expound the system of ideas he had developed, the same truths of all time but interrelated in a single branching structure, more easily comprehensible to minds trained in Western patterns. All the ideas are concentrated around a central one: the most complete evolution possible for humankind and for the individual. The universe is presented as an orderly organism, whose functioning is based on the interplay of two fundamental laws: the Law of Seven (or the Law of Octaves) and the Law of Three (or the Law of Triads). The unity of the universe takes form in descending order of worlds-within-worlds, progressing, like notes of a scale, from galaxies through star clusters and solar systems to planets and satellites. This descent branches into ever-increasing multiplicity, 'mechanicality' and limitation.

Within this orderly system, each 'note' of a larger octave branches into a whole 'inner octave', as white light (a 'note' in the electromagnetic 'scale') branches into the colours of the rainbow. This universal image is not derived as a simile from music, but rather the reverse: music is one form and expression of the basic universal laws.

Such was the breadth and range of ideas and related practices that Thomas de Hartmann and his wife were confronted with when they met Gurdjieff in the winter of 1916–17. What it did for them they tell in their own words.

In 1932 Gurdjieff closed the Institute he had developed near Fontainebleau in France and travelled again for some time. In the

mid-1930s he returned to working with groups in Paris, and contin-
ued throughout World War II and after. He died in Paris on 29
October 1949 and was buried at Avon, near the Château du
Prieuré.

Thomas de Hartmann, 1923

On Thomas de Hartmann

. . . for a long time I have known that our interior world is the soil in which the seeds of art take root. Without this seed in which the magic part of life is hidden and from which a work of art can be born . . . there is no Art, there is no Music.

Thomas de Hartmann

Thomas Alexandrovich de Hartmann was born in 1885 on the family estate, which bordered on the village of Khoruzhevka, east of Kiev in the Ukraine. He showed his inclination for music at the age of four and liked to express himself by musical improvisations. Fairy-tales haunted him from his childhood and were to become a recurring theme in his work. Perhaps influenced early by his German great-uncle, Eduard von Hartmann, author of *The Philosophy of the Unconscious*, he had a deep longing for 'something' unknown in ordinary life, a longing that never left him.

His early memories were of growing up among cultured people, close to the land and surrounded by the peasants and craftsmen of Old Russia. He was always grateful to have experienced the interdependence of life so close to nature, and to have known the spirit and style of living of the people, so well described, he said, by Chekhov.

This happy base of life continued until he was nine, when the death of his father, who was a captain in the Imperial Household Guards, obliged his mother to enrol him as a boarding student in the military school in St Petersburg from which his father had graduated. There his special talent was soon recognized and he was permitted to spend all his spare time on musical studies.

He was only eleven when Anton Arensky accepted him as a pupil for harmony and composition, and Thomas continued to study with him until Arensky's death in 1906. It was at Arensky's that he first met Sergei Taneiev, with whom he later studied counterpoint. He also worked with Anna Esipova-Leschetizky on piano technique.

In 1903 Thomas received his diploma from the St Petersburg conservatory, then under the direction of Rimsky-Korsakov. In the same year he graduated from military school as a junior Guards officer, with years of active service ahead of him. None the less, he found time to compose and to enter into the musical and theatrical life of St Petersburg. The first notable public performance of his work took place in his graduation year, when he wrote the incidental music for the Imperial Theatre's production of the Dumas tragedy *Caligula*. He also wrote piano preludes and settings for songs of Russian poets, which were published by Jurgenson and Zimmerman.

A year or two later, when Arensky was writing to Taneiev about de Hartmann, he commented:

> Take note that at the end of his very first composition, a prelude in A-flat major, published by Jurgenson, there are five or six notes that do not exist on any piano whatever. The keyboard would need to be extended about seven inches to accommodate them. Now he knows his instrument better, and plays it very well, but his attention is still inclined to wander.

Nevertheless, Thomas prospered under Arensky's tutelage. His most striking success was his ballet, *The Scarlet Flower*, premièred in 1907 by the Imperial Opera of St Petersburg in the presence of the Tsar, with Legat, Pavlova, Karsavina, Fokine and Nijinsky in the cast.

In the previous year he had married Olga Arkadievna de Shumacher, and he and his wife were happily surprised when, in recognition of his talent, the Tsar authorized Thomas's release from active service to the status of reserve officer so that he could devote his full time to music. This enabled him to fulfil his great wish to study conducting in Munich with Felix Mottl, a personal pupil of Wagner and musical director of the Opera.

From 1908 to 1912 the de Hartmanns spent the main part of each year in Munich, where Thomas was deeply influenced in new directions:

> To my great surprise, I took myself to account and began to realize that all that had attracted me in my youth, all that I had dearly loved in music, no longer satisfied me and was, so to say, outdated.
>
> At that moment, two events took place in Munich, and it was these which left a trace on my artistic path. The first was a great exhibition of paintings by van Gogh, Gauguin and Cézanne, at that time still completely unknown, and the second, soon afterward, was my meeting with the Russian painters Yavlensky, Verevkina and especially Kandinsky, with whom I remained friends until his death.

The intensity and depth of this relationship, and its meaning for his life, is hinted at in a remark about Kandinsky by his wife, Nina, in later years:

> As far as I can remember, among all his circle of friends, there was only one whom he ever addressed by the familiar second person singular, and only one who addressed him likewise: the Russian composer Thomas von Hartmann. Even with his closest painter friend, Paul Klee, Kandinsky, who was revolted by all excessive familiarity, kept always to the formal plural – even after several decades of deep friend-ship.

In those years in Munich Thomas wrote a choreographic suite, *Daphnis, Narcissus, Orpheus and Dionysus*, which was presented at the Odeon. Also at the Odeon, at Kandinsky's urging, Alexan-der Sacharoff performed his newly created solo *Danses plastiques* to music written for him by de Hartmann. During his last two years in Munich Thomas planned and sketched the music for Kandinsky's experimental stage project, *The Yellow Sound*, which did not find a producer before war intervened. He was also an integral part of the avant-garde publication *Der Blaue Reiter* (The Blue Rider) by Kandinsky and Franz Marc, for which he wrote an article, 'On Anarchy in Music'.

After the death of Thomas's mother, the de Hartmanns returned to St Petersburg in 1912. With a fresh 'palette' of his own, Thomas was busily occupied with new compositions when he met Gurdjieff in December 1916. He recognized at once in Gurdjieff the teacher who could bring him what he had long been searching for, a search shared by his wife. The two of them gave up their life of comfort and luxury to work with Gurdjieff, and followed him wherever life took them for the next twelve years.

In 1929, as with numerous other senior pupils, Gurdjieff made it necessary for the de Hartmanns to leave his Institute and become completely self-dependent. Thomas made a living writing scores for commercial films under a pseudonym while he continued to compose his own works. He and Olga survived World War II in Garches, near Paris. They lived in a deserted house because the Germans had occupied their own, but a piano was there and, inspired by Verlaine, Proust and James Joyce, Thomas set their works to music and also worked on his opera, *Esther*.

After the war the de Hartmanns began to have a lively and successful musical life in France, with performances of Thomas's songs, chamber works, concerti and symphonies in concert hall and on radio. They had begun a warm and close friendship with Pablo Casals, which promised many happy exchanges, when another turn of fate uprooted them again. Gurdjieff died on 29 October 1949. The decision was taken with Jeanne de Salzmann that the de Hartmanns would move to America to support the Work there.

The last few years of Thomas's life were based mainly in New York. He organized the first private publications of selections from the Gurdjieff/de Hartmann music and also issued a number of records of it played by himself. The work with the groups did not slow his personal creative activities. An invitation from Frank Lloyd Wright brought Thomas to Wright's architectural school in Arizona, where he lectured to the students on the interrelatedness of the arts. His orchestral music was performed in several North American cities, and in New York he played his own sonatas on the radio. He died unexpectedly in 1956, a few days before an important concert of his music in Town Hall. The concert was not cancelled and, fittingly, celebrated his music and his life *in memoriam.*

Olga de Hartmann, 1921

On Olga de Hartmann

We were married in church with all the fuss of the time. The sister of the Tsar was present and the church was filled with Guards officers and high dignitaries. My vanity and pride helped me to choose the most handsome and tall best man so as not to spoil my hair when he held the crown above my head, which was the custom, and to be careful not to step on my very long train.

Olga de Hartmann

Olga Arkadievna de Hartmann was born Olga de Shumacher on 28 August 1885 in St Petersburg, where her father was a high government official. Both her parents were of German ancestry and the Lutheran faith, in the Russian capital, where the Court officially spoke French and the state religion was Russian Orthodox. From childhood until her marriage, Olga had a German nurse and a French governess, and by the time she was six she could speak and read Russian, German and French. She recalled:

> From an early age, I always had a religious feeling. When I was seven, all the other children in our school were Russian Orthodox, but my brother and sisters and I had our religious lessons in German separately from the others. One day my mother told us sorrowfully that from now on a Russian priest had to teach us Holy Scripture in Russian, but I was unwilling for us to be separated in this way from my parents, so they finally decided to become Russian Orthodox also.

Although her parents led a very active social life in high society, they gave a great deal of attention to the children. At the age of twelve Olga liked to play chess with her father when he came home from work. In their spacious apartment one whole room was a library, with books from floor to ceiling. There, in the evenings, her father would read aloud to them from Russian literature and, sometimes, from Goethe and Schiller in German. The family always spent the summer together in a property they had in Finland, inherited from their mother's uncle, who had been a great traveller.

As they grew up, Olga's mother gave parties for the children and all their young friends. During these they played charades, danced, and improvised plays and operas. Their parents also took them often to the theatre and concerts, and to all the premières of operas and ballets.

It was during the intermission at a concert featuring Thomas de Hartmann's music that Olga was first introduced to him. 'I had a funny feeling when I met him,' she wrote, 'as if I knew him from long ago.' In fact, the threads of connection stretched further than she knew at that time. During the reign of Tsar Alexander II there was a special commission in the government to organize the liberation of the serfs. The senior senator, who replaced the Tsar at meetings in his absence, was Olga's grandfather. Serving on the same commission was the General Secretary of the government, the grandfather of her future husband.

From the time of their marriage, Olga shared in all her husband's activities. In the summer they now went to Thomas's family estate in the Ukraine, where two of the younger servants – children of older family servants – became their personal attendants and returned with them to St Petersburg, Marfousha as cook and lady's maid, and Osip as butler.

Olga and Thomas became the closest of friends with Sergei Taneiev, the great teacher of counterpoint. Olga had a lovely natural voice, and Taneiev advised her to take singing lessons from B. Curelli in Italy, which was arranged while she and Thomas were living in Munich and for which they went to Naples for several months. Later, when Taneiev's opera trilogy *Oresteia* was being produced in Moscow, Olga sang a leading part. She also took lessons from the concert singer Zoë Lody in the repertoire of arias from *Rigoletto*, *Lakmé*, *La Traviata* and *Madame Butterfly*, and in a benefit performance of the Imperial Opera she was chosen to sing Violetta in *La Traviata*.

It was in Munich that the de Hartmanns began to be interested in esoteric questions. Olga wrote:

> At that time everyone was reading Blavatsky. One evening, with Kandinsky and some others, we decided to try running a plate with an arrow on it around the German alphabet, like a modern-day Ouija board. We asked it questions, expecting the plate to stop on letters which I had to write down and afterwards decipher. But nothing meaningful was spelled out. Someone suggested trying in Russian. Again we asked questions, and at once it became quite thrilling. A ghost told us her name, Musutsky, and that she had lived in the town of Ufa, near the border of Siberia, and was buried there. She asked us to pray for her and said that a cousin of hers – she began to spell his name: S–h–a–, but here she was interrupted and got no further.
>
> Kandinsky decided to write to the priest in Ufa and ask him if he knew of anyone by the name she had given. In a month's time he had the priest's answer: there were among his parishioners many Musutskys, but there was only one with a relative by the name of Shatov. We were really astonished.

The de Hartmanns began to look for some interesting and knowledgeable person to throw light on their questions, and they continued their search when they returned to St Petersburg. There they encountered various dubious groups, in one of which the leader sought to control the members by hypnotizing them. Thomas and Olga quickly left, together with another member of the group, Andrei Zakharov, who became their close friend.

When war mobilization stationed the de Hartmanns at Tsar-skoye Selo, Olga was alone all day while Thomas was on military duty. With a friend, she occupied her time by organizing and equipping a building there as a residence and school for some sixty boys, aged ten to fifteen, whose fathers were also reserve soldiers. A benefit concert, assisted by people from the Imperial Opera, helped her to finance this project. It was at this time that Thomas was talking privately with Zakharov and meeting Gurd-jieff for the first time. Their book picks up the story.

The last chapter tells what she chose to write about the rest of their life together until Gurdjieff died in 1949. After her husband died in 1956, she continued tirelessly in her efforts to help supervise and support the development of Gurdjieff's Work in North America. As time allowed, she also promoted performances of her husband's orchestral and piano works, culminating in an oratorio-style presentation of his opera *Esther* at Syracuse, New York, in 1976.

In later years, for health reasons, she moved to Nambe, near Santa Fe in New Mexico, where she died in 1979.

Our Life with Mr Gurdjieff

I write this for you
so that you will not forget

Thomas de Hartmann

My great wish is that those who read this book will at once forget the epoch in which they live, and will try to plunge themselves into another one, more than fifty years ago, an epoch with absolutely different conditions of life, sometimes quite unbelievable now.

Russia in 1917 was torn by war and revolution.

Mr Gurdjieff was an unknown person, a mystery. Nobody knew about his teaching, nobody knew his origin or why he appeared in Moscow and St Petersburg.

But whoever came in contact with him wished to follow him, and so did Thomas de Hartmann and I.

Introduction

For a long time I wished to write about the years I spent with Mr Gurdjieff – not just seeing him from time to time, but living with him day by day and night by night from 1917 to 1929. Although I did not see him any more after that time, he always remained my teacher.

I could not write; I was afraid it would be too personal. Now I see that I am obliged to do so, especially because my wife and I are almost the only ones left from the first years of that period of Mr Gurdjieff's Work, and also because, however small, everything concerning him is of tremendous value.

Perhaps some people will not understand my reason for writing, but that does not matter; if what I have to say is not written now, it will be lost forever.

Thinking especially of those who have not known him, I will try as faithfully as possible to render a living picture of Georgi Ivanovich Gurdjieff – the man we called 'Georgivanch' in the familiar Russian way.

At once a major difficulty arises: how to do it? The outer behaviour of Mr Gurdjieff was so different on different occasions – depending on the person concerned, the level on which this person stood, and which side of him Mr Gurdjieff wished to approach at a given moment – that it seemed as if Mr Gurdjieff was very changeable. But it was not so. He was always the same – only the impression he deliberately created was different.

Mr Gurdjieff wished – perhaps it was his higher task – to bring to life in ordinary man 'something' of which man has hitherto been unaware.

How he did this we can understand only from his Work, about which I shall speak later. Meanwhile I wish to stress the point that in his 'divine acting' with people, Mr Gurdjieff consistently followed the same line of Work from the time we met him in 1917, although he always, so to speak, dressed it differently.

How then can I describe him?

It seems to me that the only solution is not to describe Mr Gurdjieff himself, but to tell about the way he worked with us, because only by speaking of our own experiences with him is it possible to convey any idea of his Work and its relation to man. And that is the aim of this writing.

Looking back on our life with him, I find that, little by little, all that he said and did comes to my mind. Putting these memories together like parts of a jigsaw puzzle, often with a new understanding now, his ideas emerge clearly, one after another, until at last the entire tremendous picture is visible.

But the ideas of Mr Gurdjieff, when considered by people who do not actively work on themselves, are like the truth Christ expressed in the words 'Faith without works is dead.' I think that the word 'faith' here is to be understood as something rational, not as blind acceptance. And concerning the word 'works', it does not mean 'good works' as ordinarily understood; rather, this word has the meaning of an active, evolutionary, creative work in connection with ideas. With Mr Gurdjieff, everything was living and active; his ideas cannot be separated from life.

He himself is life, evolution. He is his Work. And for me his ideas were exemplified by his work with people.

Only after all these years do I begin to understand what his Work as a whole meant, and what an enormous effort he had to make to instil in us the germ of a new understanding and a new approach to life. Whether my own interpretation is absolutely correct or not, I do not know; nor can anyone know, for only a man on the same level of being as Mr Gurdjieff can really and fully understand the meaning of his Work.

'Georgivanch' is no longer with us, but his Work with us will continue as long as we do not forget his words: 'Remember why you came here.'

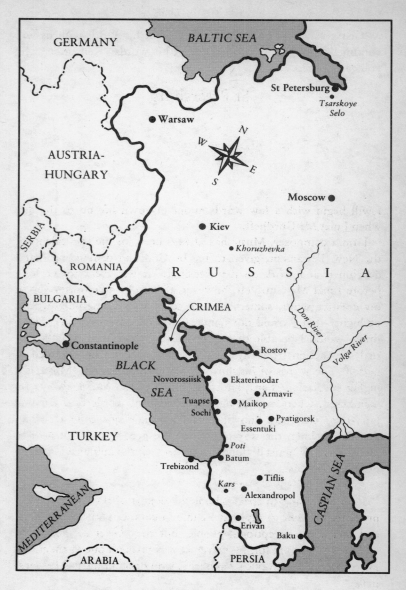

Western Russia and neighbours at the start of World War I

4

I

St Petersburg

I will begin with a few words about my own life up to the day when I met Mr Gurdjieff.

I am a composer. Music has always been for me the 'talent' of the New Testament, given to me by God and demanding that I develop it and work on it unceasingly. It was clear to me long before I met Mr Gurdjieff, however, that to be able to develop in my creative work, something was necessary – something greater or higher that I could not name. Only if I possessed this 'something' would I be able to progress further and hope to have any real satisfaction from my own creation, and not be ashamed of myself. The words of Beethoven often came to mind: 'Music is a higher revelation than philosophy or science.' And I always remembered, when composing, the wonderful words of a Russian fairy-tale: 'Go – not knowing where; bring – not knowing what; the path is long, the way unknown; the hero knows not how to arrive there by himself alone; he has to seek the guidance and help of Higher Forces . . .'

And so my life was a search.

I am not going to speak about the details of the early years of my search except to say that I came in contact with many 'ways' and met some exceptional people, but they never seemed to be what I was looking for. However, it was through one of them that I met Andrei Andreyevich Zakharov, who brought me to Mr Gurdjieff.

Zakharov was an extremely pleasant and highly educated man,

who became a great friend of ours. By profession he was a mathematician. Our conversations, however, were always about what was for us the most important thing in life: the search.

This was in 1915, during World War I. He often came to visit my wife and me in Tsarskoye Selo, just twenty-two versts* south of St Petersburg, where I was stationed by the army as a reserve Guards officer. Then in the autumn of 1916 he told me that he had met a teacher, a real teacher, but he did not reveal his name nor how he had met him.

One day when I was taking Zakharov to the station, he began to speak about this teaching, which, he said, could be an answer to our great question. 'The gist,' he said, 'is this: man on his present level of being does not possess an immortal, indestructible soul, but with certain work on himself he *can form* an immortal soul; then this newly formed soul-body will no longer be subordinate to the laws of the physical body and after the death of the physical body will continue to exist.' After a long pause following this statement, Zakharov added, 'But there is something which will perhaps puzzle you. You see, it is generally supposed that higher knowledge is given gratuitously; but in this case, if you and your wife should wish to join this Work, you would have to pay a certain amount.' He named the sum of money. Although it was quite large (2,000 roubles) it was possible at that time for us to pay it.

As I had often been disillusioned, and noticed that my wife was not listening closely or seriously to what he was saying, I began to speak with Zakharov alone. And as she did not know about the teacher whom Zakharov had met, I decided not to tell her about him until I had seen him myself. I asked Zakharov several times when he would introduce me to this man, but he always answered, 'I have already promised you, when the time comes I will tell you.'

In the middle of December Zakharov told me that if I still

---

* Verst: a Russian measurement of 3,500 feet – about ⅔ mile, or slightly more than 1 kilometre.

wished to meet 'this man', I would have to be at the Restaurant
Palkin the next Sunday between six and seven in the evening. This
was a very large restaurant on the Nevsky Prospect, the main
street of St Petersburg, where the Liteiny Prospect joins it, but it
was one to which no Guards officer would ever go. Zakharov
would come there to take me to see Mr Gurdjieff.

I went. Zakharov finally appeared and we started towards the
big Nikolayevsky station, on the same Nevsky Prospect. Suddenly
he stopped before a building and led the way to the second floor,
where there was a café. To say the least, it was a café for an
extremely mixed crowd, which walked the Nevsky day and night;
and if anyone were to find out that I had been there, I would have
had to leave my regiment.

We went in, ordered coffee and waited.

After a while I saw coming towards us Dr Leonid Robertovich
Stjernvall, whom I had met before socially, and two men in black
sealskin coats, both very typical Caucasians, with black eyes and
black moustaches. They were very well dressed, but so Caucasian!
. . . I wondered which one was he. And I must say that my first
reaction was anything but one of rapture or veneration . . .

All three approached and we shook hands. Which one of the
two was he? My uncertainty was quickly dispelled by the eyes of
one of the men. The man with 'those eyes' sat at the narrow side
of the table; on his right sat Dr Stjernvall with the other man, and
on his left myself and Zakharov. There was a moment of heavy
silence. My eyes could not avoid noticing the detachable cuffs,
which were not very clean. Then I thought: You have to speak . . .
I made a great effort and forced myself to say to him that I wished
to be admitted to his Work.

Mr Gurdjieff asked the reason for my request. Perhaps I was not
happy in life? Or was there some other special reason? I answered
that I was perfectly happy, happily married, that I had enough
money to live on without having to earn my living, and that I had
my music, which was the centre of my life. But, I added, all this
was not enough. 'Without inner growth,' I said, 'there is no life at
all for me; both my wife and I are searching for a way to develop.'

By this time I realized that the eyes of Mr Gurdjieff were of unusual depth and penetration. The word 'beautiful' would hardly be appropriate, but I will say that until that moment I had never seen such eyes nor felt such a look.

Mr Gurdjieff listened and then said that we would speak later about the question that interested me. 'Meanwhile,' he said to Dr Stjernvall, 'let Ouspensky tell him everything that has been said up to now, and let him also read the story "Glimpses of Truth".'

I decided to ask Mr Gurdjieff whether I could perhaps bring some money for his Work. He answered, 'The time will come when, if I should ask you to give me all that belongs to you, you would gladly do so. But for the time being, nothing is necessary.'

This ended the conversation, and Zakharov and I left. For a long time I could not speak. Not until we reached the corner of the Liteiny Prospect did I tell Zakharov about my strong impression and about Mr Gurdjieff's eyes. 'Yes,' he said, 'I understand. And certainly you will never see such eyes again.'

Having given this short account of my first meeting with Mr Gurdjieff, I would now like to tell you something else about it – that surely it was planned by Mr Gurdjieff himself. Everything was done by him to create unfavourable conditions for me, beginning with my going to the Restaurant Palkin and then to the café where, at one point, Mr Gurdjieff said, 'There are usually more whores here.' Everything, including this coarse observation, was supposed not to attract but rather to repel a newcomer. Or if not to repel him, at least to make him hurdle the difficulties, holding fast to his aim in spite of everything.

After this meeting, my life became a sort of fairy-tale. I had read fairy-tales since early childhood and their meaning stayed with me always: to go forward and never forget the real aim, to overcome obstacles, to hope for help from unknown sources if one's aspiration were a true one. Also, it seems that if you keep striving for one great purpose, you will win things you never dreamed of in addition, but woe to you if you allow yourself to be diverted, if you are tempted by something cheap.

The wish to be with Mr Gurdjieff now became the only reality. Ordinary life, which had been reality, continued, but it seemed almost unreal. So I had taken the first step.

After that meeting I had to find Ouspensky. He lived on Troitskaya Street, not far from the Nevsky. When I rang the bell, a soldier wearing a pince-nez opened the door. It was Pyotr Demyanovich Ouspensky himself. He had been mobilized by the army but was being released because of near-sightedness. Now he need wear his uniform only a little longer.

From the start he made a very strong impression on me; he was simple, courteous, approachable and intelligent. Without wasting time he began to tell me what he later wrote in his book *In Search of the Miraculous*.* In an amazingly simple and clear way he knew how to explain the complicated scheme of worlds, planets, cosmoses and so on, so that all this could be assimilated by anyone seriously interested in these aspects of Mr Gurdjieff's teaching. At the end of our talk he gave me the typed notes of Mr Gurdjieff's first meeting with 'somebody', as taken down by one of his pupils. This was the story 'Glimpses of Truth'.†

As soon as I returned to Tsarskoye Selo I gave these notes to my wife to read. She read them through at once, unable to tear herself away, and when she had finished she exclaimed, 'Such a man I would like to meet!'

But when I told her that I had already met him . . . well, she was quite put out. I explained the reason – that we had already met so many people we did not like that this time I had decided to see for myself first to spare her a disappointment. Needless to say, her wish to meet this teacher was stronger than any other emotion, and we waited impatiently for the day when Mr Gurdjieff would return to St Petersburg so that we might go to see him together.

By the beginning of February Mr Gurdjieff had not yet returned

* P. D. Ouspensky, *In Search of the Miraculous: Fragments of an Unknown Teaching*, New York, Harcourt, Brace, 1949; London, Routledge & Kegan Paul, 1950.
† 'Glimpses of Truth' has been published in *Views from the Real World: Early Talks of Gurdjieff*, London, Routledge & Kegan Paul, 1973; New York, Dutton, 1973.

from Moscow and I was due to leave for the front towards the end of the month. The revolution advanced slowly but surely. Everyone we knew in the city still lived as usual, but rioting had begun in the suburbs.

At last Mr Gurdjieff arrived. We were called to come to a meeting, which took place on 9 February in the apartment of Mr and Madame Ouspensky. There were comparatively few people at this meeting. They occupied chairs in front of a sofa on which, later, Mr Gurdjieff sat. Most of these people were already acquainted with the ideas now available from the book *In Search of the Miraculous*. This meeting was not a lecture and very little was said, but my wife and I both felt a strong atmosphere of inner questioning. From time to time someone would break the silence with a brief inquiry. The mood was not one of lukewarm people interested in the occult teachings fashionable at that time. These were people for whom the answering of inner questions, the finding of a way to real, active work on themselves, truly formed the centre of their lives.

To give you the impression that this meeting made on my wife, I pass the pen to her.

In February 1917 we lived in Tsarskoye Selo, the residence of the Tsar, because my husband had been recalled to his regiment as reserve officer and was to go to the front at the end of the month. It was a cold winter day and we sat in our study, occupied with our individual work. My husband handed me a typescript and asked whether I would like to read it. I began to read it at once, and when I reached the place where it said that nobody can initiate you but yourself, I stopped and told my husband, 'If we could find the man who said this, I would gladly follow his teaching.' In reply my husband told me that he had not only found this man, but also met him. Instead of being glad, I flared up, reproaching him for not having told me. It was our first quarrel ... But my desire to know more about this man was stronger than my irritation and when I calmed down I discovered that he was soon to return from Moscow and my husband would be able to see him, and to take me along.

Finally the day came. The meeting was arranged for half past eight in the evening in the apartment of Mr and Madame Ouspensky, whom I did not yet know. It also happened to be the birthday of my younger sister, Zoya, and my parents were giving a ball for her, which, of course, we had to attend. So I put my fur coat over my ball dress and remained in it all evening.

As we were at the meeting for the first time, we sat a little apart from the rest of the group. The room was not very large. In front of a Turkish sofa about fifteen people were sitting on chairs. The man we longed so much to see was not in the room. Everything seemed quite strange to me, and I was struck by the sincere and simple way in which the people spoke. Dr Stjernvall, who appeared to be at the head of the group, asked the people what they could say in answer to the question that had been put to them last time. The question was: 'What is the main thing that hinders a man from advancing on the way to self-development?' There were several different answers. One said it was money, another fame, yet another love, and so on.

Quite unexpectedly – like a black panther – a man of oriental appearance, such as I had never seen before, came in. He went to the sofa and sat down with his legs crossed in the Eastern manner. He asked what they were speaking about, and Dr Stjernvall reported the question and the answers.

When he mentioned love, Mr Gurdjieff interrupted him: 'Yes, it is true, love is the strongest obstacle to man's development.'

At that moment I thought: again the same, always we have to part, we cannot think of self-development and stay together; and I was quite disturbed.

However, Mr Gurdjieff continued: 'But what kind of love? There are different kinds. When it is self-love, egoistical love, or temporary attraction, it hinders, because it ties a man down and he is not free. But if it is real love, with each one wishing to help the other, then it is different; and I am always glad if husband and wife are both interested in these ideas, because they can help each other.'

I could scarcely look up. Nevertheless, I had a distinct feeling that Mr Gurdjieff was looking at me. Today I am certain that he said this especially for me. I was in a very strange state, I was so happy. Then we had to leave and go to the ball. As I entered the ballroom of my parents' home, everyone was already dancing. I suddenly had a definite feeling as if something had hit me in the chest. The people who were dancing seemed to be puppets.

Within a few days I had the opportunity of speaking with Mr Gurdjieff alone. I did not wish to very much, because people told me that Mr Gurdjieff would ask me what I expected from him; so I wavered, but finally decided to go. Before I could even say anything, Mr Gurdjieff asked me how I had felt when I went home after the meeting. I did not know how to express my experience. I did not even realize that it was an experience, but I told him about the strange feeling I had had when I entered the ballroom. He answered that it was good, or that he was glad. I do not really remember, except that he was satisfied and said that if we wished, my husband and I could always come to see him whenever he was in St Petersburg. I told him that my husband had to go to the front and that neither of us would remain in the city much longer, as I wanted to follow my husband as far as I would be allowed to go. I also asked whether it was not possible for my husband to avoid going to the front. 'No,' he said, 'when you live among wolves, you have to howl like a wolf; but you should not be taken over by the psychosis of war, and inside you should try to be far removed from all this.'

He asked me only, 'Do you wish in general to come? What do you expect?' I told him that I could not tell him – he would laugh at me. He said in a very nice tone that one might use with children, 'No, tell me. I will not laugh. Perhaps I can help you.' So I said, 'The only thing I wish from you is that you don't spoil my happiness with my husband.' Mr Gurdjieff did not laugh. 'You probably have an apartment with seven rooms,' he said, 'but if you become interested in the questions that bring your husband here, you will perhaps have an apartment with a hundred and seven rooms, and perhaps be even happier than you are now.' I understood at once that my happiness with my husband would not be spoiled – only that my horizons would be much, much broader.

In the corner stood a ladder. Mr Gurdjieff pointed to it and said, 'If you begin to go up, step by step, then once you come to the top you will never fall down again. So it is in your development. You have to go step by step and not imagine that you can be at the top of the ladder at once.'

The next time I spoke with Mr Gurdjieff I was not as afraid as the first time and I told him, 'Mr Gurdjieff, I thought very much about the ladder. But I know I will have no force, even no desire, to climb to the top. So I decided it was better to try to help my husband and you to reach the top of the ladder, by pushing you from behind, because I see that you and my husband wish it so much.' Mr Gurdjieff again was not angry with me at all. He only told me, 'I am very glad that you are not egoistic, and that you think more about us than about yourself. But, look, you can push us perhaps from the second step to the third, from the third to the fourth, but then you cannot reach us. So, in order to push us higher, you also have to go up one or two steps.'

Looking back on this episode, I see so clearly how clever Mr Gurdjieff was. If he had told me to read books, make efforts or do the exercises that he gave to others, I surely would not have done anything or only have done it half-heartedly. But when he pictured for me that I would stay down and my husband would go up, that I would no longer be able to follow him or to be with him, or even to understand him, that frightened me so much that I at once began with all my force and understanding to follow everything that Mr Gurdjieff asked.

Now to continue my own story: we saw Mr Gurdjieff once more in St Petersburg, a few days before I had to leave for the Austrian front in the Ukraine. Before parting from Mr Gurdjieff, I asked his advice about my military service. He told me: 'You are an officer and you must go to the front, but never let yourself be seized by the war psychosis. Remember yourself . . . Don't forget to remember yourself. You will see that revolution will break out totally one of these days and everything will be finished. Staying at the front then will make no sense from the military point of view. Try to get away and come where I shall be.' After a short pause he added, turning to Dr Stjernvall, who was there: 'He has to be entangled. Entangle him, Doctor!' Then, addressing me again: 'Remember yourself, don't forget to remember yourself.'

Self-remembering is the central idea of Mr Gurdjieff's teaching. As for 'entangling', this connects with another of his ideas – that faith in his teaching is not required. Quite the opposite is necessary, in fact. The teacher, while constantly directing and observing the pupil, at the same time changes his course, diverts him, even provokes him with apparent contradictions, in order to lead him to find out for himself what is true. This is possible only if the pupil has within him the strongest urge to persevere, a burning wish that will not permit him to be stopped by any obstacle.

I should like to relate how 'remembering myself' saved my life at the front. I was attached to the staff of our regiment and we were in the trenches. One day, about four in the afternoon, I was sent with a report to headquarters. I got on my horse and rode along a flat highland from which the road descended into a valley. Soon I heard scattered artillery shots, repeated every three minutes. I met a soldier who told me that the Germans were 'tossing them' into the valley along the road I had to take. It was impossible to turn back and not deliver my report, so I continued on my way.

The words of Mr Gurdjieff, 'Remember yourself', came to my mind. Although I had heard them only once and then without explanation, I understood their meaning in my own way and found myself in a new state of deep calm as soon as I began to repeat them and cling to them.

I could see craters made by freshly exploded shells on the road before me. As I continued my ride, I repeated to myself, 'I remember myself.' This did not hinder me at all from seeing what was going on around me. Suddenly I heard the crescendo of an artillery shell as it screamed towards me. It blew up very close, but just because of its very nearness, neither my horse nor I was hurt. When an Austrian-type shell exploded on level ground, the initial angle of direction of the splinters was very high; that is why they did not hit anyone that close. But my horse shied and fell into a shallow ditch. I jumped off, repeating all the time, 'I remember myself.' The horse got up, ran a short distance, and stopped. I was inwardly calm, but I had to decide quickly in which direction to run, since another shell would burst in less than three minutes. There is a theory that shells never fall twice in the same place. Should I then go and lie down in the crater where the shell had just landed? No. Should I try to catch the horse? If I could, I would get away from this dangerous spot – and that is what I did. The next shell didn't wait, and it fell and burst near the last crater. 'Remembering myself' had kept me calm and allowed me to make the right decision at the crucial moment.

Events prevented us from seeing Mr Gurdjieff again until 28 August 1917, this time in Essentuki in the Caucasus. After leaving him in February, we went to Kiev for a last visit with my sister before going to the front. The next morning there was a general strike: no trains, no electricity, no newspapers, nothing! For six days we lived in an unknown situation. Finally a newspaper appeared and we learned that the Tsar had abdicated, and that we now had a temporary government headed by Alexander Kerensky.

It would take too long to narrate everything that happened during those months from February to August; but through every event there ran, like a red thread, my efforts to reach Mr Gurdjieff. There was every kind of difficult circumstance; indeed, it was precisely because of hindrances that my wife and I were able at last to join Mr Gurdjieff in the Caucasus.

A mutiny of soldiers that threatened my life resulted in my being sent to St Petersburg, but since that city had become the centre of the revolution, I had to find a way for us to escape from there. Since my only thought was to go where Mr Gurdjieff was –

to the Caucasus – I hit upon the idea of getting permission to go to Rostov, near the Black Sea, because the revolution had not yet touched the south of Russia. There I could continue work on my military inventions, one of which had already been accepted by the army. But to be assigned to that particular place seemed unlikely. Then fate, or accident, helped me; it was like a fairy-tale. I met one of my relatives in the street. When he asked me what I was doing in St Petersburg, I told him my story and, as he was the adjutant of one of the Grand Dukes in charge of artillery, I had the necessary papers the very next morning.

We wished to take the first train going to the Caucasus. My five old Russian trunks were already packed. With the help of my husband's orderly, Osip, and my father's doorman, we drove in five droshkies straight to the Nikolayevsky station. The station was in fearful confusion and disorder. Trunks were piled everywhere. Osip had to leave our trunks with the baggage men, but he managed to get a first-class compartment for us. Our chambermaid, Marfousha, who was Osip's wife, would be travelling with us to Essentuki. Osip, with their two children, would get off the train at Moscow to place our most precious silverware in safe keeping at the Moscow Historical Museum, where the director was our friend. From there, he would go to our estate, where the children could stay with Osip's mother, and he would follow us later.

We left at once, but instead of going to Rostov we went straight to Essentuki. The morning after we left St Petersburg, soldiers came to my parents' home to arrest my husband!

II

Essentuki: First Expedition

It was already dark, about eight in the evening, when we arrived in Essentuki. To our great consternation only two of our five trunks had arrived. The others had somehow been stolen along the way, for we never did receive them. But at the moment of our arrival we had no time or thought for searches. We took what was left of the luggage in two carriages and drove with Marfousha to a little house, where we rang the bell at the gate. It was opened by a man dressed simply in a Russian belted shirt and a worn coat, unshaven and smelling of sweat, like a labourer. It was difficult to recognize him as the invariably smart and elegant Zakharov.

Mr Gurdjieff came out and greeted us. He told Zakharov to carry all our things over to a neighbouring house, where a room had been prepared for us. Then, in a very kind way, he invited us to come in. We found ourselves in a spacious room with men and women sitting around a dining-table, on which there was no tablecloth, only empty teacups and an oil-lamp – there was no electricity because of the war. The women had scarves tied around their heads like peasants. My wife told me later that it reminded her of a scene from Gorky's *Underworld*.

Mr Gurdjieff asked his wife, Julia Osipovna Ostrovsky, to give us something to eat, and she went and busied herself in the kitchen. She was tall of stature, exceedingly finely formed: a very beautiful woman – but not at all like those women of the cultured class who habitually interest themselves in new philosophical

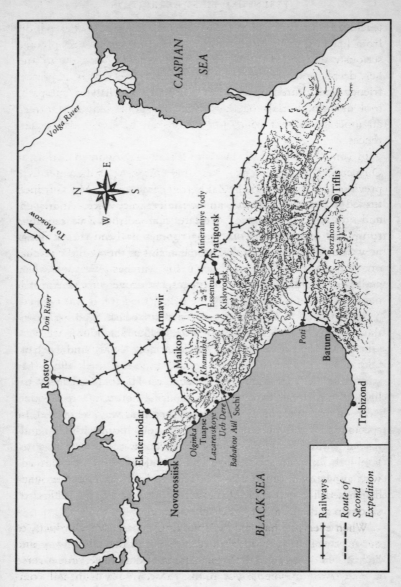

Caucasus mountain range and region

teachings. Our first impression was that she was rather remote from her husband's affairs. But we came to see how deeply and seriously she valued the Work of Mr Gurdjieff. We grew to love her, deeply and sincerely, and she began to feel for us as present friends and future pupils of Mr Gurdjieff. Much later our paths took us through trials together, which brought us close and formed an inner bond that could not be broken by day-to-day occurrences.

In came Dr Stjernvall, his wife Elizaveta Grigorevna, and the Ouspenskys with Lenochka, Madame Ouspensky's daughter by a previous marriage. When Zakharov came back, Mr Gurdjieff turned to him and said with an especially sweet voice, 'Andreyich, and now the *samovarchik*.' We later learned that Zakharov had to prepare the *samovarchik* many times a day and that it was a very troublesome business. The little pieces of wood and coal that one puts underneath do not burn easily; one has to blow on them and, if one turns away for a moment, the flames go out and it is necessary to start all over.

Soon Mr Gurdjieff's wife returned with some food and, with the reappearance of Zakharov with the samovar, we were all served real China tea. Mr Gurdjieff then said, 'Now, Andreyich, to your place.' Zakharov went into a corner and knelt there. My wife couldn't help asking, 'What are you doing that for?' 'What bloody business is it of yours?' barked Zakharov in a rude voice. Everyone burst out laughing. It turned out that this was an exercise specially devised by Mr Gurdjieff for Zakharov, who was by nature a particularly gentle and considerate man. He was absolutely unable to be severe when necessary, or to shout peremptorily with appropriate roughness or to raise his voice in objection when displeased. He was given this exercise nearly every day. 'Now go sit down and take a rest,' said Mr Gurdjieff.

When everyone had finished drinking the tea, Mr Gurdjieff, to our great surprise, suddenly ordered: 'Take the table away and line up.' In one second the table disappeared and everyone formed a line in the middle of the room. 'March!' Mr Gurdjieff commanded, and they all began to march, to turn, to run and to do all kinds of exercises. This lasted quite a long time. Finally, he told them to rest.

Mr Gurdjieff had noticed during tea that I took mine with two pieces of sugar, so now he said, 'You must not eat sweets or you will have sugar-disease.' He most certainly was not speaking of diabetes, though it is true that I was rather portly and that sweets, which I loved, were not good for me. But his reason for my not eating them was to produce an inner struggle with a strong habit. Mr Gurdjieff often gave this exercise – to struggle with habits – to those who were beginning to work on themselves.

Next day, tired from travelling, we got up late. For a long time we discussed our impressions of the previous evening and, although nothing extraordinary had taken place and as yet we understood little of all this, we both felt we had seen real evidence of inner work.

In the evening Mr Gurdjieff took my wife and me for a walk. We went a long way into the town to buy a *kulich* – a cake. On our return Mr Gurdjieff began to accelerate his pace, increasing it all the time. Finally he was practically running. We tried not to lag behind and ran some distance in this way. We knew he was testing us, to see what we could endure and how we would take it.

Back at the house Mr Gurdjieff made us all repeat gestures and grimaces that he made. Suddenly he shouted 'Stop!' and everyone froze with the grimace that he wore at that moment. My wife and I did not know then about this 'stop exercise' and others of this kind, but we stopped also and Mr Gurdjieff called to me to notice how my wife held the expression on her face without thinking about how ugly she looked.

During the evening there was some talk about Mr Gurdjieff going to Persia and about how he would earn the necessary money by 'breaking stones on the road'. That put us into a state of anxiety. Persia? . . . How could I, as an officer, go there in war-time? It would mean becoming a deserter . . . Next morning, the third day after our arrival in Essentuki, Mr Gurdjieff announced that he was leaving that evening for Persia. Not a word about how, nor any other details!

We had come in order to be with Mr Gurdjieff, regardless of difficulties. Now anxiety, doubts, insecurity about the future brought us many questions. What should we do? On top of everything else, we had to think about our faithful Marfousha and her husband. I had told Osip to join us in Essentuki after he had put our valuables into safe keeping – which we supposed was still possible – and had arranged with his mother to take care of their children on our estate.

In a few hours, however, we discovered that Mr Gurdjieff, his wife and Zakharov were going the following morning only to Tuapse, on the coast of the Black Sea. He told us that, if we wished, we could come along. Without a moment's hesitation, we decided to go and to stay with him as long as possible. Later, we realized this was the right thing to do. Going to Tuapse was the first 'lamppost', to use an expression of Mr Gurdjieff's.

So we sent word to Osip to stay on our estate until further notice, and the next day, with Marfousha and all our belongings, we took the train to Tuapse and established ourselves in a little hotel. The following morning we went to see Mr Gurdjieff in his hotel. We found him lying on his bed, covered by a carpet. In the room with him were also his wife, Zakharov, and Madame Ouspensky's daughter, Lenochka. Nobody spoke. We sat down and were silent. I felt the heavy atmosphere that overwhelms one when one does not know how to be. Mr Gurdjieff certainly knew how to create such an atmosphere . . . Finally I could not bear it any longer and asked him about his plans concerning Persia and how we could manage to follow him there.

'As I have no money to go there in the ordinary way,' he replied, 'I will make a contract to break stones on the road. I have already told you that. It is a most disgusting job. It is not possible for you, because after a day's work the women must wash the workers' feet, and Zakharov's feet, for instance, will smell awfully bad. Lenochka – well, she can wash feet, but your wife cannot.' Again the heavy silence descended and for most of the day this

pressure continued. My wife was in despair. She accused me of
not speaking to Mr Gurdjieff in the right way, of not realizing our
dangerous position – my military papers were not in order since
we had gone straight to Essentuki without stopping in Rostov.
The next day she stayed in our hotel, saying she did not wish to
go with me again to see Mr Gurdjieff.

Then the tension began to relax because Mr Gurdjieff told me:
'I know you have to go to Rostov for your papers, and perhaps
when you return I will not yet have left for Persia.'

So my wife and I went to Rostov by the first train. It happened
that the commanding officer of the military garrison there was
my former tutor, Chernoyarov, who liked me very much. Without delay he ordered my papers to be signed, giving me leave for
two more weeks. The next day we were back in Tuapse with Mr
Gurdjieff.

In our absence Mr Gurdjieff had bought two young black horses
and a *lineika*, a type of four-wheeled wagon with benches back to
back down the middle and a seat for the driver in front. In the
evening we went with him into the hills to try them out, along
with his wife and Zakharov. Afterwards he said that, if we wished,
we could accompany him on his journey, but everyone could
bring only the most necessary things – one suitcase per person –
and must be ready to start the next Sunday. We immediately
decided to go, leaving our maid Marfousha in the hotel with the
rest of our belongings.

When Sunday came, we found that the Stjernvalls, Alexei
Yakovlevich Rakhmilevich and Lenochka were coming along too.
Rakhmilevich was a well-known lawyer, and one of Mr Gurdjieff's
earliest pupils. Mr Gurdjieff told us we would have lunch in a
restaurant and then start in the direction of Sochi, further east on
the shore of the Black Sea. All the luggage was loaded on the
lineika and soon was piled three feet high, so there was no room
for anyone to sit except the driver – Mr Gurdjieff himself. He
would take Zakharov with him atop the luggage. The rest of us
were to walk, taking a short cut straight over the mountains,

because the main coastal road was too long and winding. Then we were to wait for the others at the place where the short cut crossed the main road. Since Mr Gurdjieff's wife was walking with us, my wife was reassured that he would not 'just drop us' on the road. She did not yet have full confidence in Mr Gurdjieff but she still wished to follow him as long as she could, because everything she had heard in his talks interested her intensely.

The distance on the short cut was much greater than we had expected. It was hard climbing and very hot. Neither my wife nor I was prepared for such a trip and our inappropriate clothing made it still more difficult. She was wearing fashionable high-heeled shoes, with much cross-lacing, and I was wearing my officer's uniform with wide Cossack-style trousers, tight at the ankles, and high boots more suited for riding.

Finally, at the junction with the road, we found an inn, old and far from clean. Being tired and thirsty, we went in for tea. It was already dark and Mr Gurdjieff had not come. Luckily, we had money, so we thought we would stay the night if necessary.

At last Mr Gurdjieff arrived with Zakharov. Then we all had something to eat, and we hoped to sleep, but Mr Gurdjieff said, 'The night is so wonderful, the moon is shining. Is it not better to continue?' So we went on.

Now real effort began.

Mr Gurdjieff told us merely that he wished to cover a good distance, but as to where and how far, he said not a word.

My feet began to be swollen and sore. My wife had begun to develop blisters in her high-heeled shoes even before we got to the inn, and her feet ached terribly. Still, we wished to go on.

We passed through places of extraordinary beauty. The road wound over mountain slopes covered with ancient trees. The moon was full and at some turns in the road we could glimpse the sea glittering in the moonlight. We went on and on, following the *lineika* closely.

It was now about two in the morning and we had started at two in the afternoon. Mr Gurdjieff said, 'Let us look for a place to rest.' But each time a suitable resting place appeared, he made the horses run a little faster and we had to catch up with the *lineika*. Much later we came to a rough little clearing where heaps of stones were surrounded by scrubby bushes. Here at long last Mr Gurdjieff stopped and told us to unharness the horses. We filled a pail of water for them, and a pot to make tea for ourselves, from a spring by the roadside. We needed a fire for the tea and wood for a fire. A fine rain had begun and to find dry kindling we had to struggle through thorny bushes in the dark. It was a real endurance test. But finally the fire was burning and the tea ready, and we each had a cup, with a piece of bread. I had to drink mine without sugar – I, who always liked it very sweet.

After tea Mr Gurdjieff told us to go to sleep. But where to lie down? There was no place but on the stones. Then he said to me, 'And you, Thoma, will be on guard duty during the night.' So I never closed my eyes. Of course, there was not much left of the night. At dawn Mr Gurdjieff got up and called, 'Get up! We have still a long way to go today.'

We packed the partly opened luggage, harnessed the horses and began to walk again. My wife was unable to put on her shoes because her feet were bleeding and swollen. She tied pieces of cardboard on her feet to serve as sandals, but of course these did not last long and she had to walk barefoot.

Another surprise awaited me: since I had not slept the whole night, Mr Gurdjieff told me, as a special favour, to climb up and sit on top of the luggage. The day was hot, the sun began to burn and after a night without sleep I could hardly keep my eyes open, but if I let them close for a moment I nearly fell off the *lineika*. It would have been easier to struggle with the desire to sleep while walking. Mr Gurdjieff knew this very well and was asking of me a super-effort. And I tried to make such an effort. I felt that all that had taken place and what was to come was again like a fairy-tale, in which it was necessary to do the almost impossible in order to achieve one's aim. But these things could occur in this way only in a little group of people led by Mr Gurdjieff – that is, led by a real teacher.

Now where were we going? It was said, to Persia . . . so we took it at that.

At last Mr Gurdjieff took pity on me and told me to walk. My military trousers had already hurt my legs, rubbing them quite raw, and my feet ached in my unsuitable boots.

It was midday and we were passing through a long, straggling village called Lazarevskoye. Mr Gurdjieff told his wife and Zakharov to take the large earthenware pot with a lid and go to the inn to get food, and told the rest of us to walk on. Soon they overtook us and we stopped in a wonderful little meadow covered with silky green grass and shady trees, with a mountain spring nearby. We unharnessed the horses, gave them water and food, drank the spring water ourselves with great pleasure, and sat on blankets. Then came the food in the earthenware pot. It was lamb with green beans, and we had as much of it as we wished.

Now Mr Gurdjieff told us we could rest. We lay down and fell asleep immediately. What a sleep it was! For the remainder of that day's journey we were not a bit tired.

We stopped for the night not far from a small village in a tiny glen that was surrounded on three sides by great trees and impenetrable bushes. We saw that there were apple trees too – the remains of the settlements of the ancient Circassians, independent tribes who had embraced Islam and once dominated this part of the Caucasus.*

We built a fire at once and gathered enough wood to keep it burning all night long. After tea and something to eat, we arranged to watch the fire in turns, because there were wolves, jackals and bears in the surrounding woods. Everyone prepared to sleep except Zakharov, who had the first watch. We spread our thin mattresses under the trees and lay down. What a beautiful night it was, dark as it can only be in the south! The stars were bigger and brighter than we had ever seen.

The Caucasus . . . wolves and jackals . . . knowing nothing of what tomorrow would bring – we were, nevertheless, happy in a way we had not known before.

---

* Rather than submit when the Russians conquered their territory in 1864, the Circassians precipitated a mass migration in their hundreds of thousands in the direction of Turkey. Only half survived to reach their goal and their former lands had remained almost uninhabited since then.

During the night we saw the glow of the animals' eyes, and heard their howling. If we had had no fire, they could easily have killed our horses. In the morning we were told that wolves had killed a cow from the village that same night when it ventured into the fields.

But one of our horses had developed a different problem. She had eaten too much grass, which had swelled her belly painfully. In such cases it is necessary to ride the ailing horse at a gallop, back and forth for several versts, in order to get rid of the gases. And this Zakharov had to do without a saddle during his watch.

It was my wife's turn to be on guard before sunrise, and after her, Mr Gurdjieff himself. I was already up and I still remember the kindness of his voice when he greeted her, 'Good morning, *djan*' ('dear' in Armenian). He evidently wished to reassure her in this terribly strange situation.

When the sun was up we were ready to start. This time Mr Gurdjieff put us all astride the luggage and slowly we moved on. About noon we reached a deserted posting-station. In this area no railway had yet come and travelling was still done by post-horse. But after the revolution all organization everywhere was disappearing and here only the empty buildings remained. This one was a nice peasant house with a stable for the horses. The trees in the garden were covered with ripe figs. We stayed there for two days and had a real rest.

Here I would like to stress certain points. Mr Gurdjieff demanded from us a very great effort, especially difficult because we did not know when it would end. We suffered and would have been only too happy to rest; but there was no protest in us, because the one thing we really wished to do was to follow Mr Gurdjieff. Beside that, everything else seemed unimportant.

This sudden plunging of the whole man into the Work was very characteristic of Mr Gurdjieff. During our stay in the post-house we slept well, even napping after lunch, and had wonderful food and wine, which we bought from a nearby estate. I went there once with Mr Gurdjieff. On our way back we sat by the roadside and he said, 'When working with pupils, I am like a coachman. If the horse follows the road, I give him free rein. If he goes to the right towards the ditch, I pull the left rein. If he goes to the left towards the hillside, I pull on the right one.'

I attach great meaning and significance to these words of his because they seem to embody the very essence of his way of working on us.

After two days of rest we started on again. The road became more and more mountainous. Several times Mr Gurdjieff asked Zakharov and me to push the heavy weight of the *lineika* from behind. As the road became steeper and steeper, this effort became harder and harder, until he added, 'So that your thought is not uselessly idle, count one, two, three, four, and back again.' In other words, he asked us to divide our attention.

We walked the whole day but, strangely, there was no sign of the tiredness of the first days. In the initial effort Mr Gurdjieff seemed to have pushed through some resistance in us, so that physical effort was no longer frightening.

The weather began to change, and it was very damp and slippery in the woods. So another physical strain was added. Now Mr Gurdjieff said he intended to reach a definite place, a lumber mill that belonged to his cousin, the contractor Turadzhev. Finally, very late at night, we reached it and passed the night in little cabins probably used for storing wood.

We got up early; it continued to rain. About noon we came to a very beautiful place near Sochi, a village called Uch Dere, on a hill surrounded by mountains that descended on our right to the Black Sea. It reminded me of Cannes or Nice. There were some country houses with rose gardens, and the roses were the largest I had ever seen. It was all as beautiful as Paradise.

We passed a little shop and, as we had had nothing to eat since early morning, we bought bread and sardines. While we ate, Mr Gurdjieff went into the shop, where he stayed for a long time. When he finally came out, he told us to open a large wooden gate almost opposite the shop. There a road led to a country house on a slope running down to the Black Sea. Mr Gurdjieff had rented this house. It appeared that we had arrived in . . . Persia.

I think Mr Gurdjieff is the only man on earth who ever led people on an expedition that, when looked at from outside, seemed so unnecessary and ended with 'nothing'. But it was full of meaning and value for those who took part in it and who 'remembered why they came'.

After a preliminary short session of work on attention, self-observation and 'discovering America', as Mr Gurdjieff called the discoveries we made in ourselves, he gave us another kind of work.

By speaking of going to Persia and by creating all kinds of emotional and physical difficulties, he was creating in strange surroundings a ladder of obstacles over which we had to pass to reach a certain little *do* in ourselves – the *do* in the scale of our general development.

These were the 'scales within scales' – 'inner octaves' – about which Mr Gurdjieff spoke so often. If we look literally for scales, we will never find them. Our whole earthly life is perhaps not one full scale, but only part of one, made up of a great many little scales with their semitones, *mi–fa*, which we must pass. So by completing one tiny scale, our group came to the beginning of another scale, about which I will speak in the following chapters.

This first expedition was for us a miniature foretaste of another that took place a year later.

III
Typhoid

So in Uch Dere we opened the wooden gate and found ourselves in Paradise. But we were not given long to admire it, because Mr Gurdjieff immediately plunged us into a whirlwind of new work.

When we went to put our luggage in the room he had assigned to us, my wife and I found that to enter our room we had to pass through his own room. In the daytime this would be no problem, but at night? However, we noticed there was a window quite close to the ground, so we could manage to use it instead of a door.

Zakharov and I were immediately given the job of cleaning out the sheds; there was one for horses and another filled with hay. We had to toss this hay into the loft. It was full of thorns but we had to thrust our arms deep into it. We did not pay attention to the scratches, however, for the intensity and tempo of work had been established. Before sunset the hay was moved. Returning to the house, I saw a tree of beautiful Hungarian plums, which are very sweet and have a pit that comes out easily. A few days earlier Mr Gurdjieff had warned us about eating fruit, recommending that we eat pears and not plums. I was sure he meant that we should avoid the fruit bought in the market, because it could be contaminated by handling and there was a serious typhoid epidemic in the area, but I felt that fruit that was from a tree would be safe.

The following day we went about ten versts with Mr Gurdjieff to buy live chickens, and on the way back I had to hold them in my hands as there was no basket. This was another awful job requiring constant attention, because one or another of the chickens was always struggling to get away – and then, go catch it! I held them by the legs and very soon my hands were covered with fresh chicken droppings. It was not at all pleasant and, to add to my discomfort, a physical weakness was coming over me. When we got to the house, Mr Gurdjieff killed and dressed the chickens himself. Zakharov and I stood nearby, ready to help him if needed, for we thought we could learn something from whatever he did.

During the night I began to feel quite ill, with a pounding headache and a sort of dysentery, but the next day Mr Gurdjieff forced me to overlook my illness and to stay on my feet and be active. Much later, when I had recovered, he told me that because of this activity, I had stored up certain forces that had helped me to fight my serious disease. I went with him to bring fruit from Sochi that day and we stayed there for lunch. On the way back I lay down in the *lineika*; the illness was progressing. Mr Gurdjieff asked me what was the matter and I told him how I felt, and that I was trying to connect myself with him in my thoughts. 'Good, Thoma, good,' he said.

Next day, after a sleepless night, my head burning with fever, my wife saw that it was absolutely necessary to find another house for us nearby. It was really not possible for anyone as ill as I was to stay in a room with only one bed and no comfort whatsoever; and then we could have with us our maid, Marfousha, who was still in Tuapse.

Luckily, just across the road my wife found an empty house, which the caretaker said belonged to Dr Botkin, the Tsar's private physician. Dr Botkin had followed the Tsar into exile in Siberia. (He was later killed at the same time as the Tsar and his family.) The caretaker was occupying the house, but he said there was another little house in the garden, which we could rent if we wished. It was a wonderful little house, literally submerged in enormous roses, with steps covered with green moss leading down to the sea and a lane lined with cypresses. I was nearly unconscious when we moved in, but I saw those wonderful roses and for me this paradise of beauty has remained associated ever since with an unbearable headache.

My wife had telegraphed Marfousha to pack our things and come at once, and very soon she arrived. I started to lose consciousness, so what followed I gathered from my wife when I regained full consciousness three weeks later.

Next morning Mr Gurdjieff came to visit us and, seeing that I was much worse, told my wife to take Marfousha and go to buy food and everything necessary while he stayed with me.

When they returned Mr Gurdjieff was sitting on the veranda, his face as white as his suit, and to the anxious questions of my wife he answered: 'Now he sleeps. I have no more fear for his head, but we have to take him to a hospital as we have absolutely nothing here, not even a thermometer. Later you will see that this is important for other reasons also.' He added, 'I will go immediately to Sochi to find a hospital and later we will take him there together.'

Mr Gurdjieff left. I woke up and . . . it began. In my delirium I wanted to run away. At one time, when my wife went to fetch something from the next room, I jumped out of bed and was halfway out the low window before she could stop me. She had literally to drag me back. With Marfousha's help, she put me back in bed with a hot-water bottle, though for that she could find nothing better than an old wine bottle. When she lifted me up in bed I caught her wrist and almost broke it. And when she wouldn't let me get out of bed, I took the bottle and tried to hit her on the head with it.

In the evening things went from bad to worse. Zakharov came to help and even he, together with the caretaker, my wife and Marfousha, could not hold me down in bed. My wife was in despair, not knowing what to do, and Mr Gurdjieff did not come and did not come. Zakharov kept going out to the road to watch for him, and finally, about midnight, he returned. I was asleep, but when Mr Gurdjieff came into my room I woke up at once and threw myself at him with such unexpected violence that I overturned a table with burning candles on it and Mr Gurdjieff nearly fell down. But the moment he put his hand on my forehead, I became quite peaceful and, although I did not fall asleep again, I was quiet.

Mr Gurdjieff decided that as soon as the sun was up they would take me to Sochi and that he himself would drive, going very slowly to avoid the bumps.

My wife and Marfousha packed everything and dressed me. At five in the morning Mr Gurdjieff arrived with two carts. He put a mattress in one of them so that I could lie on it full length. He carried me to it and tied me down with a clothes-line, my head towards the horses. He drove and my wife sat at my feet. Marfousha and the luggage followed in the other cart. When I moved, Mr Gurdjieff just said, 'Thoma, Thoma', putting his hand on my forehead, and I would become quiet. But at one time I was so unexpectedly restless that I broke the rope. Slowly, we made the twenty-two versts to Sochi; some of the passers-by threw flowers on me, thinking that I was dead, for my lips were blue and I looked quite stiff in my military uniform.

Because of the raging epidemic of typhoid, not one of the hospitals in Sochi had an empty bed. Mr Gurdjieff had been able to find a room only in a home for convalescent officers. We spent the night there and in the morning doctors came to visit the patients. After examining me they told my wife that they could not keep me a moment longer because I had typhoid, which is highly contagious. My wife had to look for another place, but there was none. The situation was desperate until finally one of the doctors located a free bed in a little country hospital several versts from Sochi, and we had no choice but to take it. It was a tiny hospital and my bed was in a room with three others.

Mr Gurdjieff left as soon as I was installed, but my wife stayed with me. Of the men in the other three beds, one had scarlet fever; another, diphtheria; and the third, typhoid. The doctor saw to it that I was bathed immediately to lower my fever and given all necessary medication, after which I fell into a profound sleep. Then he told my wife that he could not allow her to stay in the hospital and asked where he could reach her in case of emergency, but she refused to leave. He insisted that there was no room for her, not even anything to sit on, and in no case could he permit anyone to stay in a hospital for contagious diseases. She replied that she would *not* leave and, if necessary, would stay in the garden. The doctor finally said it was no use quarrelling with such a stubborn woman and let her stay. Before he left, he even put a stool at my bedside. Earlier, Mr Gurdjieff had urged her to go to a hotel, where he had reserved a room for her, and get some sleep, for she had not slept for four nights. But she remained in the hospital. Much later Mr Gurdjieff said that it was then that he had begun to look at her differently.

It was September and by nine o'clock it was pitch-dark. About eleven the doctor's assistant told my wife that my pulse was too low and I needed an injection of camphor, but that he had none and could not find our doctor or any other doctor, although he had telephoned everywhere. Again the situation was desperate. The assistant said he could give me the injection himself if he had camphor. He pointed towards a feeble light in the distance among the trees, which he said was a military hospital where they would certainly have camphor. Since he had no right to leave the hospital, could my wife go and get it? The night was dark as only nights in the south can be, but she ran. They listened to her at the military hospital, but refused to treat anyone under another doctor's care. Finally, after frantic persuasion, they understood that it was a matter of life and death, and one of the nurses agreed to go herself and administer the injection if she saw that it was really necessary. Of course, she found that it was and I was saved.

In the morning when the doctor came in, my wife asked him how he could have left without giving the assistant instructions. He answered, 'I allowed you to stay *only* because I felt sure that your husband would not live through the night and I hadn't the heart to send you away. Now, on the contrary, you saved his life.' From then on he became our friend and did everything he could for us.

My wife managed to persuade one of the convalescent patients to move to a hotel room (which she paid for a week in advance), so that we could have a room to ourselves in the hospital and bring Marfousha to stay with us. It was very important to move me because of possible contagion from the others in the room I shared. It was wartime and there were few sanitary precautions in such a little hospital. There were not even sheets to cover the hay-filled mattresses, and it was almost impossible to buy anything. After a long search, my wife bought some silk from a Chinese street merchant and made sheets and pillow cases; we did not need blankets because it was so hot.

Mr Gurdjieff, Dr Stjernvall and a Mr Mobeis visited me. Mobeis was a marine officer, one of the pupils who had come from St Petersburg. He spent the night in our room, for Mr Gurdjieff now insisted that my wife get some sleep, after thirteen nights of watching over me.

I was only semi-conscious and kept asking whether it was night or day, what was the time and so on, for I could not sleep. Mr Gurdjieff asked Dr Stjernvall to write a prescription he himself dictated and then told my wife to go to the pharmacy to get the medicine. When she gave the prescription to the chemist, he looked at it blankly and said that it did not specify any medicine, but just the sugar coating used on pills. She told him to make up the pills just the same. She understood what Mr Gurdjieff intended, and he laughed when she reported the chemist's comment.

But the pills helped me marvellously.

I had nightmares continually. One of them was that red musical notes were running through the room and would not leave me in peace. My wife tried to persuade me that there was nothing in the room, but it did not work. Suddenly Marfousha said to my wife, very reproachfully: 'How is it that you don't see them when the room is filled with them?' My wife thought: 'Goodness me! Now Marfousha is going mad.' But Marfousha took her apron in one hand and with the other collected some imaginary things around the room; then she went out and came back telling me that she had thrown all the red notes away, so now I could sleep peacefully. I slept and did not see them any more. A simple peasant, who could scarcely read, understood the problem better than my wife.

It is interesting to experience the divided state of delirium. In one sense I knew that there were no red notes and that Marfousha was pretending they were there, but her clever action quieted me completely.

All that I remember from that period is, naturally, like a dream, and only certain moments come back to me: the view from the window on the right, where, by day, I could see the tops of yellowing autumn trees . . . the sound of the whistles of the Black Sea Railway locomotives . . . a bowl of *kisel* jelly with Bulgarian clotted cream . . . But I clearly recall how happy I was when Mr Gurdjieff came to visit me. I always asked him to put his hand on my forehead.

Before long, Mr Gurdjieff went away with the other pupils to an estate of former St Petersburg comrades of mine in the cadet corps. The estate was situated in Olginka, near Tuapse. It was very hard for my wife to be left alone, with me still so sick.

One day when she returned from shopping I asked her in a different voice: 'Where am I?' and from that moment I began to recover. I was terribly thin and weak, so that she even had to turn me over in bed, saying that it was like holding a little chicken that was nothing but skin and bones. As it was difficult to buy anything nourishing, my energy came back very slowly, but the morning tea with sugar and two biscuits tasted wonderful, and we were happy that I was finally myself again.

Further difficulties were looming.

One day we received a letter from the manager of my estates. He said that the Bolshevik Revolution had broken out and, because everything was being confiscated by the Bolsheviks, he was sending us the money we had been receiving monthly for the last time.

The same mail brought me a letter from the Engineering Administration of the White Army, asking what I would like to receive in payment for an invention of mine that had already been accepted and used by the army. It was a device similar to a periscope for sighting and firing rifles from the trenches without having to poke one's head over the top for snipers to shoot at. Three hundred thousand of them had already been made. What irony! By the time I received this letter the White Army was no longer in control, and I certainly would not receive any payment from the Bolsheviks.

My wife and I were alone and weary in a little country hospital, not knowing what to do or when I would be able to move. And what of the future? We clung to one idea: sooner or later we would join Mr Gurdjieff again. That meant going to Tuapse as soon as I could walk.

One day in November, when I could hardly stand on my feet, my wife returned from the post office with the news that the last train from Sochi to Tuapse would leave in three days, because, with the onset of winter, the railway line was usually blocked by rockfalls and avalanches.

On 15 November the Sochi medical commission examined me and concluded that I needed a long convalescence before returning to military service. The doctor warned me to be very careful and not to move quickly, for I was still terribly weak. But we decided to take the last train. My wife went to buy the tickets and to reserve seats so that I would be able to lie down, but that was impossible. Finally the post office staff promised her that they would make me a bed of mailbags in the mail car if we could be there when they loaded it at five in the morning, before the public arrived at the station. We were certainly there on time and the postmen themselves carried me to the bed they had made, where I could stretch out, with my wife and Marfousha beside me. These were among the many good people who helped us.

In Tuapse we went to a hotel and luckily got the last room, but it had only one bed. What a wonderful sensation it was for me to lie in a real bed, a clean bed. Although my wife and Marfousha had to sleep on the floor, they too felt as if they were in a palace.

The next day we located Mr Gurdjieff and he advised us to go to Essentuki as soon as I was able to travel. We had friends there and would find doctors and the medicines I needed. So in a few days we left for Essentuki. That journey was a nightmare. We had to change trains twice. We left Tuapse in a roomy compartment. But when our train reached Armavir, our first transfer station, it turned out that the train to Mineralniye Vody was crammed with soldiers; there were no first-class cars and everything was in complete chaos. I thought that my being an officer might only make things worse for us, but luckily there was a very kind woman soldier in the crowd who helped by ordering some soldiers to get up and let the sick 'comrade' have a seat. Nine of us were crowded into that compartment and my wife and Marfousha had to stand in the corridor, which was jammed with passengers and luggage.

We reached Mineralniye Vody after dark and there we had to wait three hours for the train to Essentuki. My wife and Marfousha managed to fix a bed for me on a bench at the station; they covered me with my wife's mink coat, for the nights were now cold. When we finally reached Essentuki in the morning, we faced a similar problem: not a single room in any hotel or in any of the many guest-houses.

Usually after the summer season Essentuki and all the other resort towns in the Caucasus were emptied of everyone but the home-owners and other inhabitants. But now they were over-crowded as never before. Moscow and St Petersburg were feeling the pinch of famine. Aristocrats, high government officials, the wealthy, all who could, were pouring into this region, where the land was good, provisions still plentiful and they could escape the pursuit of the Bolsheviks. We somehow managed to find a temporary room in a private house.

My military leave had expired long before, so officials could ask to see my papers; now we realized how wise Mr Gurdjieff had been to insist on my going to a hospital. My hospital papers stated that, having had abdominal typhoid, I now suffered from anaemia, exhaustion and a weakened heart, and needed several months' rest. On 18 February 1918, with these same papers, I would be released from military service by a commission in nearby

Pyatigorsk. I could then burn my uniform and become a civilian and a musician again. I would keep only my sword.

The search for a place of our own in Essentuki led my wife and Marfousha to look on the outskirts of the city on the other side of the railway line, and there at last they found a tiny house. It lay in the back part of a property where the house in front was occupied by the owner, Mandzavino, who also owned a fancy goods store in Kislovodsk. Beyond our house in the garden were empty stables. Still further back stood an unfinished, typically Caucasian, two-storey house, with all the rooms giving on to a veranda – although as yet this house had no windows or doors. It was as if it had been waiting for us. And not only for us, because after Mr Gurdjieff came to Essentuki in January 1918, he founded his Institute there in the unfinished house.

IV

Back in Essentuki

Meanwhile we began to live a peaceful life after so many difficult months. We telegraphed to Osip to join us as soon as he could, and at last our little home was complete again: Marfousha resuming her place as cook and personal attendant to my wife, and Osip as butler and my military orderly. When I had gone to the front at the end of February, Osip had refused to allow any other soldier to be my orderly, saying, 'I will not let Mr de Hartmann go to the front with a stranger!' He had gone through everything with me behind the trenches and, when the soldiers mutinied, we escaped together on foot all the way to Kiev to join my wife. He and Marfousha were both children of older servants on our estate and were devoted to us as to their own families.

The thought of Mr Gurdjieff and his plans never left us; was he going to Persia – or would he stay in the Caucasus? In a few weeks a postcard from him arrived, saying that he would like to come to Essentuki and asking if we could find a place for him. In another day or two we received a letter in which he enclosed 1,000 roubles – still a large sum though inflation had begun – saying that he sent the money in case we needed it. We were deeply touched by his thoughtfulness. Later that same day we were happily surprised to see Mr Gurdjieff standing at our door. For the next few nights he slept on the sofa in our tiny living-room.

He liked the place; the owner rented him a big room in his own house, with the right to use the kitchen. Several days later Mr Gurdjieff's wife arrived, and soon afterward, the Stjernvalls.

I thought that interesting philosophical talks would begin now, but nothing of the sort happened. We just went for walks every day with Mr Gurdjieff to the centre of Essentuki. He bought sunflower seeds, always giving me a handful, and would spit out the shells in front of passers-by. Not a word was said about philosophy. And I, impatient, walked at his side, not knowing how to ask a question.

He often came to see us in the evening and sometimes Dr Stjernvall came with him; then at last the conversations became interesting. One evening Mr Gurdjieff spoke at great length about the lack of precision in our language, how we are unable to transmit an idea or philosophical concept accurately – scarcely, indeed, to communicate at all with each other. Later, Ouspensky developed this idea wonderfully, underlining the fact that our language is based on associative thinking, each word being coloured by all kinds of individual and subjective images, sensations and thoughts. His exact transmission of Mr Gurdjieff's ideas is all the more admirable in that, during the Moscow and St Petersburg period, we were categorically forbidden to take any notes whatsoever.

Later, in Essentuki and Tiflis, however, Mr Gurdjieff told us to write down what was said by him or to fulfil a writing task that he would give us, as, for instance, to find a suitable name for the Institute and define its aim. This was a real head-breaking job, which thoroughly brought home to us the conversations with him about the inexactitude of language. The most interesting thing was that during this long search for possible definitions, our inner work was creating within us a taste for exact language. Even though we could not achieve it, at least we acquired an understanding that there are ideas, thoughts and sensations that are almost impossible to put into words.

One evening, just before leaving our little house, Mr Gurdjieff said quite casually: 'This is the last evening I will come to you, because I shall soon begin to work with the doctor.' Oh, God, how much these words hurt me! I thought he was about to begin extremely important esoteric work with Dr Stjernvall and that I would not be included because I was still very 'young' in the Work. All the next day I had no peace, and when I could bear it no longer, I told Mr Gurdjieff how sad I was that I could not take part in the new work. 'Why sad? You have to catch up!' was his answer.

When a vivid confrontation such as this one occurred, the mask fell from his face and I felt the deep inner bond already established with him, a bond that grew stronger with the years. It was never a hypnotic tie, because all Mr Gurdjieff's teaching leads men towards being free of suggestion. This inner tie (let us call it a magnetic tie) was an invisible bond with Mr Gurdjieff, who was then the person *nearest* to one, in the true sense of the word. It was as if one then saw the 'real' Mr Gurdjieff, with whom one wished to stay forever. This was not the 'everyday' Mr Gurdjieff, who was sometimes agreeable, sometimes very disagreeable – a man one often wished to run away from, and with whom one stayed only because one's own work depended on it.

I recall that Mr Gurdjieff once said that the soul, which has to be awakened in us, will be connected with the physical body by a magnetic bond. Through his work with us he temporarily took the place of our soul and so a magnetic bond had to be formed with him, which we recognized and which produced this feeling of nearness.

One morning when I passed through the centre of Essentuki, I noticed a poster advertising a special evening at the social club and had the desire to sit peacefully in the corner watching people dance. Later in the day when I walked with Mr Gurdjieff and Dr Stjernvall, I spoke of this quite casually.

'Doctor, you hear? He's inviting us to the club this evening. What? Will you invite us for supper? Let's go, Doctor. Thank you for your invitation!'

This was bad. A supper during the inflation cost a tremendous amount of money and I no longer had any money coming in each month. But there was nothing for it but to go ahead with this plan, because I hadn't the courage to say no. That evening I took 500 roubles (in former times a supper in the best restaurant would come to no more than two and a half roubles) and went to the club. It was almost empty; there was no dancing and only the restaurant was open. Now my hell began. Mr Gurdjieff played with me as if I were a child to whom he wished to teach a lesson. 'Well, Doctor, since he's treating us, come on; it would be nice to start with some vodka and hors d'oeuvres. Then later . . .' It went on and on. I vividly remember to this day the oranges he ordered, because then I knew that my 500 roubles would never pay the bill. I did not have the courage to tell Mr Gurdjieff I didn't have enough money and ask him to lend me some until we got home. How could I get out of this situation? It was agonizing. Finally I decided to tip the waiter and send him to my wife for more money. She was frightened when a stranger knocked at our door in the night. But finally the money was brought and I paid for everything. The bill came to about 1,000 roubles, enough for us to live on for half a month.

Next morning Mr Gurdjieff came to see us and gave me the money I had spent on the supper. He said, 'Sometimes you act like a lamb and the tigers will eat you up. It is good that you have a tigress near you.' This was another extremely painful moment – not from the ordinary point of view, but because I realized that I did not know how to behave like a grown-up man. Mr Gurdjieff had told me so several times, but only now did I believe it. That morning Mr Gurdjieff was not at all as he had been the evening before; there were no reproaches, no raillery. All he said was that what had happened had been done for my sake.

Quite unexpectedly, for us in any case, a cart arrived one day with eight people of Mr Gurdjieff's family: his mother; his brother, Dmitri, with his wife and small child; his sister Sophia, with her fiancé; and a niece and nephew from two other sisters. Mr Gurdjieff rented a house for them not far from us, where they could live until they were able to establish a new life.

His father did not come. He wished to stay in his home in Alexandropol, where he was, unfortunately, killed later by the Turks on the porch of his house.

One day Dmitri Ivanovich brought in a large wine-skin, and that evening we all gathered and drank a toast to Sophia Ivanovna and her fiancé, Georgi Kapanadze, who were soon to be married. (I had not seen Dmitri since my first meeting with Mr Gurdjieff. He was the 'other man' who came along.) When the wedding took place, Mr Gurdjieff arranged the wedding dinner – not in the spacious house of Mandzavino, but in our little home, where everything was simple. We had a fine feast. A group of musicians called *sazandari** was invited to entertain us, which made it possible for us to hear real Eastern music.

Next morning the bridal couple came to the second floor of our house, where Sophia sat down on a carpet and began to spin. This is an Eastern custom, symbolizing that the bride, from the very first day and afterwards, will work unceasingly. She was preparing yarn in order to weave a shirt for her husband.

Life went on. We soon learned that Mr Gurdjieff had arranged to rent the big house at the end of the garden, since the owner had decided to finish it. In February he had his wife write letters to his people who were still in Moscow and St Petersburg, telling them that anyone who wished to work could come to him in Essentuki. Meanwhile we had to prepare everything to be ready to receive them. Beds, tables, chairs and other necessities had to be bought. Time passed. The owner finished the house. The furniture began to arrive and soon the house was liveable.

It was there, also in February, that I had my first experience of music with Mr Gurdjieff in one of the numerous rooms where the pupils from Moscow and St Petersburg were soon to live. In the evenings he began to come with a guitar that belonged to Mandza-

* *Sazandari*: musical ensemble of Transcaucasia; usually three performers playing *tar*, *kiamancha* and *daira*, one doubling as a singer.

vino and, lying on the *tahta* (an Eastern divan with cushions), he would play.

There was no music like waltzes and mazurkas, which later on he used for our 'Sacred Gymnastics' and which, when I asked about them, he said came from a study book for guitar. This music was quite another one. He played not in a usual manner, but with the tip of the third finger, as if playing a mandolin, rather slightly rubbing the strings. There were only melodies, rather pianissimo hints of melodies, so that one had to listen closely to catch all the varieties of musical vibrations.

These were surely reminiscences of melodies from the years when he collected and studied the ritual movements and dances of different temples in Asia. At the time he could not note down these numerous melodies on paper, but kept them in his memory.

All this playing was essentially an introduction for me into the new character of the Eastern music that he wished later to dictate to me. For us, Essentuki can surely be called the cradle of Mr Gurdjieff's music. Neither in Moscow nor in St Petersburg was there any talk about music. But, of course, we can talk about it only in relation to the years after 1916, since what came earlier is really unknown to us.

One morning I went into the street and, to my surprise, saw my friend Zakharov and Madame Bashmakova, a middle-aged lady from the Petersburg group, approaching our house. They were followed by some unfamiliar people, who, I now discovered, were from Mr Gurdjieff's group in Moscow. Among them was Alexander Nikanorovich Petrov, one of the chief pupils there. Physically, he was like a healthy young bull, and, as I came to learn, he had a very intelligent mind and was highly gifted in mathematics and engineering.

That evening we all gathered in one of the rooms of the new house and Mr Gurdjieff said: 'Nikanorich, give us a lecture.' And Petrov, without any preparation, spoke on the theme that one has to enter with all one's being into the Work. He was a wonderful lecturer, with a clear, distinct voice that was just as effective in a big hall as in a small room, and his speech flowed logically, without hesitation.

It was generally in the evening that Mr Gurdjieff himself would speak to us and give us tasks. Already one of the rooms was called 'Mr Gurdjieff's room'. It had a carpet, where we all learned to sit cross-legged in the Eastern way, while he sat on a sofa, also cross-legged. After a while other carpets began to appear on the walls around us and the room took on the aspect that Mr Gurdjieff's rooms generally had: always covered with carpets. But in the beginning there was only one carpet and one sofa, and, in the pupils' rooms, a bed and a chair, nothing more.

From the very beginning the conversations related to attention. Mr Gurdjieff told us very seriously that attention is absolutely indispensable for any work we wished to do with him. If we did not understand that, nothing could bring us to the aim for which we came to him. All of us there already felt that we were more than just a body. We knew that 'something else' was in us, and we wished to know: what is that? What have we to do with that? How can we call to it? How can we bring it out? How can we rely on it and not depend only on the body? All this was really a burning question for us, and Mr Gurdjieff made it clear that if we didn't study attention – not study in the ordinary way, but putting all our attention on developing that attention – we would arrive nowhere.

For this he gave us exercises at every moment. All the next day we had our task, where attention had the central place, whether it was in the kitchen or the garden or with the horses when they appeared. Mr Gurdjieff planned everything that went on in the house, and nothing, but nothing, could occur without him knowing it, seeing it or being all the time present.

We rose early, had tea, and each person was given a pound of bread for the day. About one o'clock we had lunch. There were little tables on the terrace, four chairs at each. With coloured tablecloths? Each place set with knife, fork, spoon and napkin? No such thing! On each table was a single deep earthenware bowl. Everyone had a wooden spoon and all four at the table ate from the common dish.

The menu was as follows: a savoury *borshch* or some other thick soup with vegetables, followed by a large piece of meat for each of us, with potatoes and beans or another vegetable. In the evening we had tea with the remaining bread.

At that time, although my wife and I lived in our little house, Mr Gurdjieff asked us to have our meals with the others. It was terrible for my wife, who simply could not eat from the same dish with other people. I do not know how she arranged it, but Mr Gurdjieff allowed her to have her own plate. He probably did not wish to press her too hard, as other difficulties were in store.

One day I began to eat 'slowly and consciously', as described in some books I had read before meeting Mr Gurdjieff. Pondering on the physical process of the transformation of food and how it ordinarily cannot serve its highest end, and on what was said about evolution, I had persuaded myself of the necessity of conscious eating. In many religions prayers before meals are to remind us of this need. I had taken only four spoonfuls slowly and consciously before the common dish was empty. Mr Gurdjieff usually walked among the tables when we ate, noticing everything. On this occasion he stopped by my side and said only: 'So, Thoma, so.'

Mr Gurdjieff used to say, 'Man should eat, not as an animal, but consciously.' I think he meant by it that we should not 'identify' with food, as always happens when a hungry person finally reaches it.

I can still see him vividly, sitting in an armchair, his muscles completely relaxed as always, the whole weight of his body submerged in the depths of his chair. Slowly he lifts to his mouth a very good pear, not peeled. Unhurried, he takes a bite of it as if striving to absorb its entire aroma, its entire taste. And so he continues until it is finished.

I was able to watch his way of eating many times. It always seemed to me that he was demonstrating how we should eat.

*

Soon after the Moscow people arrived Mr Gurdjieff began to make heavy demands on some of them. We often did not understand, but the explanation can be found in the fundamental principle of the Work of this second period: to try to stay with him in spite of all obstacles and to remember why we came to him.

He often said that, in life, great unhappiness or even insults can move people forward. On the way we were following, the teacher deliberately contrives such insults but, under his observation, they cannot bring objective harm to those he is working with. 'Where Georgivanch is, there the fleas do not bite', he said, meaning that the blows of fate through everyday adversities do not touch the one who is working with him. In our case the suffering was intentional, to test our resolve to hold to our aim. And the more the person was advanced, the more Mr Gurdjieff would press him.

At Uch Dere Mr Gurdjieff had pressed Zakharov so strongly that he finally couldn't bear it any longer and left and went to Tuapse, where he passed through a serious illness. He even went back to St Petersburg, but had taken the first opportunity to return to us in the Caucasus. Here new difficulties confronted him. Still weak as he was after his illness, Mr Gurdjieff did not receive him tenderly and said he could not support him at the house. Zakharov had to move into a small room elsewhere in the neighbourhood.

When I dropped in to see him, he was lying on his bed fully dressed. He looked poorly, still not fully recuperated after his illness and very depressed by everything that had happened.

In two or three days he was among us again.

Earlier in the year Mr Gurdjieff had bought cheaply somewhere a huge bale of tangled, multicoloured silk. It was a shrewd investment. Goods were now in short supply and silk commanded a high price. Even before the arrival of the Moscow and Petersburg people, he had begun to disentangle it himself, working very quickly with great dexterity, often making me hold the skein between my two hands. Dr Stjernvall was trying to do the same with the help of a chair back.

After the others arrived, the work went faster and soon many skeins were ready. From those skeins the silk had to be wound on small paper tubes. We were all asked to bring all the white paper and pencils we could find. I said timidly that I had music paper of a rare size, which I intended to use for the orchestration of my ballet. (I had given one quire of this paper to Prokofiev, who had come especially from Kislovodsk to get it from me.) 'Well, then, why didn't you say so? Bring it here,' said Mr Gurdjieff. And this precious paper was at once cut into little squares, the squares wrapped around pencils, and the silk thread wound on the paper tubes. It was a tedious job, winding round and round . . . Everyone else was very patient, but I could not bear it. Whether I thought then about the way of a 'clever' man I do not know, but I decided to invent a winding machine when Mr Gurdjieff was away.

One of the pupils had been led to believe, naïvely, that Mr Gurdjieff was going to conduct experiments in magic, perhaps even call forth planetary spirits. For this it was necessary to have frankincense, which the pupil had managed to obtain. He showed it to me in a little wooden box with a tight-fitting lid – just the thing for the flywheel of my future machine!

I borrowed the box and found some thick wire in the cellar to serve for axle and handle. For a bobbin to hold the paper tube itself, I adapted a pencil, with safety pins at both ends. The box and the bobbin revolved in holes punched in pieces of stiff cardboard fastened to a small board. With trepidation in my heart, I started to wind the first skein . . . The machine worked splendidly!

Just then Mr Gurdjieff came into the house and caught sight of my factory. 'Wiseacre!' he said. 'You always have to invent something.' But the machine continued to work without interruption and soon the tubes of silk were ready.

One evening Mr Gurdjieff brought in a large box that had many compartments and said to me: 'So, Thoma, go tomorrow to Kislovodsk and try to sell this silk.'

'But, Georgivanch,' I answered, 'Kislovodsk is filled with my Petersburg acquaintances. I cannot sell there!'

'On the contrary, so much the better. With so many acquaintances, you will sell the silk more quickly.'

So the next day I took the train to Kislovodsk. I arrived at dusk, but I did not go to my friends, who did not need silk thread, because I did not wish to start gossip. Under cover of darkness I went around to the little shops. Finally I entered a big one. It was the shop of our landlord, and to my great surprise I saw Mr Gurdjieff standing there. The landlord bought a lot of silk and then Mr Gurdjieff said: 'Now let's go home.' What a relief!

I will never forget this experience through which Mr Gurdjieff hit another of my weaknesses: I had never before realized my almost insurmountable sense of class pride, which made me ashamed to sell the silk. At this time no one yet understood that everything in Russia was turning upside down. I realized what a wonderful lesson Mr Gurdjieff had given me; many people of my class were forced by circumstances to do similarly embarrassing things, but I had to accept it as a task and not under pressure of circumstances. And Mr Gurdjieff never again sent me to sell silk in Kislovodsk.

Marfousha and Osip had left their two children at home with his mother on our estate in the Ukraine. Since the revolution was spreading, Mr Gurdjieff told us that it would be sensible to send our faithful servants home now, as later it might become impossible. With great sorrow we did so, sending as much money with them as we could.

Soon Mr Gurdjieff told us that he needed our little house, and suggested that it would be much better if we came to live in the big house. For me, accustomed as I was from childhood to living in common in the cadet corps and in military service, it was not such a terrible thing, even though my memories and associations of it were unpleasant. But for my wife, who was always accustomed to our living together in a home of our own, however small it might be, such a move was very difficult. It was now clear to us that what Mr Gurdjieff wanted was not our house, but that we ourselves should take part completely in the life of the big house. We accepted this, moving into one room on the upper floor, and gave up our little house to him.

Mr Gurdjieff changed the arrangement of the rooms quite often, and then all the furniture and carpets were carried up and down . . . and so much the worse for the person who had grown attached to his surroundings.

V

Forming the Institute

Soon we began 'Sacred Gymnastics'. We started with simple exercises, going on to more complicated ones of concentration and memory that absorbed the attention of the whole person. For example, simultaneous extension of arms and legs; or placing oneself on all fours; or, while kneeling on one knee, having to jump directly up by pushing off the ground with the upper part of the foot; or the second part of the so-called 'Mazurka'. These exercises were obligatory for all, but some others were very tiring and were performed only by men. Mr Gurdjieff always pushed us to the utmost in these exercises, after which we would fall on the carpets like sacks, without needing to be reminded to relax.

There was one exercise in which all the men had to fall in a heap and squirm around like snakes in a tangle of arms and legs. Suddenly Mr Gurdjieff would cry 'Stop!' and take someone aside to let him view the group. I think that no sculptor ever had such a chance to admire the beautiful, complicated and unforeseen postures that resulted from the sudden 'stop'.

I did the Sacred Gymnastics at that time, for Mr Gurdjieff himself played on a guitar borrowed from our landlord, since it was impossible to get a piano. He played very well.

Although by nature I was a musician, I had spent years in a military school and had come to hate all physical exercises, which I found dry, tedious, depressing and mechanical. With Mr Gurdjieff the Sacred Gymnastics were never dull, quite new, and I felt a vital aim in them. And there was always inspiration in the atmosphere during work with him.

He sometimes gave individual exercises to certain people. N.F. Grigoriev was a young man, nineteen or twenty years old, who had weak lungs. To help him, he was given an exercise of movements for his shoulders, combined in a special way with tension and relaxation while inhaling and exhaling.

Lina Feodorovna had a little daughter, eleven or twelve years old, who was by nature very gifted in movement. One day Mr Gurdjieff sat her down facing him on a carpet and told her to watch his face closely and imitate exactly what he did. He began by completely relaxing the muscles of his face until it became perfectly neutral. Then his face began very gradually to spread into an affectionate smile, which grew and grew until it reached its fullest extent, where it paused, and then began to fade away, equally gradually, until his face was once again perfectly neutral, as at the start.

In all this, Mr Gurdjieff spoke very much about relaxation and urged us to work at it often by ourselves or check one another at odd moments to see how tense we were in our arms, our legs, our body. Sometimes he made us all lie on the floor and told a woman to verify among the women, and a man among the men, till we were absolutely relaxed, as much as we possibly could be.

One day he told us, 'Lie on your stomach with your nose to the carpet!' And then he said, 'Look! We studied it already. Who knows it, all right. Who has done nothing, that's your business. Now I will walk on your backs. If you do not know how to relax, well, your bones will crack!'

He took off his shoes and I felt on my back four steps going across. Probably he had one foot on the floor and with the other made as if he walked. I don't know. I don't even know if we were more relaxed or more tense. But certainly no one had his bones cracked.

The time came when Mr Gurdjieff decided to enlarge the musical programme. Among those who had recently arrived was P. V. Shandarovsky, a man who had come from the 'outside' on his own initiative and who later played an important part in our life. He behaved very well, was very modest and did not ask to be received in the Institute. He said he had come hoping to find in Mr Gurdjieff his teacher. He was a well-educated man, still young, and played the violin quite well. He read me his translation of Hérédia. He had been interested in occultism and magic for a long time and told me about an experiment with the Lord's Prayer that he had once practised.

Mr Gurdjieff allowed him to come in the evenings for the Gymnastics and, later, for lectures. He was very punctual, continued to be very modest and at last Mr Gurdjieff accepted him in the Institute. This man, Shandarovsky, now had to play his violin, a real Guarneri, for the Gymnastics.

One day a second violin was borrowed from Mandzavino, and Mr Gurdjieff said to me, 'Learn to play bass notes by this evening.' Even though I am a musician and composer, I had never held a violin in my hands, but once Mr Gurdjieff wanted something, it had to be done. And so, when we were called together that evening, I was playing chords on the violin. Then Mr Gurdjeiff began to play something on the guitar, and Shandarovsky and I had to copy it, Shandarovsky playing the melody and I the accompaniment. It was not long before we were able to reproduce what he wanted.

A few days later he began to teach singing to everyone who could possibly produce a more or less correct musical sound. They sang what we played on the violin.

Another evening, when the pupils arrived, Mr Gurdjieff took the guitar and made us all sing. We soon memorized the melody, and the more we sang, the stronger the irresistible penetration of the wonderful melody became, and the more the feeling of religious devotion rose. But not only in us; Mandzavino and his wife, who lived in the house nearby, could not help but come to ask: 'What is this unknown religious song you performed?'

I remember that Petrov was quite extraordinarily tone-deaf and unable to produce even a single exact note. He was one of Mr

Gurdjieff's favourite pupils, with whom he worked much on self-concentration and self-observation.

In my presence Mr Gurdjieff, guitar in hand, obtained from him a precise singing of a precise note. That was many times repeated with the suggestion that Petrov should attentively observe all the sensations in his throat. And a little later, on the basis of these sensations, he had to reproduce the same note. And he reproduced it not only that evening, but days later, each time I asked. Moreover, in this fashion he learned what is called 'absolute pitch'. And I am a good judge, since from birth I have had absolute pitch and *do* in my mind cannot be mixed with any other note. This was a demonstration of a new method of solfeggio, based, not on mechanical factors, but on conscious self-concentration and self-observation.

Mr Gurdjieff knew how to bring a man from his ordinary state to a higher level. At such times all worldly desires for wealth, luxury, food, wine, women became dim and so extremely shallow as to be non-existent. There was no sense of loss, because a new light began to shine and one could almost touch the goal to which Mr Gurdjieff was leading one.

But then, in a flash, Mr Gurdjieff would change, acting the part of a man who had all these cravings . . . and one again began to sense all of them with pleasure and – oh horror! – even to be overwhelmed by them.

How is it that at such a moment the thought never occurred to us: why did Mr Gurdjieff manifest this way? On the way to Uch Dere the previous autumn he had said to me, 'With a *svolotch* I am a *svolotch*.* With a good man, I am a good man.' In other words, amid the multiplicity of our little 'I's are many *svolotches* of every kind, endeavouring to outwit our good 'I'. We should accept our reactions as reflections of ourselves in a mirror, but be much cleverer than they.

* *Svolotch* has a variety of insulting meanings, all implying 'the lowest of the low'. 'Dirty swine' translates the thought, but misses all the punch.

And now, in Essentuki, he told us: 'I can lift you to Heaven in a moment, but as quickly as I lifted you up you would fall back down, because you would be unable to hold on', and added, 'If water does not reach 100 degrees [C], it is not boiling.' So in our development, by our own understanding, we had to reach the boiling point or nothing would be crystallized in us; if only one degree were lacking, we would fall back again.

We also began to see more clearly the roles of personality and essence. Mr Gurdjieff often said: 'What is good for personality is bad for essence.' At the same time he never sought to destroy anything real in a man, only to put everything in its place. Under the mask of a bad personality, Mr Gurdjieff became our tempter.

As tempter he provoked in us a strong inner experience of feeling and sensation, which in life expresses itself as what some call 'negative emotion', and then he strove to enable us to transform it by seeing it and reasoning about it. With some he aroused insult, anger, rage and so on, until the person could not help knowing this in himself. Others he loaded with praises – 'You alone truly understand what you know', 'Only you can I trust' – until all their pride, ambition and self-esteem were loosened to the point where they could not help seeing their own worthlessness. Through seeing himself a man can awaken to his authentic mental centre and begin to acquire genuine responsibility.

The true meaning of temptation comes from schools where it was created for Work. Through such Work man's essence can be developed in a school under the guidance of a teacher. When the personality is made to suffer, it produces a 'ferment'; one must not avoid this suffering, because this 'ferment', this 'spark', this 'fire' feeds essence: 'What is not good for personality is good for essence.'

All this is extremely difficult, but man has a kind of deep sense that what is sent to him is always within his capacity to bear. For those who really wish to work, the attitude must be one of acceptance.

With Mr Gurdjieff we had always to be able to respond in the right way to his demands. This becomes possible if a man is 'present', if he has a conscious feeling of his self, of I AM . . .

*

We are fortunate to have kept in our notes what Mr Gurdjieff told us one evening about the conscious feeling of one's real self. It was during the time when he was planning to open his Work to public knowledge and participation in some sort of formal organization. We were sitting around the dining-table when someone asked what the Institute could bring a man. As he did so often, he began to walk up and down around the table while he spoke to us:

The Institute opens new horizons for a man and gives a durable sense to a man's existence. A man begins to see clearly that everything that he previously counted so precious and big is only a house of cards, only ideals artificially built by him or by others, and from this nothing stays. But a man clings to it all because he is afraid to stay in front of an emptiness, an abyss . . .

He understands clearly that it is necessary to throw all this away, to blow down this house of cards and then, brick by brick, to build something that nothing can blow away. He knows this with his mind, and wishes it, but he is afraid to give up all his past; perhaps he will not even find a brick! What then? What will happen? He thinks it is better to have an actual house of cards than nothing . . . But a risk is necessary. Without having blown away the old, nothing new can begin.

Sometimes in a sudden flash one sees all this nonentity so clearly! And then a man who feels it has the right – no, he is *obliged* – to throw all that past away, even to stamp it all under his feet, because it is no longer necessary for him. And then how insignificant do all people appear to him, with their little ideals, strivings, sufferings, passions and so on. How he wishes to shout to them that all that does not exist: there is no such suffering, no such love, nothing of it, all this is invented by themselves! And it seems then to him that wings grow on his back, and he does not know why he begins to love everyone, understand everyone, and wishes

to tell other people, to explain to them all that he understands and thinks. And at the same time, when it is you,
you feel that you do not know *how* to speak to them so
that they will understand. And, because of that, you remain
silent . . .

Then, something occurs, something from the outer life,
and where do all those good thoughts and feelings disappear to? . . . You begin to see only that outer life. You
suffer, because you begin again to see only through this
dark glass. You remember all that took place a few minutes
before and you even remember your sensations and
thoughts, but you can do nothing . . . Something inside
physically gnaws at your heart, physically aches as a tooth
aches. And hours and hours are necessary, with much reasoning and many examples, to push away your thoughts
and feelings, to throw all this away from you and to be
able again, without aching, to feel your Self . . .

And here is the question: how to bring it about that
these bad things will not occur again? We can, perhaps,
even reach the point where nobody from outside can tell
what is going on inside ourselves . . . But for what serves
all this outside, when inside there is all the time the same
gnawing? To understand, to see, not to show – that is
possible. But how to pull out the root itself so that nothing
of the same ever occurs again?

VI

The Work Deepens

One morning I came upon Zakharov at the table downstairs. In front of him were slips of paper. I asked, 'What are you doing?' He answered, 'I'm learning to write my signature in such a way that they won't be able to find out who I am – in case of Bolsheviks.' We both burst out laughing.

What was actually in question was the making of a sign to identify our organization. Mr Gurdjieff had given us the task to think of a suitable name for our society, considering the fast-changing political situation. Ouspensky suggested 'The Society for Struggle against Sleep'. Mr Gurdjieff laughed, but said it was too obvious. After long discussion, the title finally selected was *Essentuksky Obshchezhitiye Mezhdunarodnavo Ideino-Trudovovo Sodruzhestva*, which means roughly 'The Essentuki Home of the International Fellowship for Realization through Work'.

Now came the problem of making a sign for our front gateway, and, for some reason or other, Mr Gurdjieff chose me for the making of signs, as he did later also in Tiflis.

From Petrov, who was a marvellous calligrapher, I learned how to write a particular style of lettering, thoroughly Russian, but with elements of ancient Hebrew characters. Then I made a sign and lettered our name in a rose colour, and decorated it with pentagrams in green – the only two colours of paint that I could find.

When I had finished, Mr Gurdjieff came along with Petrov to look at it. He said to Petrov, 'Here, on this side, draw an enneagram.'* But he did not wish any kind of mystical m ng to be taken from the whole inscription.

We hung it over our front gate. It had one surprising result. One of our acquaintances came to call. He had seen the symbol with horror and had gone at once to consult a 'specialist' in all sorts of dark, mystical societies, and was trying to explain to us the fearful dangers lurking behind such inscriptions. As he left us, he implored us to escape with him while there was still time.

I will never forget how one intelligent and gifted young man among us was given a very difficult inner task to carry out at this time, to which it was added that, if he did not succeed in what was demanded, 'he would be sent off to the Turkestan Correctional Section of the International Fellowship for Realization through Work'. He told me about this and I said with a smile that it was doubtful that the Correctional Section existed, but that the demand of the task must certainly be fulfilled.

One evening a notice appeared in the downstairs corridor, beautifully handwritten by Petrov, which said that the International Fellowship for Realization through Work had been formed and that Mr Gurdjieff was not going to work with anyone outside this society.

Every day there were new notices: that this Fellowship would have full members who would take part in the Real Work; that there would also be candidates whose participation in the Work would be limited; and that there would be those who could not hope to take part in the Work before they became candidates. The first full members to be named were Ouspensky, Petrov and Dr Stjernvall.

The breaking of all ties was demanded, meaning that one must not be identified with – blindly attached to – one's husband or wife, parents, children, friends and so on. This announcement had an

---

* Enneagram: the central symbol of the Gurdjieff system, showing the interplay and unity of the two fundamental laws of the Universe, the Law of Seven and the Law of Three.

enormous effect on my wife and me. Not to be attached to each other – what did it mean? Not to be concerned with one another – that made us ponder in order to reach a new understanding. At this time I felt I would go wherever and do whatever Mr Gurdjieff demanded, without giving it a second thought. But this was not at all the attitude required in the Work, each step having to be thought over carefully.

As for my wife, although she was very deep in the Work, her love for me was stronger, and she even felt ready to part from me if it were necessary for my work. But Mr Gurdjieff always told us: 'I need both of you or neither.'

Then came a notice requiring everyone to give up all possessions, which had to be listed in writing. I could do this with great ease, as material things did not have much importance for me; but my wife will tell you herself what an intense inner struggle she went through at this time.

I was very much annoyed that my husband gave up everything without thinking about the situation that could arise if, for one reason or another, both of us, or even I alone, did not wish to remain with Mr Gurdjieff, and we did not have a penny until we had found some way of earning money. It is true that we had many friends then living in the resort, and I knew some of them would gladly help us, if only in order to see us leave Mr Gurdjieff, though that was the last thing I wanted to do. So I decided to speak frankly about it to Mr Gurdjieff. I found him talking with Dr Stjernvall and wished to back out and speak to him later alone, but Mr Gurdjieff insisted that I tell him what I had come for. So I told him that in order not to feel obliged to stay with him simply for lack of money, I wished to hold back 3,000 roubles of the money we were going to give him. He turned to Dr Stjernvall and said with approval in his voice: 'Oh, that's it. Very good, very good, give her what she wishes.'

In a few days another notice announced that the women had to give up all their jewellery. They could keep only a wedding ring and a watch. It was a fresh blow for me . . . what was I to do? I

*was very strongly attached to my jewellery, which had been my
mother's and my husband's mother's, and I realized that I would
never be able to replace it. I did not wish to give it up, but I had
to decide to do so or to leave. My husband did not hesitate for a
moment, but for me it was a tragedy. On the one hand I could not
even think of going away. On the other hand I did not wish to
part with my jewels. I was in real torment, caught between conflict-
ing emotions, and I cried all night long . . .*

*Then the words of Mr Gurdjieff in one of his talks came to my
mind: 'When we die, we won't take our belongings with us . . .
but something else, if we develop it.'*

*I put my jewels, about which I no longer cared, in a box, and
when morning came I went to Mr Gurdjieff's house, knocked and
entered.*

*He sat at a table, his head resting on his hand. 'What is it?' he
asked. I told him that he had asked us to bring our jewels to him,
so I had brought mine. He hardly moved and said: 'Put them
there', pointing to a little table in the corner. I put the box on the
table and left.*

*I had just reached the garden gate when I heard him calling me.
I returned. He said, 'Now take them back.' . . .*

*Many years later someone told me I had played a bad trick on
her. 'Why?' I asked. 'Well, you told me that story about your
jewels, so when Mr Gurdjieff asked me to give him something
valuable, I gave it. But he never gave it back to me.'*

We had to pass through the experience of renunciation demanded
in all monasteries, in all religions. But what we had to give up was
only our wrong attachment to things.

Much later I saw that those demands of Mr Gurdjieff's had a
double purpose. He already had in mind a plan for a second
expedition and the liberation from attachment would be of greatest
importance to everyone taking part in it. This expedition, which
finally brought us to an area safe from the Bolsheviks, was carefully planned in advance.

The first expedition had been preparation for this one. Incidentally, I should like to say here what Mr Gurdjieff once told Ouspensky: 'Sometimes, revolutions and all consequent difficulties can help real Work.'

Each little detail was considered by Mr Gurdjieff and worked out with the greatest precision. For example, the papers we had written stating that we were giving up all our personal belongings were used later to convince the new Bolshevik authorities that we were not unsympathetic towards the idea of common ownership of property. So they legalized our group as a scientific and non-political society. In this way we were able to exist peacefully, without arousing suspicion. Mr Gurdjieff went even further, and asked Shandarovsky, who was a lawyer, to go to the local Bolshevik administration and accept work, as they needed lawyers.

We were all horrified by the idea that one of us White Russians was asked to help the Bolsheviks. However, Shandarovsky went and at one of the Soviet meetings made such a wonderful speech on the theories of Proudhon and Fourier that he was immediately chosen as an instructor.

In the meantime Mr Gurdjieff gave us some new exercises, in one of which we were given special movements for arms and legs that stood for the letters of the alphabet. We practised them for a week; then suddenly Mr Gurdjieff announced that within the Institute we were to speak only by means of these movements. We were not to utter even a single word, no matter what happened, not even in our own rooms. We could speak outside the Institute, but we could not go out without permission. Life began to be very complicated. How difficult it was to remember not to speak, especially in private! During those days my wife and I had to go to Kislovodsk, which meant we had to dress appropriately for the outside world. In order to ask each other if we had forgotten something, we had to perform a long series of gestures, but it never occurred to us to speak in our room, even in a low voice so that nobody could hear. If we had done so, we would have felt that we had failed in our effort, that we had cheated ourselves.

It was wonderful to have this attitude in our work with Mr Gurdjieff. Understanding that everything was done for our sake, we fulfilled the tasks. It was not blind obedience, for we saw the purpose. And how clearly we began to see our mechanicalness! We had to be aware of ourselves. Every moment we caught ourselves about to speak, but we remembered in time and stopped. It was difficult . . .

Every evening after supper we gathered in Mr Gurdjieff's room. Sometimes he would explain an exercise we had tried; sometimes he would give a new one, which we had to try to do at once. He spoke very little and we could never ask questions. Sometimes Mr Gurdjieff would send away practically everybody and give special exercises to individual pupils – 'inner' exercises; but I do not feel free to speak about them.

In the morning Mr Gurdjieff often sat at the table on the veranda downstairs, his head always on his hand and, if it was winter, wearing his astrakhan hat and coat. He just sat there, in silence, near the door, where, from time to time, notices were posted on the wall telling us what we were to do or not to do, what was planned for the day and so on. These notices were very often a shock to some of us, though probably not for everyone, as I realize now. Mr Gurdjieff sat where he could watch how his pupils reacted to these shocks.

One morning as I was going downstairs I saw Mr Gurdjieff sitting at the table near the staircase. Opposite him on the wall was a new notice. It read: 'Th. A. de Hartmann is now a full member of the International Fellowship for Realization through Work.' When I turned to Mr Gurdjieff, his eyes somehow radiated encouragement. For me it was a very profound experience of happiness. I could not restrain myself: tears gushed from my eyes.

In the evenings Mr Gurdjieff always asked us what we had fulfilled of the tasks during the day, and gave us other tasks for the next day . . . Once he gave a task which none of us could understand. But we would never have asked Mr Gurdjieff to repeat it or explain it. That night, Petrov, Zakharov and Ouspensky came to our room, and we asked each other, 'Have you understood what Mr Gurdjieff meant?' One said 'x', another 'y', a third 'z', and only later, after all that, we came to the right meaning. We were all very proud that if Mr Gurdjieff asked, we would be able to answer in the right way.

The next evening arrived. We waited and Mr Gurdjieff gave us tasks for the next day, but didn't ask at all about the task we had struggled with the night before . . .

Two weeks passed and in the evening, as always, we sat and Mr Gurdjieff, as if nothing was unusual, said, 'Ah, I forgot to ask you about the task I gave you two weeks ago. Petrov, can you remind me what it was?' And poor Petrov, quite unhappy, in a low voice said, 'No . . . I have forgotten.'

Mr Gurdjieff changed his face and his voice at once and very sorrowfully said, 'Look, I brought you today something about which you have to think, but now I cannot tell you, for if the other is forgotten, it will not stick together.' He meshed his fingers together as illustration and got up and went away. We were all disappointed but none of us, although many remembered the question very well, would think to say, 'Mr Gurdjieff, I remember', because we would never wish to put Petrov in the position where it seemed that only he had forgotten.

Late in the evening Mr Gurdjieff went, as always, to a café; he took with him this time only Petrov . . . This was a kind of 'reward' and was Mr Gurdjieff's way of dealing with people, even if they had forgotten something, when he saw how truly unhappy they were.

One day after Gymnastics Mr Gurdjieff began to speak about confession, real confession, and how it was practised in esoteric schools. Real confession had no relation to confession in the churches, for its essence consisted in the necessity for a man to see his own defects not as sinful but as a hindrance to his development.

In esoteric schools there were men of high attainment who studied the nature of a man as a whole. Their pupils were people who wished to develop their being. They spoke sincerely and openly about their inner search, how to achieve their aim, how to approach it, and of their characteristics that stood in the way. To go to such real confession one had to make a major decision: to see one's real defects and to speak about them. Mr Gurdjieff told us that this was absolutely essential – especially for one to see his chief feature, the one around which (as around an axis) turn all his stupid, comical, secondary weaknesses.

From the first days Mr Gurdjieff had spoken with us about this chief weakness. To see it and to realize it is very painful, sometimes unbearable. In esoteric schools, as I have mentioned, when the chief weakness is made clear to a man, it is revealed with great care, because the truth about himself can sometimes bring a man to such despair that he might end his life. A spiritual tie with the teacher prevents such a tragedy. Holy Scripture speaks of the moment of realizing one's chief defect when it says that when you are struck on the right cheek, you must then turn the left one. The pain of discovering your chief defect is like the shock of receiving a slap in the face. A man must find in himself the strength not to run away from this pain, but boldly to turn the other cheek – that is, to listen and accept further truth about himself.

One day Mr Gurdjieff called us to his room one after another. We sat on the carpet before him and he began to talk about how to reach that depth in oneself from which alone it is possible to face oneself sincerely. He was unusually kind and gentle with both of us. It was as if the everyday mask fell from his face and before us was the dearest man in the world. At such moments the strength and power of the inner spiritual tie with him was felt very intensely.

The next week he again called some of our people privately, but for some reason did not call me and, as I thought, even avoided me during the day. I felt I had to speak with him and finally found him alone on the big terrace. 'Mr Gurdjieff,' I said, 'in St Petersburg you said that we needed to risk only five kopeks*

* Kopek: a small Russian coin; one-hundredth of a rouble.

in the beginning; in other words, we needed to have only a mini-
mum of faith in your teaching to begin to apply it in our life. But
if your advice proved to be good and we found it helped us, we
should then risk ten or twenty kopeks more; that is, we should
trust you more and more. Have I now to place complete confidence
in you and fulfil unquestioningly all that you advise me to do?'

He shook his head a little, paused a moment and then said:
'Certainly, on the whole it is so. But if I begin to teach you
masturbation, will you listen to me?' And he left me without
another word.

I place great significance on these words, because they point to
the essence of his Work. It is not the way of unquestioning obedience; the pupil has always to remember his own principal aim.
Even the teacher's intentional provocation must be powerless to
make him deviate from what he knows to be his true path.

Much later Mr Gurdjieff said that our conscience must guide us
in our actions and that conscience is innate: we do not have to
acquire it; we have only to awaken, because almost always we are
asleep to it.

VII
Facing the Public

Mr Gurdjieff decided we should actually experience a fast, about which he had already spoken to us, but he added special conditions. He told the women to move to the upper floor and the men downstairs. During the period of fasting, men and women were not allowed to speak to each other, except for one hour once a week, when we could go out and walk together. It was very difficult for my wife, not only because she was separated from me, but also because any discipline went against her temperament. It was less difficult for me because of my early training, from the age of nine, in military school.

After a few days I could walk and talk with my wife. Just before the appointed hour Zakharov and I began a very interesting conversation, in which I became so absorbed that my wife, who had been missing me very much, was kept waiting. At last I went to her and a very bitter conversation began. She told me that she did not wish to interfere with my work, that she saw how the Work was dividing us and that it would be better to part . . . The conversation itself was not important; the important thing was the suffering and pain we both were experiencing. Then, just as our talk reached its unhappy climax, as if by magic, there was Mr Gurdjieff on the street corner. He did not seem at all pleased and, to our chagrin, told us curtly: 'I don't need you separately. Both of you or neither.'

When we returned home it was already dark. We were both heartbroken. My wife went upstairs, I stayed downstairs.

Later in the evening Mr Gurdjieff gave an order: everyone was to return to his quarters, though the fast was still to be carried on. We were overjoyed. My wife told me that she had thought we were going to be separated forever, but had decided to stay at the Institute in order to see me sometimes and to continue herself to follow Mr Gurdjieff's Work.

All this is a striking example of how experiences of real suffering can be provided without causing harm. When we accepted such suffering willingly and consciously, we had the possibility of creating in ourselves the real 'Master'. We certainly did not understand then the connection between all the demands that were made on us. We knew that situations were intentionally created by Mr Gurdjieff, but at the same time we felt them to be real.

As the fast was nearing its end, Mr Gurdjieff watched our states very carefully. I don't know how or where he found them in those hard times, but he managed to obtain some oranges, which he gave to those who were the most weakened.

To me was given something else. It seems that on Thursday at two o'clock I fell asleep and slept soundly for some time. I was awakened by a tender hand. It was Mr Gurdjieff, who said to me, 'Go into the corridor. There is something there waiting for you.' The 'something' was a big piece of white bread, smeared thickly with butter – another unobtainable delicacy. He told me to eat it very slowly.

Mr Gurdjieff announced that every Sunday there would be lectures on philosophy, mysticism and occultism, and that they would be open to the public. Petrov had to write announcements of the dates and the place on small pieces of paper (paper was very scarce), and these were put up in prominent spots around Essentuki by Grigoriev and two girls, who carried paste and brushes in a little pail made from an old tin can.

Several days before the first of these lectures Mr Gurdjieff called us together and told us that we must become acquainted with the origin of this Work. The beginning, he told us, was a prearranged meeting in Egypt at the foot of one of the pyramids.

There three persons met after long years of separate work in places where initiation centres were still maintained. The first of these three was a man of science, who was able, through Western knowledge, to verify and evaluate in a scientific way all that was apparently miraculous. The second man was a connoisseur of religions and their histories. The third man could be called a 'man of being'.

The result of the meeting of these three men was the formation of organizations of people in suitable places and in suitable conditions. 'Such as', said Mr Gurdjieff, 'our group in the Essentuki branch of the International Fellowship for Realization through Work.'

The real purpose of the Work in Essentuki could become clear only if a man gave his attention to the idea of the crystallization of the soul. The products of food, both coarse food and air, are necessary; but without impressions, the great achievement, the crystallization, cannot take place. In this effort a man can rarely succeed by himself. Almost always someone of great wisdom, a teacher, has to be near the pupil. Material of the special quality received from impressions has to exist in the pupil if the teacher is to help this transformation to take place. To build up a sufficient quantity of this material, which the pupil has to collect by his own efforts, some kinds of isolated 'reservoirs' are necessary, where special conditions permit this material to be deposited.

Perhaps now we can better understand why Mr Gurdjieff called his yoga 'khaida yoga'. In Russian khaida is a peremptory call, as when somebody gives an order and wishes it carried out at top speed. Khaida yoga is, therefore, a 'quick yoga', which gives the pupil the possibility of learning much in a short time. Mr Gurdjieff felt that a man should not have to depend only on life to bring him all kinds of impressions of happiness and unhappiness, sorrow and joy. Mr Gurdjieff wished to create special places where he could consciously provide them. Work would help, so to speak, the growth of the 'Kingdom of Heaven' within us, the growth of the divine quality that distinguishes men from animals.

But as the basis of Mr Gurdjieff's Work was to create every

kind of impression in a pupil for this transformation, he could accomplish it only through playing roles. For instance, if he wished to make someone experience injustice, he had to play the part of an unjust man – and he knew how to do it superbly! Then one had to hold back from reacting badly and not be resentful. Mr Gurdjieff told me once that it caused him pain when I was resentful. In other words, a man had to accept intentional suffering.

Mr Gurdjieff could not say: 'Don't you see that it is done on purpose?' The whole sense of his Work would then have been lost. There is a constant temptation for the teacher to show his true self, the way he is in reality. But Mr Gurdjieff knew full well that then everyone would run after him and become his adoring slave. He did not wish to create slaves but, on the contrary, conscious, voluntary individuals, the seeds of which he sought to plant in his pupils.

The day before the first public lecture Mr Gurdjieff decided to have each of us prepare for it by writing in our own words the story of one of the three men who met at the pyramids. That evening we were to read our papers before our whole group. Trying to write these accounts showed us clearly how awkward and helpless we were.

In the evening an iron bed was placed in the upper corridor and on it many mattresses. We had to climb on top of this construction, sit in the Eastern manner and read what we had written. My wife wrote of the 'man of being' and her essay was chosen as the best.

From today will begin a series of lectures organized by our new society. It is important to say a few words about our society, its beginnings, its history, its reason for being and its ultimate results. Its history is very complicated and to convey even an approximate picture, it is necessary to begin way, way back.

Twenty-five years ago in Egypt, near the pyramids, three tourists met accidentally, and from their ensuing conversation it was clear that all three had nearly the same world outlook and understanding of the meaning and aim of life.

One of them was a Russian prince, another a professor of archaeology and the third was a young Greek guide. The Russian was wealthy and from an ancient lineage. In his youth he had lost his wife, whose death so strongly touched him that he pulled himself away from ordinary life and began to occupy himself with spiritualism. He began to travel and met some exceptional people who were interested in esoteric teachings. He went to India many times and lived in the temples. His unhappiness over his wife's death pushed him to travel all the time. His meeting with the professor and the Greek took place on his second trip to the Egyptian pyramids.

It was science and only science that brought the professor to the pyramids.

The Greek guide came because he wished to be different from what he had been until then.

Before their meeting, all three had spent many long years searching, and that is why they had all arrived at the same conclusion – that 'something' absolute existed, but they did not have enough knowledge to come to an understanding of it. They always ran into difficulties because of this lack of knowledge. That had proven to them that it was first of all absolutely necessary to obtain this knowledge – a knowledge that encompassed all sides of life. The fact that they had each equally striven for this made them realize the necessity of changing the nature of their search. First of all, they had to understand their aims and then begin from the beginning with their search for knowledge.

To know all was too much for just three men. All religions, all histories, all special knowledge about life was too much for three people to arrive at during their short lives. But without this knowledge, they would always encounter obstacles on their way.

So the idea came to them to draw to themselves people of different knowledge. Again, another difficulty arose because if the new people they attracted did not have the same interest in, and aim for, something higher, even their special knowledge would not help. Different specializations would bring them nothing without this.

They made a plan to find these necessary people, and to direct and prepare them with their advice in their material as well as spiritual lives.

With this aim, the three men parted and went different ways, and the final result was that about fifteen people came together. Among them were Orthodox, Catholic, Muslim, Jew and Buddhist. They knew mechanical sciences, chemistry, horticulture, astronomy, archaeology and philosophy. There were also women among them. Each one was obliged to specialize in his or her field.

They all went to Persia, as planned, and from there, with all their cumulative knowledge, a number of them went in 1899 to India through Kashmir, Tibet and Ceylon. The others went to Palestine through Turkey and Arabia. They chose as their mutual meeting place Kabul, in Afghanistan. After many years had passed, twelve of the fifteen met again. Three had died during their travels.

They decided to travel to Chitral. On the eve of their departure, the Russian died; and then, as they were on their journey, a few were taken as slaves by the wild tribes who lived in the mountains through which they had to pass. These members never reached the aim they had set for themselves.

Some time later four men only of the original twelve reached Chitral, having fulfilled the aim that they had set for themselves. Three years later they returned to Kabul. There they again began to draw corresponding people to themselves to live together. This was the beginning of our Institute. People collected around them very quickly, and each one who came told the rest the results of his or her difficult search.

Five years later they transferred their activity to Russia, but because of the political conditions of the time it was impossible for them to continue their work there.

From Kabul on, it was necessary for these people to live together. It was indispensable to them not for communal material reasons, but as a means to arrive at 'something higher' much faster than if they each individually made quite separate and unrelated efforts.

The day of the first public lecture arrived. On the ground floor of the house Mr Gurdjieff arranged a buffet: tea with a little sugar, very sweet tea with saccharin, and little homemade sweet rolls, which were a very great luxury. Chairs were brought to the upper veranda to make a suitable auditorium.

That same day Mr Gurdjieff put Petrov, though one of his favourite pupils, through an inner experience that shattered him. Half an hour before the lecture was to begin this strong, healthy man came into our room and began to cry despairingly. My wife and I tried to quiet him. Meanwhile, beyond our curtained window that opened on to the veranda the audience was beginning to gather.

The first lecture was read by Ouspensky and was brilliantly presented to a crowd that exceeded our expectations. This lecture was followed by another one on 'The Ray of Creation', written and read by Petrov, whose inner state we could easily imagine. Nevertheless, it was delivered excellently.

In the audience that evening was a deacon of the Church of Old Believers, who probably came to see whether he might find some anti-Christian heresy. He listened very attentively but, perhaps satisfied, attended no further lectures.

A general of the Tsar's staff, a professor at the military academy, where they prided themselves on their ability to lecture, also attended. He greatly admired these lectures and was amazed at the way Petrov could, with such 'dry philosophical material', as he expressed it, produce so vivid an interest in the audience. That evening Mr Gurdjieff took Petrov to a restaurant. It was a great reward at that time just to be able to speak with Mr Gurdjieff alone. This was another instance showing how, having given a man an intense and difficult experience which was willingly endured, Mr Gurdjieff would never let it pass unnoticed.

*

The next public lecture was fixed for the following Sunday and we awaited it with great impatience. We hoped Mr Gurdjieff himself would speak. We thought we might hear something we had not yet heard, perhaps even something about the supernatural. Our interest in magic and all other phenomena of this sort had not yet subsided in those days. We hoped, we waited ... but again Mr Gurdjieff forced us to remember our aim and why we were there.

On Thursday posters were put up everywhere in Essentuki advertising a lecture by the notorious 'Dr Black'. In other words, the lectures were given an intentionally suspicious character. The reputation of 'Dr Black', a charlatan, was very well known from satirical poems published in pamphlets of this period with titles like 'The Trial of Johann Huss' and 'Dr Black, Bearer of Bad News'. But perhaps the doctor did not exist, for he never appeared.

Why was this done? Why in the early days in St Petersburg did Mr Gurdjieff tell Ouspensky that a meeting was to be held in a fashionable lady's drawing-room, only to let him find when the time came that, in spite of having gone over the arrangements together, it took place in a room in a public school? Why was it necessary to invent such things for Ouspensky? Why had it been necessary to organize for me, a newcomer, the meeting in that dubious café on the Nevsky? Why now this 'Dr Black'? Why always a suggestion of charlatanism for prospective pupils at the very first meeting?

All this can be explained only by Mr Gurdjieff's determination to make us work, to remember our true aim, which, if serious, could not be shaken by any kind of action on his part. Teachers usually surround themselves with an atmosphere of great seriousness and importance to give newcomers a good impression. With Mr Gurdjieff it was just the opposite: everything that could repel, even frighten, a new man was always produced. A newcomer had the opportunity to meet Mr Gurdjieff and to talk with him, but at once there was put before him some obstacle to be surmounted. On the other hand, Mr Gurdjieff never let a newcomer go away empty-handed if he came with real questions and spoke about something that was of genuine importance to him.

Another Sunday came when Ouspensky lectured. During the tea break Mr Gurdjieff was approached by an elderly man with a long beard. He asked about yogas. This man was the type who has a superficial interest in Hindu teachings. Mr Gurdjieff pretended that he had never even heard the names of the various yoga methods. Then this intellectual began self-importantly to explain 'hatha yoga' and so on, but Mr Gurdjieff interrupted him quickly and said: 'Well, and my yoga is called *khaida* yoga.' I don't need to say how astonished the intellectual was to hear about a new yoga. He understood nothing. Mr Gurdjieff, however, had expressed in this way an idea full of meaning, if he could have grasped it.

Soon another notice was posted in the house saying that in two days we would begin new work of a special inner character. The day was divided into hours, and each hour was to be devoted to inner exercises, which we had expected for a long time. But we received only a very deep and bitter disillusionment, again undoubtedly intended by Mr Gurdjieff.

He had been trying Petrov almost beyond endurance. At last Petrov could not hold out any longer. He forgot himself and answered Mr Gurdjieff angrily. Mr Gurdjieff turned and left the house, and an hour later it was announced that all further work was to stop for everyone because one of the senior pupils had manifested himself in this way towards his teacher.

Everyone felt a profound sense of guilt. We knew that no apology would change the situation. We had to look within, to ask ourselves if we always had before us the purpose for which we had come and if this aim occupied the first place in our lives ... Mr Gurdjieff fully achieved what he wished to produce in us. We all passed through a very acute emotional crisis.

VIII
Preparing to Move On

Every day there was working and waiting. We acquired two horses: a handsome chestnut-coloured one named Rusty, and Dralfeet, big and brown, who was seriously inclined to bite. We also bought a mule, Bardadim, a gentle creature without any distinctive personality; and a female donkey, Mashka, young, full of life, provocative, but essentially inoffensive and harmless. We men had to take turns cleaning and looking after all four.

We needed to fatten up our animals. It was already July and the grain had recently been harvested from the fields, so we obtained permission from the authorities to graze them on the stubble. Because of sloppy garnering, many ears of wheat were lying about. Mr Gurdjieff wasted no time in taking advantage of this.

Every morning at sunrise one of us set off for a field several versts away to pasture the animals and collect loose grain. It was a very long process. The creatures wore hobbles to limit their movement, but the donkey, Mashka, knew how to throw these off and then she had to be chased down. Poor Zakharov once spent two hours trying to catch her.

By the time it was my turn I knew what I had to figure out: first, where to find some large sacks to bring along, in which to collect the loose ears of wheat; second, how to ride four animals at once! No one else could help, as it was early dawn. Riding on Rusty, I had to hold the others by their halters, the two donkeys on one side and Dralfeet on the other. There were gates to lead them through – which also had to be closed. Before mounting

Rusty, I tapped Dralfeet's nose sharply with my finger several times, as a reminder: 'Don't you dare bite!' In the end everything went smoothly. Dralfeet didn't bite. The horses grazed well. The sacks were filled with wheat. Only once did Mashka get loose, but I was able to catch her quickly. In short, I was able to return by noon.

Mr Gurdjieff was pleased with the sacks of wheat. As a reward, he brought out a large wine glass filled with vodka, which turned out to be made of denatured alcohol. For once in my life I got to taste such vodka. It tasted awful! But, on the other hand, it added to my life experiences and left me with a great hope – that never again would I have to repeat this experience.

One day Mr Gurdjieff told Petrov to write a letter for Shandarovsky to the Essentuki Soviet, which was then called the Council of Deputies. Whenever an official paper had to be submitted somewhere, it was always given to Petrov to copy. His beautiful calligraphy invariably impressed all institutions, headed so often by former junior civil servants, telegraph workers, accountants and so forth. The letter was a formal request for aid in organizing a scientific expedition to the region of Mount Induk in the Caucasus.

Our expedition would ostensibly have a twofold aim: we would search for gold in a river near the mountain and also for dolmens – strange stone constructions, which are found throughout the Caucasus. There were reasons for thinking that in ancient times these dolmens had a special significance; to explain that significance would be of great scientific interest.

Mr Gurdjieff had long been interested to study these dolmens for himself, but political events had prevented it. He had now come to the conclusion that he might be able to satisfy this wish while we made our escape across the mountains.

This request was handed to the Soviet authorities. It made a very good impression on them, as the Bolsheviks were then in a mood to patronize all scientific undertakings. The Essentuki Soviet passed it on to the higher Soviet in Pyatigorsk, which had the authority to assist the expedition materially.

At the same time a notice appeared in the Pyatigorsk newspapers describing the aims of the expedition. The whole story was in the form of a reporter's interview with one of the members. The delicate question of how the expedition intended to go in spite of the civil war was raised as though it were merely incidental. I see Mr Gurdjieff as if he were in front of me now, dictating this question and at once his answer: 'The expedition intends to go to a remote wilderness, inaccessible to military activities of the civil war. Therefore this scientific work and its discoveries cannot be hindered.' No question of our loyalty or political reliability arose.

Some of the equipment for the expedition soon began to arrive from Pyatigorsk: two smaller carts to add to our *lineika*, a big tarpaulin, two large blue and white officers' tents, hatchets for all the participants, and small spades and picks, which Mr Gurdjieff immediately distributed to all the men and women. And there was something else: a broad red fireman's belt with black stripes and brass rings, which Mr Gurdjieff wore on the day of departure.

Neither Ouspensky nor his wife were able to join the expedition. Madame Ouspensky's daughter, Lenochka, was expecting her first child, so her mother couldn't leave her during such incredible times. And Ouspensky couldn't abandon his wife. But although he was not going to come with us, he was active in the preparations. He told Mr Gurdjieff that, for washing the gold, alcohol would be necessary and in no small amount. Mr Gurdjieff understood and immediately dictated an appropriate request, which was given to Shandarovsky. And, to my astonishment, several gallons of pure alcohol, at that time almost unobtainable, and some denatured alcohol were brought into our house in Essentuki. All this alcohol was quickly put into small bottles, which were then given to each of us. Certain bottles were marked 'Medicine for the treatment of cholera'; others, 'Medicine for the treatment of malaria'. The bottles of the first category were of pure alcohol and those of the second were of the denatured alcohol, which had been filtered through hot bread and baked onions so that it could be safely drunk.

Preparations for the expedition continued. Although Mr Gurdjieff knew very well how to do things quickly, he also knew how to wait, for a long time if necessary, for the most opportune moment. In this case he again proved to be right.

Appropriate passports, *laissez-passers*, recommendations and identification papers had to be obtained. We also had to arrange for the use of some railway baggage cars in which to travel with our equipment and our horses and donkeys during the first part of our journey. The story of how we got our passports will illustrate Mr Gurdjieff's ability to see and plan ahead for everything that we would need and for what would normally have been impossible to obtain.

About six weeks before we were to leave Essentuki Mr Gurdjieff had astonished and even shocked us all, as I already mentioned, by telling Shandarovsky to go to the Soviet authorities and apply for a government position that required legal training. Since Shandarovsky was a good lawyer, he was not only appointed to the position, but was soon promoted and before long found himself in charge of the office that issued passports and other such documents. Of course Mr Gurdjieff at once told him to issue Soviet passports to all of us, describing us as citizens of Essentuki: one was a teacher, another a gardener, one was retired, one a simple worker and so on. Had we ventured into the remote frontier regions with only our tsarist papers showing us to be doctors, engineers, Guards officers and so on – considered by the Bolsheviks to be 'enemies of the people' – we would have been shot on the spot.

When our new passports were in order and everything else was ready, Mr Gurdjieff told Shandarovsky to ask for two weeks' leave. This was readily granted. The next day our expedition left Essentuki and Shandarovsky never returned.

Meanwhile the ladies had made roomy linen rucksacks, with leather shoulder straps where possible, and linen hip straps. We would be able to take with us only what we could carry on our backs. The last few days before starting everybody was busy trying to select from their belongings the most necessary things for the journey. We could not be sure that anything we left behind would ever return to us again. It was difficult to get all those chosen things into our rucksacks and to decide finally what to leave out. In addition to our old summer work clothes, we had to take something we could wear in places frequented by the 'respectable intelligentsia' or former 'people of consequence' and not appear poorly dressed. Everything had to be thought out and each eventuality foreseen. The men had to carry seventy-pound packs, and the women, fifty-pound packs. To accustom us to carrying such loads Mr Gurdjieff would sometimes make us walk back and forth in our garden in the evenings with our rucksacks on our backs filled with the required weight in stones.

One evening Mr Gurdjieff showed everybody how to locate the Great Bear and the North Star, since some of the ladies did not know how to find them. This would, of course, be useful to us on the expedition.

Another evening he showed us how, as he expressed it, 'to walk consciously'. He told us that in the mountains on very dark nights we could at any point stumble down a precipice or come upon some other danger. To walk in this way one puts the weight on, say, the left leg, freeing the right to touch and sense the ground ahead. Feeling the ground firm, the weight is then put on the right foot, sensing ahead with the left, and so on. We had to practise this, and how helpful it proved to be in the mountains!

Along with the material and practical needs of this expedition there were also moral preparations, which culminated in a very serious talk by Mr Gurdjieff. For all who would take part in it, the rules were Draconian.

Walking as he always did around our dining-table, he told us that since he did not know exactly where we were going, and since circumstances were such that nothing could be determined in advance, this would be the first time he would ask from us strict and unquestioning obedience in carrying out his orders. Everyone would have to think very seriously before deciding to go. We were no longer to be husbands or wives, brothers or sisters or children to one another. A mistake on the part of one person could endanger the whole group. If this happened, Mr Gurdjieff would be

*obliged to sacrifice someone's life, no matter who it might be, for
the safety of the whole group. And he took out a big revolver and
put it on the table. I was terribly frightened, because I thought
that even unwittingly someone could make a mistake and Mr
Gurdjieff would be obliged to kill the one who did it.*

*All night I spoke with my husband, not giving him any sleep,
saying, 'I am not ready to give my word for something that could
bring such a possibility of risk or misfortune to the whole group.'
My husband tried to persuade me that the other trip we had made
with Mr Gurdjieff showed us that nothing special would happen
and that I shouldn't leave him and go and stay with my parents.
Finally, when it was almost sunrise, I decided to go and, like
everyone else, I had to tell Mr Gurdjieff that I accepted his conditions.*

Everything that had happened since the beginning of the war,
such as my long illness, had exhausted my wife. I was worried
about her. She implored me to ask Mr Gurdjieff to let us go away
for a week or two by ourselves to rest and gather strength for the
expedition. I went to speak with him; I remember it was on the
street. 'Mr Gurdjieff,' I said, 'I know that everything you do and
all you require of us is done for our sake, for our development.
But my wife is at present so tired . . .' and I told him her wish for
a rest. Mr Gurdjieff did not get angry, but with great gentleness
looked at me and said: 'You just told me that you understand that
everything I ask of you is for your sake. So, then, why do you ask
me this?' It was obvious that my wife would have to make another
super-effort and that the time for rest had not yet come. And she
proved to have energy enough.

It was not only people that Mr Gurdjieff prepared for this trip.
Once I saw him in the street holding Rusty on a long rope. With
the other end of the rope he was beating him on the belly, where-
upon the horse would rear up on his hind legs. We could not
imagine why Mr Gurdjieff would do such a thing.

A few days later soldiers came to commandeer our horses for

the Red Army. The donkeys they did not touch, but Rusty and Dralfeet they led away. Mr Gurdjieff sat calmly on the garden bench, watching what was happening and interfering in nothing, in spite of the fact that our lives depended on the horses. My wife was even angry because he passively let the horses be taken. All he did was send one of the senior pupils to the commission to ask the reason for the requisition. The pupil had not even time to get there before the soldiers brought the horses back, warning that they were very dangerous. Rusty had learned his lessons very well: as soon as a soldier tried to approach him and take hold of the reins, he at once reared up and fell over on his back, pinning the soldier underneath. Dralfeet had bitten another soldier on the belly. 'Keep them,' they said, 'we don't need such horses', and they gave us a paper protecting them from further requisition. Of course, Mr Gurdjieff made us manage the horses as they were and master them – or at least get them to do what was necessary.

Shortly before our departure Mr Gurdjieff decided to have a rehearsal of travelling with the *lineika* and the two smaller carts. The horses were harnessed to the carts, the donkeys to the *lineika*. In the first cart sat Dr Stjernvall and his wife; in the other, Zakharov and the young boy. In the *lineika* the other women sat with me. Mr Gurdjieff was coachman. He knew very well how to turn such an occasion into a merry and comical event.

Our vehicles looked like a parody on some sort of English dog-cart. The whole episode gave me the impression of something out of Dickens's *Pickwick Papers*. Right at the end of the line came Petrov, on foot, holding our three dogs on a rope. As we went along, we broke into a trot and at that pace we rode right round the outskirts of Essentuki – Petrov running after us.

I shall never forget the eve of our departure. Perhaps I should explain here that our stay with Mr Gurdjieff had never been associated in our thoughts or feelings with the idea that all the past was lost or that through Mr Gurdjieff we could escape from the Bolsheviks. That the Bolsheviks would really stay in power in

Russia never entered anyone's head. My wife and I had very important and powerful friends, such as our last Prime Minister, Count Kokovtzov, and several others who wanted us to go away with them in comfort.

When the bustle of our final preparation began, the things that we were to leave behind were packed in big trunks. Some of our possessions, of course, had already been stolen during the journey from St Petersburg, but the rest of them, including my personal music manuscripts, were in trunks heavy with linen, silver and clothing. Mr Gurdjieff decided to put them, along with many of his own carpets, in the cellar of his brother's house and hide them behind the woodpile. They were moved there in the dark of night and Mr Gurdjieff himself took one of those heavy trunks on his back and carried it down as though it were nothing.

IX
Second Expedition

The sixth of August 1918 was fixed for the starting day. Besides Mr Gurdjieff, we were five women, seven men and two children, fourteen and twelve years old. Early in the morning of that last day all our rucksacks and supplies were ready. We had sacks of flour, potatoes, salt, tea and coffee. We had tents and carpets for sleeping in the open air. We were all dressed in our expedition clothes: ladies in simple skirts and blouses, men in Russian linen shirts like tunics. Mr Gurdjieff himself wore a linen tunic, with his fireman's belt. Hung on our belts we had bags with the two bottles of 'medicine', axes and a saw or some other tool, and a thermos or a little cooking pan. All this paraphernalia and the added weight of our rucksacks reminded me of a medieval suit of armour.

We took all our luggage, carts and horses to the railway station, where we were assigned two baggage cars. The horses and the two small carts were put into one of them, with a few of the pupils to look after the animals. The rest of us would go in the other car with the *lineika*, which would also serve as a bed for Mr Gurdjieff.

There was still an hour before our departure and Mr Gurdjieff agreed that we could walk in the park. It was the hour for music and there were crowds of people. I had a very painful meeting with the Bulgarian general Radko-Dmitriev. During the winter I had made acquaintance with this hero of the Bulgarian-Turkish war. Now, seeing my travelling outfit, he was interested and asked me where I was going. I told him I was off on a scientific expedition. 'If I were younger,' he said, 'I would ask you to take me with you.' Three weeks afterwards, when the reign of terror began in Essentuki, Radko-Dmitriev, General Russky and many Guards officers were arrested. They were taken up the nearby Mount Mashuk, where they themselves had to dig a ditch; there they were shot, and then thrown in and covered with earth, half dead. As I was a Guards officer, if we had stayed in Essentuki I would surely have shared their fate.

We finally left Essentuki in the two baggage cars. Our train was a slow freight and stopped at every station. As nobody but soldiers travelled at that time, we were attracting a great deal of attention, so we were forbidden to leave the cars or even to look out. We just sat quietly in the dark corners.

Not until the next day did we reach Armavir, where we had to be shunted over to another track. My aunt – my mother's sister – lived in Armavir and I wished to see her, for I knew that it would be the last time. We were told that our cars would not be moved until the next morning, so Mr Gurdjieff allowed my wife and me to go. The town was in Bolshevik hands. There was no transport, so we had to walk. As Bolshevik soldiers were patrolling the streets, we tried not to attract attention; we dirtied our fingernails, turned our coats inside out, my wife put a shawl over her head and I wore a workman's cap. We blew our noses in our fingers and our pockets were filled with sunflower seeds, which we constantly chewed and spat out in the manner of working people, as Mr Gurdjieff had taught us. In this way we went safely to see my aunt and quickly returned to the station.

To our horror, the cars were no longer there. We searched every track in the large station, but still could not find them. Then we learned that our cars had already been hooked to another train, which had left. We were afraid even to ask too many questions and felt like rats in a cage when, to our inexpressible joy, we saw Shandarovsky looking for us. Our two cars had been left outside of town on another track and would depart only next morning. As a commissar, he had received permission to get two sacks of sugar from a nearby store, although at this time to buy sugar was almost impossible. Our relief was such that it seemed a trifle to go with him to the store and carry the sacks more than three versts to the train.

It began to rain; we had to take off our coats to cover the sugar, which was so precious. Late in the evening we arrived at the cars, wet to the bone, and found everyone angry with us because we had left. They were anxious for us and did not know if we would return in time. The sight of the sugar put everyone in a good mood, however. By candlelight Mr Gurdjieff divided it among us and we each had to hide our share as a great treasure, which in reality it was.

The next morning the train went as far as Maikop and stopped. For a long time we could not leave the car because we did not know what was going on outside or if the train would go further or not. Mr Gurdjieff sent Dr Stjernvall to the local Soviet office with our papers, asking for permission to continue our trip.

Near us stood a Red Army train, where some of the soldiers from boredom were playing a card game in which those who lost had to make fools of themselves by getting down on all fours and barking 'Bow-wow!' like a dog. To the delight of the soldiers and for our amusement, Mr Gurdjieff speedily organized us to join the card game. Having lost at cards, amid general laughter, we went down on all fours and barked. The result was that the soldiers immediately considered us as 'their own kind' and we could be at ease with them.

Dr Stjernvall was gone a long time, but finally returned bringing the news that most of Maikop was surrounded by fighting Cossacks and Red Army troops, and that it was impossible to go further. The Soviet proposed that we stay in a deserted farm three versts from Maikop. Certainly nothing better could be expected.

Our friendly soldiers helped us unload all our gear from the train and showed us the way to the farm. It was a beautiful place, left by its owner a long time before, but the house and the other buildings were in good shape. There were empty stables, cowsheds, and barns filled with hay on which one could sleep. The farm was situated on the edge of a wood through which there was a little path leading to the beautiful White River. There was even a place on the river where we could swim, complete with diving board.

Far away, one could hear gunfire, and sometimes shots whistled over our heads, striking the mountain on the other side of the river and causing stones to fall into it. But we paid no attention. It was a heavenly oasis during such a terrible time.

In Essentuki Mr Gurdjieff had said that on the ocean, even during great storms, there are quiet areas where there is no turbulence at all. And so it is during revolutions. There are places where people can live quite peacefully and the turbulence does not affect them. In these years of upheaval Mr Gurdjieff brought us from one quiet spot to another. We did not realize it, but it was so, and only later did we appreciate his inspired guidance. Meanwhile, before our own real 'battles' – our inner struggles – began again, we had an easy life in a beautiful spot for about three weeks.

This part of the northern Caucasus was the most fertile land in Russia. The climate was wonderful, the summer hot and quite dry; the population was rich, and in the market one could get all the provisions one wanted. There was even a factory near us where they made 'coffee' from acorns. We went there not only for the acorn powder but to sharpen our axes.

From the first day Mr Gurdjieff divided our company into small groups of four or five persons. In each group one person had to buy and prepare food. For our group it was my wife who had this task. The food was cooked in the open air, in a pot hanging from a tripod over a camp-fire.

Soon Mr Gurdjieff told me to have my meals with him, so then my wife had to cook only for herself and two men. Then one of them was told to eat with Mr Gurdjieff, and she was left with a man she did not particularly like. Some days later, even this man was put in another group, and my wife had to cook only for herself. It was hard to be alone at meals, because all day long we were working around the farm and only at mealtimes did we come together.

Each evening Mr Gurdjieff assigned two of us as night-watchmen. After a day of heavy work it was very difficult not to close our eyes until the next morning when Mr Gurdjieff awoke, although he was up very early. What lightened these nightly vigils was hot coffee, with one of our precious pieces of sugar. How we learned to economize them and make them last! At the same time, we came to appreciate the beauties of the south Russian nights. The sky was our clock. The appearance of the constellations showed us that midnight had passed; then that it was two o'clock; then that the sun would soon rise. We prepared the camp-fire for the others, who would shortly awaken, and then went to one of the empty barns, where we slept until noon.

On days when we had not been on night-watch the morning began with the grooming of the horses under the supervision of one of the ladies appointed by Mr Gurdjieff. 'Goddess of the cleaning of the horses' he called her. She did not touch the horses herself, but was responsible for their perfect grooming. And so, when we were scrubbing away with all our might, this lady would appear and say: 'Look, here you have not scrubbed enough . . . a little more there . . . here too – not clean enough . . . nor there . . . and there . . .' This was calculated to irritate us, but we would not show our annoyance. Besides, life at the moment was so wonderful that it was impossible to be angry.

We encountered a number of interesting people, among them a Finn, who was a Buddhist monk, trying to get home to Finland from India. He was the head of some sect and lived in a nearby villa with his pupils. He was a tall man, middle-aged, with a long beard, dressed in a shirt that came down to his ankles and was belted at the waist. When we went to visit him, he welcomed us very cordially. He was busy cutting tomatoes and other vegetables into little pieces and putting them in a barrel to salt them. These people were vegetarians.

There was another quite unusual stranger. He was barefoot,

wearing a worn-out cape and linen trousers that were torn and came only to his knees, revealing very elegant legs. He was tall, with curly blond hair framing his face, and had quite a long beard. He told us about himself, speaking very sincerely. He had been an officer of the Guards, which meant that he was an aristocrat, but he had chosen to be a wanderer and had no wish to return to his former life. We felt in him an absolutely honest and good man, so Mr Gurdjieff permitted him to join us so that he would not go alone. He stayed with us until we reached Sochi, then continued on his way alone. Who he was we did not know, but in spite of his rags he was an impressive figure – like Nathaniel in *Thaïs*, by Anatole France.

We had one disagreeable experience. A soldier rode up on horseback, with an officer's epaulette hanging from his saddle. Whether he wished to appear an ardent revolutionary or really had just killed an officer we did not know. He asked us who we were, why we were there and so on, but he must have been satisfied with our answers, for he galloped off and bothered us no more.

When the Bolsheviks realized that the White Army was advancing, they proceeded to draft every man in the neighbourhood into their ranks. In order that our men should not be called, Mr Gurdjieff sent us down to the river bank where we kept our horses hidden all the time. There we spent the whole day, screened by the high grass, and the women brought us food.

Finally it became possible for us to continue our journey, since Maikop was retaken by the White forces. The Buddhist monk told us with horror that he had gone into Maikop to find out how things stood and, on entering the town, had seen a gallows with bodies hanging on it. With a Finnish accent, and expressing all the horror of his impressions and the protest of his whole being against the cruelty of mankind, he said: 'See, they hang there, they hang . . .'

When the White Army took Maikop, I went into the city. Fortunately, I did not see the gallows, but I saw a two-wheeled cart covered with canvas, under which one could discern a heap of flesh and bones, the mangled bodies of people killed in the fighting. In the town, near a two-storey house on a large square, some fifty White Russians, who had been in hiding, were gathered. Out of curiosity, I entered the house, where there was quite a crowd. Soon an officer wearing a Cossack hat passed nearby, probably the commander of the regiment that had taken the town. He was at once surrounded by people asking questions about the situation and receiving orders.

I went out, and only then realized that I had been running a considerable risk: I was in a common shirt with a belt and could easily have been mistaken for a Bolshevik. I had no papers with me and even they would not have helped in such a tense moment. Thank God nothing happened.

I hurried back to our farm, noticing on the way some other signs of liberation from the Red Army. I was attracted by one merchant who had sweet pastries, customarily covered with chocolate, pink and white glazes. Formerly they used to cost three kopeks. Even the best Petersburg confectioners charged only four or five kopeks. When I asked how much for these, the merchant said, 'Three roubles apiece' – a hundred times the old price. Of course I left, but on the way home the crazy thought flashed through my mind: 'How seldom I used to eat these pastries when they only cost three kopeks!'

On my return I learned that Mr Gurdjieff had, as usual, sent the doctor to get a White Russian pass for us. He had had trouble. The authorities had not wanted to accept our passports, but luckily an admiral who was an old Petersburg acquaintance of the doctor's appeared on the scene and arranged everything at once, including the right to have revolvers and guns.

The admiral came to tea at the farm the next day. Mr Gurdjieff received him warmly, regaling him with home-made chocolate biscuits. Some middle-aged ladies also came for tea, members of the local theosophical society, who had learned about Mr Gurdjieff from the admiral. Petrov was told to lecture to them, and I can still see them under the great old oak tree: Petrov surrounded by these philosophical ladies, who listened to him with close attention. That was a strange gathering in the midst of civil war.

*

Two nights later, during dinner, Mr Gurdjieff told us that the next morning, very early, we would leave the farm. Afterwards he went with us to a lumber mill to get some poles for our tents. As I was taking one of these poles from him, it slipped and landed painfully with all its weight on my left foot. When we got back to the farm, I found that the toenail of my big toe had been split in two, crosswise.

Next morning I found my toe all bloody. It was agony to put on my boot. But then, with all the bustling about and walking up and down while packing and loading, the pain was no longer felt and was forgotten.

We moved on, just in time. The following day Maikop was again taken by the Bolsheviks, but we had departed unscathed from this area of revolution. We all had to walk, except Shandarovsky, who was still weak from typhus, which he had contracted in Maikop.

Now the road was very wide and wound between harvested wheatfields through a region dotted with Cossack villages. At one place we had to cross two lines of shallow trenches, evidence of the civil war. Then we had to ford the White River, belt-deep in water. The stones of the riverbed blocked our carts and as we were pushing them clear, my axe slipped unnoticed out of my 'armour' and remained somewhere in the river. I had been very proud of that axe. My wife managed to save hers.

Soon we came to a big and prosperous village, and when Dr Stjernvall went to the officials with our documents, we were let through without any difficulty. However, several versts further on, when we stopped for a little rest, we saw in the distance some Cossacks galloping in our direction, with their rifles at the ready. At this time such a sight was very disturbing, because one never knew with whom one would have to deal: real Cossacks or Bolsheviks. We had already arranged in advance that whenever we had to show our papers, we would first look at Mr Gurdjieff; depending on which side of his moustache he twirled, left or right, we would know which papers to show. We had our old tsarist papers and also those especially obtained from the Bolsheviks. So now we carried on with whatever we were doing and the Cossacks were received by the doctor, who brought them to Mr Gurdjieff. Very soon Mr Gurdjieff's gesture told us they were not Bolsheviks, so we brought out our White Army papers and the Cossacks went away, even apologizing for bothering us.

In the evening we came to another big village, where we were permitted to pass the night in an empty school. We were very tired. The broken nail on my toe began to ache badly. It would have been so good to lie down and rest, but instead we had to carry pails of water for ourselves and the horses. I remember how the full pails nearly pulled my arms out of their sockets. In such moments of superhuman effort one has to restrain the inner revolt that results from physical fatigue. What helped me was to look at myself as if from the outside, and laugh. This laughter helped me to put the magnitude of the effort required into better perspective – an effort that at the same time seemed to be so enormous.

If at such moments someone tells you not to be lazy and not to be afraid to make an effort, you can become very angry. It injures your self-love and provokes a reproach; you feel that no one understands your tiredness. It is important then to remember the qualities of your real 'I' – of love and forgiveness. Real 'I' cannot be made angry.

The next day, as soon as the sun rose, we prepared to leave. Again all the luggage was packed, the horses were harnessed and we pushed on. Everyone walked, except Mr Gurdjieff, who drove the *lineika*. At first our way was not difficult and the country was very beautiful in those lovely late-summer days. The road curved around low hills covered with stands of fine oak trees and passed by open fields.

In the forest I saw wild pears ripening – of a kind that I knew Mr Gurdjieff loved. They are hard and sour and pucker the mouth when unripe, but become very sweet and aromatic when they soften and turn brown. Spotting some quite close to the road, I went over to pick a few, then ran back to give them to Mr Gurdjieff. But when I had barely caught up with the *lineika*, he made the horses trot and pulled away, making me run faster. No matter how hard I ran, he played with me, managing to keep just ahead. This went on for some minutes before he stopped the horses and, smiling, let me get into the *lineika* for a while to rest. He accepted one of the pears and ate it slowly, with pleasure. No matter what was taking place, he knew how to bring it to the point where we had to stretch our usual limits by an extra intentional effort.

One evening, while looking for a place to stay, we approached an empty posting-station. Remembering the excellent stay we had had at a posting-station on our journey the year before, we entered by the gates in the high fence and found a large house with roomy sheds, a paradise . . .

But we suddenly noticed that our white linen shirts and the ladies' linen skirts were becoming strangely discoloured. Hordes of tiny black fleas had found us! Surprisingly, they weren't biting or even settling down to bite. In view of the goose-down everywhere blowing about, we guessed that the station was a nightly refuge for flocks of geese, which we had seen on sale in town, and that the fleas belonged to them! We quickly got out of the infested place and hurried to a nearby brook to get rid of the fleas. Beside it was a green meadow on which Mr Gurdjieff decided to camp for the night.

X

In the Mountains

The easy part of the journey was soon at an end. One evening we arrived in a village called Khamishki and stayed with a rich farmer, from whom we bought a sack of potatoes and a sack of apples to replenish our food supplies. When we were all settled – men in one room and ladies in another – Mr Gurdjieff told us that we would continue on our way early the next morning. As there would be only a little path instead of a road, we would have to leave the carts here, put all our luggage on the horses and donkeys, using pack-saddles that Mr Gurdjieff had brought, and carry our personal belongings ourselves; until now our rucksacks had been carried on the carts. However, as our four animals could not carry all our tents, small carpets and sacks of food, Mr Gurdjieff decided to take only a few of us and part of this luggage, and to return with the animals to fetch the rest of our people and things the next day. He said that this time he would take five men and two women; that he would choose the men himself, but the women could decide among themselves who would go or wait. At once my wife was in a quandary – whether to go or stay, since she did not know if Mr Gurdjieff would choose me. The only thing she did know was that Mr Gurdjieff's wife would stay until the next day and that meant that Mr Gurdjieff would come back in any case. If I were to go, I would have to stay in the mountains until Mr Gurdjieff returned, and she could stay with me. And if Mr Gurdjieff took me with him when he returned to get the rest of our people, she would not be afraid for my safety, since to be with him was to be out of danger. So she decided to ask to go. And I was among the five men.

That night there could not even be thought of sleep because of our inner excitement about what would come, and the whole night, by the light of small candles, we packed and prepared the sacks for the horses and for ourselves.

We started out as soon as the sun was up. The road wound upward all the time. Our packs were very heavy, the horses walked quickly and we had to hurry to keep up with them. Near midday the sun grew much hotter and there was little shade. I was getting worried about my wife. She was quite exhausted and once, when Mr Gurdjieff and the horses disappeared ahead of us, she told me that she did not think she could continue.

We had left at six o'clock in the morning. The path rose very steeply up the mountain and in spite of all previous practising I was finding it unbelievably difficult, bent double under the fifty-pound weight of my rucksack. I recall vividly how I was struggling to walk: tears were flowing in torrents. Finally, I made a decision that I would go just to the next turn in the path and, if Mr Gurdjieff gave us no rest, I would stop there and sit under a tree. Was it not all the same to go on like this or die? I was already beginning to sense myself taking the sack from my shoulders and there remained only a few more steps to the turn in the pathway when I heard Mr Gurdjieff calling me: 'Where are you? Come quicker! We are stopping here.'

We found that Mr Gurdjieff had stopped by a deserted hut near a wooded slope, where we could hear a stream murmuring. He ordered us to unload the horses and to feed and water them. We ourselves ate, then slept for two hours. When the sun's heat began to abate, Mr Gurdjieff selected Petrov, Grigoriev and myself to return with him on horseback to the village. He told Zakharov and my wife to organize watches and keep a fire going the whole night to frighten the wild beasts away. After apportioning tasks to be done while we were gone, he said, 'Now I am at peace. We do not have to deal with men anymore, just wild animals.' He promised to return next day at about the same time. My wife was quite content because I was with Mr Gurdjieff. She did not even think about herself.

Four of us were left alone: two women and two men. It was the first time I had been separated from Thoma since our marriage, except when he was at the front and then I was safe at home. I tried to calm myself with the thought that he was with Mr Gurdjieff, and that I was thinking of him and not of myself. But certainly I was thinking only of myself! How else could it be?

When our four riders had disappeared from view, we allotted the hours for each of us to be on watch during the night. As my turn was from four to six o'clock in the morning, I retired early into the hut, but couldn't stop crying. Nevertheless I finally fell asleep.

I was sleeping like a stone when I was wakened at four in the morning. It was a beautiful night, full of stars. In spite of all these extraordinarily agonizing conditions, the grandeur of Nature acted on me in an unexpected way to give me force.

Suddenly, from the direction of the village, gunshots rang out and then more of them. What could that be? The preservation instinct brought alertness and common sense. First decision: put out the fire! I woke the others and in one minute we had smothered the fire with earth. After that we all went into the hut, waiting in complete darkness for what would happen. Somewhere in the distance we again heard several shots, then all was silent.

In the morning we started the fire again, made tea and began our tasks while waiting for the others. As midday approached, we watched for signs of movement on the path from which we had come. When silhouettes appeared on the horizon, we were at once overjoyed, but instead of our caravan we saw only two black figures, two monks. We stopped them and asked them where they had come from and where they were going. Among other things they told us that, late in the night, four horsemen had appeared, coming from the forest towards the village. Fearing they were

*Bolsheviks, the peasants began to shoot at them. One of the riders
was wounded, but was rescued by the others, and then all had
disappeared.*

*You can imagine our state of fright! Time passed and our
people showed no sign of coming. We had already finished the
tasks that Mr Gurdjieff had given us, which had helped until then
to fill the dragging hours. We really did not know what to do.
Should one of us try to go back to the village to find out what
really happened? But the path was not always clear and it was
easy to lose the way. Moreover, it was dangerous for any person
to travel alone.*

*At last, about six o'clock, when our terror and indecision were
at their height, we caught sight of our caravan . . .*

*It is incredible what a tremendous role this event played during
the rest of our trip, as if all our fear and anxiety had quite
departed from us and nothing of the sort remained inside.*

We rebuilt the camp-fire and hung a kettle over it on a tripod.
The ladies made soup with potatoes and onions and some kind of
cereal. We went down to wash in the stream, nobody thinking
that there might be snakes or scorpions in the grass and tangled
undergrowth. We lay down for the night and slept soundly under
our *burkas.**

In the morning we put apples and potatoes in the hot ashes of
the night's fire. Our appetites were huge and the sacks seemed to
empty very quickly.

The pattern was now established that each time we moved
on further, the packing was divided into two parts. Two people
had to stay behind with half of it until Mr Gurdjieff returned
with three men and the animals to fetch them and the second
load.

After each night's stop, all our things were skilfully packed by
Mr Gurdjieff, who reserved this job for himself. Nothing was ever

* *Burka*: a Caucasian felt cloak.

broken. I remember that even a little glass kerosene lamp came through intact. The pack-saddles for our horses and donkeys had hooks on each side to hold baskets and bundles; the rest of our belongings were piled on top. To tie all these packs in place was a task assigned to me and Zhukov – Where is he now? How I would like to see him again! Zhukov was a hard-working, practical man, a moderate socialist and admirer of Kautsky. He was a native of Moscow, and for some reason Muscovites were not fond of Petersburghers, who were, for the most part, civil servants, Guards officers and the like. As a result, he had a certain contempt for our Petersburg people and especially for me, which was most evident during the loading process. He was very experienced in this kind of work and I was not, but, as the days went by, I learned from him how to do it well.

I discovered that the loading of the animals was a whole 'philosophy' in itself, since donkeys are very sly. The 'professor' in this case was our donkey, Mashka, and the others followed her example. They would swallow as much air as possible just before the baggage was tied on, but as soon as the packing was secured they expelled the air, their bellies contracted and the loads slid to the ground. Mr Gurdjieff told us to tap them smartly on the belly before tightening the rope, so they could not swell up. But we had to watch them all carefully, especially Mashka, or else while we were loading the second or the third, one of the others would suddenly be rolling on the ground, legs in the air, and we would have to start all over again.

We now continued on our way, which became more and more difficult. In spite of that, my wife told me that after the previous day everything seemed light and simple. We walked along a narrow path through virgin forest. Each day's journey was not long in versts, but we had to overcome all kinds of unforeseen obstacles. The path crossed a high plateau and we had not expected that there would be so many swampy places, some of them impassable. Big tree trunks had been laid across such swamps and we had to walk along them. Each time we came to such a spot we took all the equipment off our horses and carried it across ourselves. At first, when we tried to lead the horses, they absolutely refused to cross on the trunks. Then our little donkey, Mashka, leaped on to the trunk and the others followed her. In one swamp where there were no tree trunks we tried to lead the loaded horses through, but they sank into the mud up to their bellies. Naturally they became frightened and would not stay still, and it was very difficult to remove their packs so that they could pull themselves out.

We covered only ten versts that day, but nevertheless it was 7 p.m. before we arrived at a very high cliff, where we made camp between two mountains. We had climbed much higher than we realized and had a spectacular view of all we had just passed through. The mountains were so terribly high that glaciers lay on some of them. Our path ran along the slope of one of these, and later we learned that the White River had its beginning there.

We put up our tents as it began to rain with an icy wind, and went to sleep with the tent flaps blowing in our faces, letting in gusts of rain. In the night it became even colder, so that when we awoke we found our dresses and sandals frozen.

In the morning, very early, Mr Gurdjieff started back to fetch the others who were left behind at the previous camp. This time he took me along with him, as well as three of the men. With no packs it was easy for us and the horses to make the trip back.

After we had reloaded them and ourselves to make the return trip, Mr Gurdjieff told us not to try to lead the horses, but to let them find their own way; otherwise they would have difficulty trying to stay on the muddy path.

It was amazing. In quite impassable places, where the day before we had had so much difficulty in removing their packs so they could pass, they went quite simply with their load, so it took only three hours to travel the same distance that had taken us seven hours the day before. Our little donkey went ahead of the others in all the difficult places, as if she looked in advance and avoided all the pitfalls. Only after she went through very easily would the others follow her. Sometimes she went far away in the woods to avoid some particularly difficult place, jumping from stone to stone or trunk to trunk. It was fascinating to see her instinctively moving to find the right path.

We ourselves had the greater difficulty after the rain, picking our way painfully through slippery mud patches. And sometimes, in this mountain defile, the route was like a corridor of stones, with steps to climb about three feet high.

One evening when Zhukov and I were unloading the horses the friction that had been smouldering between us burst out in the open. Unable any longer to contain his ill-feeling, for some reason or other he threw a small satchel right in my face. In the exchange that followed I was lucky enough not to identify with the offence and succeeded in remaining free in myself. Gently, but without holding anything back, I was able to get across to him the incorrectness of his attitude and conduct towards me as a fellow pupil.

The result was remarkable. Almost overnight Zhukov became a different man. We hardly had time to take stock of ourselves before our former hostility was transformed into conscious friendship – which never hindered us on occasion from giving each other a rap on the knuckles.

Finally we were out of the forest and on a wide plain. After a while the path brought us to a very sharp downward slope. It was strewn with boulders two or three feet across and to descend we would have to scramble from one boulder to another. To make our way more difficult the slope was covered with dense grass that grew chest high.

Before making this difficult descent, Mr Gurdjieff decided to give us a whole day of rest. He spoke to his wife and at once flour and yeast appeared. Madame Ostrovsky kneaded dough for bread and next day, when the dough had risen, Mr Gurdjieff built a little oven of stones, on which he put a pan and began to bake the flat Eastern bread called *lavash*. In the East they bake it in big cylindrical ovens fitted in the earth, heated on the bottom with glowing wood coals. The baker shapes pieces of thinly rolled dough, folds them over in a particular way, then bending over the oven, he flips them open adroitly and flattens them with his hand on the insides of the hot oven walls. When the baking is done, he equally deftly pulls them off. And here we were, in complete wilderness with only stones for an oven, yet Mr Gurdjieff baked equally wonderful bread. We all sat around this oven waiting patiently, like children, for the bread to be ready, and warming ourselves in its heat, since the weather was becoming cold and damp. In the evening it began to rain and all around us muddy puddles appeared. But the earth remained dry under the tents because we had made small trenches around them.

I recall that night very vividly. It was cold and dismal, despite the wood fire that was kept burning. Everyone else settled down to sleep as best they could, while Mr Gurdjieff, in his grey overcoat with the collar turned up, would pace back and forth or sit near the fire, smoking and drinking coffee from a thermos that I had prepared beforehand. Everyone could sleep peacefully, knowing that someone was on guard and thinking about them . . .

When the sun rose, it became warmer. Mr Gurdjieff decided to go on. We had to take advantage of the fine weather to descend from this swampy plateau. The descent was very strenuous. We had to let the horses and donkeys find their way down unloaded and carry a good deal of the luggage ourselves, though not all of it. The rest was left behind with Zakharov and Madame Bashmakova, until we would return for them the following day.

After the steep descent, an immense green prairie stretched away to the south as far as the eye could see. No mountains were visible. We started across this prairie, called the Luganaky, on a hot sunny day, and for several versts we passed drying-up mud puddles. We had the impression that we were going through a flat field covered with waist-high grass, but that was not true because the prairie continued to slope upwards for thirty versts.

It was very tiring and soon we were plagued by thirst. Dr

Stjernvall had a canteen of water with a little metal cap and he gave us each a swallow, but it did not help much. I remembered the muddy pools with envy and recalled a story of King Darius, who, on one of his campaigns, quenched his thirst from dirty puddles and said, 'I do not know of a better drink.' Fortunately, about three versts further we came to a spring with wonderful mountain water, where we were able to drink and drink as much as we wanted. Mr Gurdjieff called a halt and we rested for a short while.

Finally, that evening, we came to the edge of the prairie and the mountains seemed very close. From this prairie we descended again into a little valley, where we found a large field with some primitive sheds belonging to Armenians who grazed herds there during the summer, but there was no one about. It was already dark, so Mr Gurdjieff decided to make a halt.

First of all, it was necessary to find water for the animals and ourselves. The moon had not yet come up. We could hear the sound of a rushing mountain stream, but could not see it in the darkness. Zhukov and I each took two pails and began to go towards the sound of the water. Here the lesson Mr Gurdjieff had taught us about 'conscious walking' was most useful. We followed this method in the blackness carefully and attentively, and had no difficulty reaching the stream. Having filled our pails we returned the same way without incident. But next morning, when we saw where we had been and the precipices we had passed, we were terrified!

The supper that evening was very meagre because there were only enough potatoes left for one more day, some onions, a little flour, but no bread. Having eaten a small portion of soup, we went to bed. We slept in one of the little sheds with the horses, and my wife said that all night she felt Dralfeet's breath on her cheek, so close was his muzzle to her face. But, all the same, there was such a charm about it that words cannot describe.

At sunrise Mr Gurdjieff, with Zhukov and Petrov and myself, returned on horseback to those we had left behind the day before.

The weather was beautiful. We travelled quickly and soon reached Zakharov and Madame Bashmakova, who had been resting and feeding on berries they found in the woods. As we loaded the horses again, three peasants from Khamishki came by. They were very friendly and at once offered us half of their round loaf of bread. Money at this time would buy nothing, so they gave us the bread only because they seemed to understand how much we needed it. Zhukov divided our half into six little pieces; although we were very hungry, we ate it slowly. After so much strenuous activity and so many days without a normal meal, its taste was indescribably delicious. Later, in Tiflis, Mr Gurdjieff said that this trip had been worthwhile if only to experience the real taste of bread. In ordinary life our taste impressions are seriously blunted.

As I ate the bread, it occurred to me to save a little piece for my wife, but then I realized that I would have to walk the whole way back and so I finished it. It was already dark when we returned and I went to the little shed where we had slept the night before. My wife told me that there had been no food at all for them that day because the young people had found some mushrooms and had put them in the soup made from the remaining provisions, but it was too bitter to eat. One of them, feeling especially hungry, tried to make himself eat it, but he could not swallow more than two spoonfuls. How right it would have been to have brought my wife that little piece of bread!

Next morning we encountered a new terrain, walking across the perfectly bare rock slope of a granite mountain. Down it flowed streams of icy water of crystal clarity and purity. I scooped some up in a glass and took it to Mr Gurdjieff. He drank it with delight and then said, 'Noble thing!' The surrounding mountain landscape was unusually beautiful and very distinctively Caucasian.

We walked in this way until noon, when we approached a broad valley, where we came across large numbers of cows, goats and sheep. They belonged to Georgian shepherds, who had brought them there from the south for summer grazing. The shepherds showed us great hospitality in the patriarchal manner that was their custom. Each of us received a big bowl of yoghurt and a piece of very dry and thick cornmeal porridge, which for them took the place of bread. This food was handed out by the host, the old father of the young men. Mr Gurdjieff spoke with them in a friendly manner and showed them his rifle, which was a 'repeater'. They were very interested. As we had a camera with us, Mr Gurdjieff told us to take a group picture of all the herdsmen. In the middle of the group stood the old father and, beside him, Mr Gurdjieff in a dashing pose holding his rifle.

After a short rest we loaded the horses. Mr Gurdjieff and our people, with the exception of my wife and myself, went on; it was our turn to stay behind with part of the luggage. Mr Gurdjieff said he would come to get us the next morning. He left us quite content, since Georgian mountaineers have patriarchal laws and would never offend or trouble a traveller who stopped with them. We spent the rest of the day collecting wood for the night's fire – fallen trees that we had to carry from the far side of the stream, which was not deep but full of stones and very rapid. We attached a rope to the trunks and were able to pull them to our side without too much difficulty.

While we were sitting by our camp-fire a monk came along. We gave him coffee with pieces of sugar. It was still some of the acorn coffee we had bought at Maikop. He carried a heavy prayer-book with him, which he set down beside him as we talked together. I couldn't help noticing that where the cover of his book had come loose a bedbug was taking a quiet stroll. He told us that travellers had been robbed and two monks had been killed on the road we were to follow. It was just then that I understood the sense of Mr Gurdjieff having his photograph taken with the chief and all the shepherds, and that dashing pose with the rifle in his hands. Such a brave man, fearless for his own life, you do not rob without reason.

The monk also said that farther on, in a cave in a wooded grove, there lived some monks who had been driven from their monasteries by the Bolsheviks and who had gathered all their religious books and church equipment there, and everything else that they could save. We felt that he and his brethren were also searching for salvation – in their way.

Mr Gurdjieff did not come to get us the next morning, so we again began to gather wood in case we had to spend another night alone. During the day some of the shepherds came to visit us and wanted to buy some of our clothing and the big gun. Mr Gurdjieff had, of course, taken the gun with him. We could only offer them our acorn coffee with sugar and they invited us again for supper. We went as soon as it began to grow dark. There was freshly killed, roasted wild goat and with it a piece of cornmeal porridge and a big piece of white Caucasian cheese – for us a very rich meal. Everyone sat on benches around a primitive table. A boy carried a pitcher of cold water and poured some over everyone's fingers; only then did we begin to eat. The old father distributed the food. Later, having thanked them for their hospitality, we left them and went away to sleep. We took turns keeping vigil and replenishing the fire.

Next morning, about ten o'clock, we saw Petrov and the schoolboy S.* in the distance riding our horses, but not Mr Gurdjieff – he had fallen ill. They came with two peasants from the village where they had stopped. We loaded the horses quickly and followed them with our sacks on our backs. Quite soon we left the woods and came out on an open pathway, high up in the granite mountains. The peaks were not far from us. After about an hour we stopped on a flat space surrounded by large rocks. We sat down in the shade of some of them. In great peace we ate what had been brought for us by Petrov and S.

Suddenly we heard several shots. We thought it was the shepherds hunting wild goats and paid no attention. Then more shots rang out and we saw bullets strike the road. We were still sure that it was shepherds hunting and I shouted in the direction of the

* In his manuscript de Hartmann frequently referred to people only by initials. Where it has been possible to identify them by other means, their names have been restored.

bullets: 'Stop! There are people here!' But more bullets came in our direction and finally we understood that someone was shooting at us. I shouted to my wife to hide behind a rock and to put her sack on top of it, as we all did.

We finally discerned on both sides of the pathway, in the mountains overlooking the little clearing, dark figures with guns aimed at us. They could easily shoot us down from 200 feet away. My shotgun had only two shots in it and had a range of 100 feet at most. There was no chance whatever to escape. I stood up and raised my gun in the air as a sign that we would not return their fire. In response, two men in tall sheepskin hats and Cossack dress appeared from behind the rocks and came towards us. Two others on horses stayed on the mountain, their guns trained on us.

When the men approached, we could not see their faces, which were blackened with soot. In their hands they carried large revolvers and from their shoulders hung whole belts of cartridges. With foul language, in a Caucasian accent, they ordered the two peasants to get out of sight behind the shoulder of the mountain and told us to stand with raised arms in the middle of the open space. I had time to throw aside my little revolver, for I did not want them to get it. My wife also had time to take a little sack of jewels which hung securely from her belt along with her thermos, axe and cooking pan. She untied it unnoticed and slipped it into her bodice. She had to tighten her stomach muscles, so that it would not fall through. Luckily, she was a singer and these muscles were well developed.

We stood there with arms raised before the guns while they searched us but found nothing. Although we knew that we might be shot, we had no fear. Perhaps somewhere very deep was the certainty that nothing so terrible could happen to us since we were with Mr Gurdjieff. My wife told me later that the only thought she had had during these minutes was for me, that I might perish now, so young and so talented.

Petrov shouted: 'May we smoke a cigarette?' and perhaps this broke the tension. Without lowering their revolvers, the mountaineers permitted us to put our arms down. They ordered us to go to the far side of the clear space, but told my wife to stay and open all our sacks. She now faced a threefold problem: to avoid showing the brigands anything more than necessary while opening the bags; to pay no attention to the choice obscenities that poured from their horn of plenty; and always to remember to keep her stomach muscles tight to prevent the little bag from falling to the ground.

The robbers searched her again, but did not notice the bag. They took the thermos apart, but found nothing. They asked her where the money was – they told her they had followed us for a long time and knew that she looked after it. She replied that we would not be so foolish as to carry money with us and that it was in the village. The robbers then began to take everything they wanted: high boots, *burkas*, raincoats – things we ourselves needed badly. My wife argued with them over every piece. When they came upon the little leather and silver toilet set my soldiers had given me when I had gone to the front, they howled: 'You are bourgeois to have such things!' But my wife persuaded them that she was a singer and that if they ever went to the theatre, they would certainly expect the singers to be well dressed. They gave in and told her to keep it.

At one point our schoolboy whispered, 'They're taking my pants. My watch is in the left pocket!' My wife took hold of the pants and said sweetly to the robbers, 'The child's passport is in these pants. Do you really need to take it?' – 'All right, take it back.' She quickly drew out the watch, masked by bending over, and gave back the pants to the robbers.

When they went to open the bags on the horses and were undoing them, my wife had time to take several items, including my raincoat (so important to me), from the heap of things they had put aside. Finally, when they had finished going through our belongings, they seemed anxious to get away. 'Get on, now, and quickly! There, below, more of our men are awaiting you!' They began to climb back up the mountain, but my wife followed them and asked them to write on a little piece of paper that they had already taken everything useful. One of them scribbled something and then they quickly disappeared in the direction of the village we had come from.

We repacked as quickly as possible and started off; only then did we notice that our hands and knees were trembling. The way was quite open to view and we watched the hilltops for signs of other figures. But nothing happened and no other robbers appeared.

There had also been another great danger, although it didn't occur to us until later: the robbers could have carried off my wife! But, happily, she was as thin as a stick at that time and Eastern men like only fat women.

Not until the road ran through thick rhododendron bushes did we begin to breathe freely. We did not stop for a second and in three hours we reached the village where Mr Gurdjieff was waiting for us with the others. We poured out our story of all that had happened to us. He listened to the end, with a peculiar expression on his face, and said nothing at all. This offended my wife very much. However, he let us stay, not in the cottage with the others, but in the garden, under a pear tree, where we had a little cabin all to ourselves. It was triangular, thatched with straw, and even had straw mats on the floor. Here we rested wonderfully for several days.

XI

Sochi

Our further journey was a far lighter burden. Between villages the way was already a well-trodden road. We travelled through woods full of flowering oleanders, deeply touched by such enchanting, gentle beauty after all the rocks. I recall one moment, about two versts from our next halting place: it was midday, the sun scorching hot, the heavy rucksack cutting my shoulders. Walking continued to be very painful because my broken toenail had started to fester. Moreover, both my wife and I now had big blisters on our lower legs, apparently from pushing through some poisonous grasses. But I was in such a state of euphoria and cheerfulness that I could go on and on. Even my rucksack reminded me, 'Don't forget yourself!'

Mr Gurdjieff had told us in Essentuki about real faith – not a dogmatic faith that must be held for fear of the tortures of hell. He said that faith is the knowledge of feeling, 'knowledge of the heart'. This knowledge burns like a bright light in the crises of life. During this journey we experienced the truth of what he said.

Mr Gurdjieff now rented another *lineika*, on which we lashed all our personal sacks, thus ending our great discomfort from the straps. Next day we were approaching Babakov Aül, a big village about twenty versts from Sochi, when a frightful downpour started. Mr Gurdjieff, with our belongings on the *lineika*, went quickly on ahead, leaving us far behind trying to hide from the storm under the trees. When we finally reached the village, we found somebody waiting for us, who took us to Mr Gurdjieff. He had decided to rest here for several days and had already rented rooms in the house of an affable and sympathetic Polish landowner and road engineer named V. Y. Philippovich, who seemed genuinely attracted by Mr Gurdjieff.

Our host had a fine bass voice and we learned that he was fond of singing, with a repertoire mainly of Polish songs. In his house was a Russian-style heating stove, on which Madame Ostrovsky, with corn flour, sour cream and butter very quickly made flat cakes, which we all ate with great relish. When Philippovich mentioned that some prosperous tea merchants had built a Turkish bath for the village, Mr Gurdjieff lost no time in arranging to have it heated for us. First the women, and then we men, enjoyed it fully, after which we retired for the night. The only bed in the house was our host's, and Philippovich gladly gave it up to Mr Gurdjieff. The rest of us slept happily and soundly on the wooden floor.

During our stay, from conversations with the local peasants, Mr Gurdjieff learned that somewhere in the surrounding mountains there was a dolmen and that certain hunters knew how to find it. The study of dolmens was one of the original aims of our 'scientific expedition', so the next day found us all going up into the mountains with these hunters as our guides.

They brought us to an area almost completely covered by a thick growth of hazel bushes and oleanders. Forcing our way through this undergrowth, we reached a small clearing, where we found the dolmen. The area looked as though it had been inhabited many years before. The hunters said that at one time peasants had used the stones as a chicken house.

This dolmen was a heavy stone box, seven or eight feet square and about the same in height, hollowed out of a single rock. The walls were seven or eight inches thick, covered tightly by a single flat stone that projected beyond the box on all sides. In one of the sides was a perfectly round hole, ten or twelve inches in diameter. With difficulty, my wife managed to squeeze through this hole, but she found the dolmen completely empty. I remember that this opening faced towards the south-east.

There was a theory that the dolmens were sacrificial altars, but this is very doubtful. Mr Gurdjieff said that they might have been road signs, pointing the way to places of initiation. He asked the hunters whether they knew of any more dolmens in those woods, but they said they had not seen any.

Then he took some measurements, from which he determined a direction for us to follow through the undergrowth. To keep our line straight, he told us to mark it at intervals with sticks, to which we attached handkerchiefs. We had to hack our way with axes through heavy, virgin forest. After some time we came upon another dolmen, completely covered with grass and bushes, but intact. Still further on a third was found, but the stone cover of this one lay broken nearby. Again there was nothing inside. This discovery of Mr Gurdjieff's was the result of calculation and astonished us as much as it did the hunters, who thought they knew their country perfectly.

The descent from the place of the dolmens was dangerously steep. Our guides took us out of the thickest part of the forest, but there was no path to follow and the angle of the hill was about forty-five degrees. We asked our guides how best to get down and they told us with great seriousness: 'By sliding on your bottom!' Mr Gurdjieff laughed heartily and this expression often turned up afterwards in difficult situations.

The next evening we reached the beautiful Black Sea town of Sochi, which was now in the hands of the Georgians. I said to Mr Gurdjieff: 'Last year you took me dying to the hospital of this same town, and now I am back here again, alive and healthy.'

'How will you thank me?' he asked.

I replied: 'By trying to understand your work with me.'

In Sochi we had rooms in the best hotels, with windows opening on the Black Sea. Before supper, washed and dressed in our best clothes, we gathered in the drawing-room of the hotel where Mr

Gurdjieff was staying. Pointing to the piano, he asked my wife to sing the 'Bell Song' from *Lakmé*, as if she had not just finished a two-month walk.

It was in these pleasant surroundings that we ate an excellent supper of *borshch*, bread and minced cutlets with potatoes, followed by sweet pastries – altogether a complete contrast to the privations we had endured for so long.

But as we left the dining-room, thinking of hours of sleep in bed, Mr Gurdjieff said: 'Thoma Alexandrovich!' – which he called me on special occasions when he wished to be formal and which never preceded anything agreeable – 'Tomorrow, early, not later than six, get up and go to the hotel on the square. Our horses are there. Give them oats and water.' So in spite of my yearning for a long, long sleep – how beautiful to sleep in a real bed, by a window opening on to the quiet moonlit sea! – I had to get up and go out to the horses with one foot in a boot and the other, owing to the festering toe, in a bedroom slipper. But the idea of fairy-tales, promising that you will reach your goal only by overcoming all obstacles and difficulties, was happily so strong in me that I felt no silent protest. In spite of all apparent tiredness, when one takes the right course one finds that inner energy increases, new force appears and it begins to be easier to make new efforts.

After this chore I changed my clothes while my wife prepared breakfast. Zhukov came and we all had tea with sugar, corn bread and the dry Caucasian cheese we had to fry slightly in a pan.

The next day our horses were transferred to a shed in front of our hotel. I continued to have the task of looking after them. Each morning, dressed in my old coat and odd footwear, two pails in my hands, I went to the kitchen of the hotel to get food for our animals. After having cleaned the horses, I returned with the pails to the hotel, passing among the tables where all the fashionable people, many of them acquaintances, were drinking their morning coffee. It is strange, but I was not embarrassed as I had been when I went to sell silk in Kislovodsk.

*

Mr Gurdjieff suddenly announced that the expedition was finished. He advised us to make our own plans for the future, as he had no more money to support any of us. I decided at once that, whatever happened, my wife and I would not leave him. So, as Mr Gurdjieff decided to stay in Sochi for the moment, we had to try to organize our life there somehow. Dr Stjernvall, his wife and Zhukov also remained. The Moscow people decided to return to Essentuki, which the White Army had now taken back from the Bolsheviks and where two of them had left their mothers. Zakharov went with them. All this was very sad, for we never saw them again. Zakharov died from smallpox in Rostov; the others went to Maikop, where Petrov became director of a state school. Mr Gurdjieff asked him to come to Tiflis when we went there, but he did not come. And when the Bolsheviks again conquered the whole northern Caucasus, he returned to Moscow. Soon, even correspondence with him became impossible.

After our companions left, we went around the city to find a place to live. Passing a very nice two-storey villa in a garden, my wife remarked that such a place would be perfect for us. The next morning she passed the house again and, seeing that there was a room with a veranda available on the second floor, rented the room at once. The owners were nice people and the landlady taught my wife to cook, to iron and to do all kinds of household chores, which was very helpful since she had never done anything of the kind before. Zhukov also found a room in the same house. The Stjernvalls stayed nearby with some friends. Mr Gurdjieff came to live quite near us at his cousin's. Again it was as if everything had been prepared in advance.

The horses were now quartered quite far away and I had to go every day to feed them. Besides this, Mr Gurdjieff gave me a new task: to unstitch both of our big tents, which were made of white canvas with dark blue stripes. This resulted in a good length of material that peasants liked for trousers. When I was finished, he said: 'Tomorrow you will go in the morning to the bazaar and sell it.'

'For how much?'

'For a very high price', and he suggested an amount.

This time I felt no hesitation or embarrassment, only fear that I might not be able to get the high price. I went to the market and saw that the best locations were already occupied. As I was a complete novice in such affairs, I spread the canvas on the grass at the edge of the market and waited. Everyone passed by and no one even glanced my way. Finally, one came over to me, then another; they looked at the canvas and left without even asking the price. Then they came back and asked. But they would not even listen when I told the price Mr Gurdjieff wished me to ask. Perhaps it was too high? Perhaps they pretended it was? I did not wish to sell for less, but as more people came and left, I finally decided to lower the price. At once one bought, then another, then a third, and even little pieces were sold in about a minute. When I gave the money to Mr Gurdjieff, he said: 'You could not sell it for the proper amount.' But I saw he was satisfied.

The next day I had to sell a large, heavy tarpaulin. I put it on my shoulder and went to the middle of the market-place. I was already an 'old hand'. Mr Gurdjieff told me to ask 500 roubles – a price that no one would consider. But finally a man in a bowler hat stopped and I quickly called to him to buy. He agreed, but asked that the tarpaulin be brought to his home. I put it on my shoulder and we started off. At that moment I heard someone call: 'Thoma Alexandrovich, what are you doing here?' I looked up and saw the doctor who had cured me of typhoid a year earlier in the hospital here. We were very glad to see each other, to the great astonishment of the man in the bowler, who found out from the doctor who I was. He became quite friendly with us and later bought our horses.

I was sent several more times to deal at the bazaar. My 'swan-song' was the sale of a light wool scarf. I had already sold it and was walking home when the old woman who had bought it caught up to me and said, 'Your scarf has little holes in it. Give some money back!'

As a result of my experience, I would advise all would-be

businessmen and financiers, right up to ministers of finance, to spend one day on the receiving end of bargaining in a bazaar. In the West it is no longer possible to experience and understand this psychology.

My wife also had quite an experience at this time. One of Mr Gurdjieff's cousins was in the final stage of consumption. Dr Stjernvall was treating him but, after staying up for several nights, he was tired and Mr Gurdjieff asked my wife whether she wished to stay one night with the sick man. She said she would, and it turned out to be his last night. He died while my wife lifted him to ease an attack of coughing. Until then she had never seen a man die and she said she had the astonishing impression that a light had been switched off.

A new life began for us in Sochi. I never again had to sell anything at the market. I now returned to music professionally and my wife began to use her singing to earn money. These activities were very successful, so our musical 'fast' had not been harmful. With Mr Gurdjieff, neither fasting nor labouring lasted very long. It seemed that each phase would never be finished, but the end always came unexpectedly soon.

Zhukov became acquainted with the director of the Sochi post office, a very kind man and a lover of the arts. It turned out that in the post office building there was a big hall with a stage and a second-rate piano, which served for local concerts and soirées. The director put all this at our disposal and Zhukov became our 'impresario'. In less than a month he had posters printed advertising a concert to be held on 15 December, which was to feature my wife under the stage name of O. A. Arkadieva, proposed by Zhukov himself. She would sing operatic arias from *Figaro*, *Traviata* and *Tosca*. And I would accompany her and also play some of my own compositions. Zhukov persuaded Philippovich to join the programme to sing a group of Polish songs and a duet from *Thaïs* with my wife.

It now appeared that Mr Gurdjieff was very right in insisting that we bring good clothing in our expedition sacks. However, the robbers had taken my wife's best dress, so she had nothing left suitable for the stage. Madame Ostrovsky provided her with an evening dress, but since Madame Ostrovsky was a much larger woman, they had to alter it. On the day of the concert, with needle and thread and pins, they made the necessary changes, and that evening it looked just as it should. Mr Gurdjieff came to listen to us. You see, in spite of all we had done together, he had never heard me play the piano or my wife sing in public until we came to Sochi.

At Zhukov's urging I started giving piano lessons to some very nice young ladies from the post office, who began to study seriously. During the Christmas season he organized a second concert for us with Philippovich, as well as a stage play that he was putting on himself. These proved to be Zhukov's last projects with us, as he then decided to move to Novorossiisk. Meanwhile he had helped very much to make life happier and financially easier for us. All this time beautiful surroundings and warm weather contributed to our general well-being, and we lived very freely.

Two or three times, always late at night, Mr Gurdjieff sent me to get *douziko* – a Greek drink of which he was very fond – not at a store, but at someone's house. I would have to find the place, climb up the outer staircase, knock and wake up the people, and all this to ask for *douziko*. It was a lesson in 'inner considering', to overcome my dread of waking and disturbing people, who could either chase me away or curse me, or both, and often did.

Sochi at this time belonged to Georgia – a new socialist state including both Armenians and Tatars – whose capital was Tiflis, or Tbilisi in the Georgian language. Mr Gurdjieff had been going almost every day to the Georgian Officers' Club in the big hotel where he had stayed the first night. The club was not only for the officers, but also for rich merchants and wealthy people from St Petersburg and Moscow who had escaped to the south. Every evening they played cards, a game called 'vint',* which was then very fashionable, and Mr Gurdjieff could play it very well. It was only later that I understood why Mr Gurdjieff was so keen on card-playing at that time; it enabled him to keep up to date concerning all political events.

The Volunteer Army was drawing near. Fighting could start at any time in Sochi, and that would be the moment for Mr Gurdjieff to leave in the direction of Tiflis, where the old regime still existed. Zhukov had already left for Novorossiisk, but we and the Stjernvalls would go with Mr Gurdjieff. The only means of reaching Tiflis at this time was by boat to Poti at the east end of the Black Sea, and from there on by train.

* A Russian card game that was a forerunner of bridge.

XII
Tiflis

In the middle of January, when the weather was very cold and windy and the sea very rough, Mr Gurdjieff came and told us to pack all our things so that on hearing the ship's whistle we could be on the pier within one hour. The next day we heard it, but on account of a heavy storm the ship was unable to dock. Two days later a whistle was heard again. It was still too rough for even little boats to come right to the shore, so we had to reach them by means of very narrow planks. On the ship itself there was no comfort because it turned out to be very small and crowded with people and vermin. We stayed on the upper deck in the rain one whole night and day. Then it turned sunny and quite cold, with a head wind. It became very dangerous, because delay meant that the fuel might not last. The captain was happy when we finally reached the pier at Poti.

Although Poti is not so far from Sochi, and further south, there was a heavy frost. A driver at the pier asked a very high price to take us to the station, but we had to hire him. We stayed the night at the station, because the train for Tiflis would not leave until the next morning. The station was unimaginably dirty and crowded with civilians and soldiers. But, luckily, one of the train-men was very nice and allowed us to go into an empty car and spend the night there.

At eight the next evening, in terrible cold, we reached Tiflis. Mr Gurdjieff was met at the station by the Turadzhevs, his cousins. My wife and I had stayed at the Orient Hotel some years before and knew that the prices there were prohibitive, so together with the Stjernvalls we hired an *izvozchik** and told him to take us to an inexpensive hotel. We crossed the Kura River, went up the mountainside and drove along the Golovinsky Prospect, the main street of Tiflis. We were taken to a very seedy hotel near the Opera House. We never thought we could endure a stay in such a hotel, but what to do? We had no protection from the bitter frost, as we had only summer coats, so we went in and rented rooms.

Our room had two primitive iron beds with mattresses and pillows stuffed with straw. No sign of sheets or blankets. In one corner was a cylindrical stove, on which had been scrawled a detailed encyclopaedia of indecent words. We had to go out to buy something to eat, and found wonderful Caucasian apples and corn bread. That was our first supper in Tiflis. The indecent stove worked well, and we lay down at once, with our coats for blankets, and slept soundly.

The Stjernvalls were less lucky. Facing on to the Golovinsky, their sleep was interrupted by street altercations and the marching of soldiers, for at that time Tiflis was occupied by English and American detachments.

The next day, on my way to see Mr Gurdjieff, I was just approaching the bridge over the Kura River when I ran into my old friend, the composer Nikolai Nikolayevich Tcherepnin. He was as astonished as I was to meet on the streets of Tiflis. We shook hands and I asked, 'What are you doing here?'

'I am the director of the Conservatory. And what are *you* doing here?'

'Well, as you see, I am standing in the street.'

'So? We just happen to need a professor of composition . . .'

Within two days I had a class in composition and a large class in theory for beginners.

Now we could afford to live more comfortably. For example, every day I now brought two dinners home from a restaurant

---

* *Izvozchik*: a carriage driver.

instead of one as before, and each morning and evening we ate corn bread with 'tea' that we made from apple skins. The winter remained cold and we had only summer clothing, but we had faith that with Mr Gurdjieff nothing too awful could happen.

Soon we could afford to look for better accommodation. We found a comfortable room with some nice people who had a piano in their drawing-room, which they put at my disposal. There I could practise and compose.

During this period when the old regime was still in control of Tiflis Tcherepnin remained as director of the conservatory belonging to the Imperial Music Society. The Conservatory of Tiflis served the whole of the Caucasus and 2,000 pupils were enrolled. In my composition class there were twelve very talented young men, among them Tcherepnin's son Alexandre (who is now a very well-known composer). In general, Tiflis was a town of great culture; there was an opera house as large as the Opéra-Comique in Paris, a drama theatre with a revolving stage, as well as Georgian and Armenian clubs with theatrical halls. In short, owing to Tcherepnin, I at once found myself in the centre of the artistic, theatrical and cultural life of the city. Very soon the director of the state opera suggested that I join the artistic committee of the theatre, which was then planning a gala spectacle with a great singer from St Petersburg as Carmen. Tcherepnin was also the conductor of the Opera House orchestra and proposed that my wife, though she had never sung in a whole opera, take the part of Micaela, saying, 'We will finally have a Micaela who really looks like a young girl.'

I asked who would design the scenery for this special performance and was told that it would be done by a very great artist named de Salzmann. This name at once awakened memories of my days in Munich, where I had studied conducting with Felix Mottl. At that time an Alexandre von Salzmann* had been a very

---

* In Tsarist Russia, after French became the official court language, aristocrats of German origin changed the 'von' in their name to the French 'de'.

well-known young painter, with whom I had struck up a warm friendship. I asked his full name and, learning that it was the same painter, went to find him. We renewed our old ties and from then on saw each other daily in the theatre. He had actually been born in Tiflis, where his father was the State architect, who designed most of the educational institutions as well as the governor's residence and the Opera House. Although de Salzmann was always cordial with me, he did not invite me to his home. Later we found out that when he had spoken about us to his wife, she had said: 'Bring him, but not his wife.' He had replied: 'No, that is not possible; ask both or neither will come.'

At that time I could not invite him to visit us because we never invited anybody – Mr Gurdjieff did not wish it. Some weeks later, however, Mr de Salzmann asked us to come to his home, where he introduced us to his quite young wife, Jeanne, whom he had met in Hellerau, in Germany. As Jeanne Matignon, she had been a pupil of Emile Jaques-Dalcroze there, and later one of his chief artistic assistants and a performer in his celebrated production of *Orpheus*. Alexandre had created the lighting system in the Hellerau theatre, based on a quite new principle. All who had seen it were struck by its beautiful effects and the rich opportunities it could offer. But the war ended all further development of such experiments and now fate had brought husband and wife to Tiflis.

Madame de Salzmann was then expecting her first child and did not go out socially. She was teaching the Dalcroze system of dancing and held her classes in the hall of the military school, which was large and had a very good piano. She was planning a demonstration, already set for 22 June, at which she was to show her class in the State Opera Theatre, since the Dalcroze Institute in Tiflis was under the patronage of the Georgian government.

We began to see the de Salzmanns quite frequently and soon our conversation turned to the subject of Mr Gurdjieff's teaching without any mention of his name. The question was raised of the necessity of a guide, a teacher, and we were able to say that we were fortunate enough to know such a man. When we saw the de Salzmanns' sincere interest and eager desire to know who this man was, we spoke about them to Mr Gurdjieff and he permitted us to bring them to him. And so at Easter time we went with them to Mr Gurdjieff. The conversation, as I vividly remember, was very interesting. After they had left, we asked Mr Gurdjieff his impression and he said: 'He is a very fine man, and she – is intelligent.'

Madame de Salzmann, having learned from us about the Sacred Gymnastics given in Essentuki, asked Mr Gurdjieff to come to see the work of her pupils. So one day we went with him to her class. The pupils, all young, pretty girls in Greek costumes, stood in a circle in the middle of a very big hall. Mr Gurdjieff greeted them, watched with interest for five or ten minutes, and left. Some days later he came again and at once ordered them, in a military tone, to straighten their lines, to dress left, to dress right. Then he put them all in one row in front of him and said: 'Before beginning any work in Sacred Gymnastics, you must learn how to turn.' He showed them how to turn in the military way, this turning being accompanied by my chords on the piano. I was very surprised by all this. When we had arrived that first day in Essentuki and Mr and Madame Ouspensky and the others had done this military turning, I had not been surprised. Here I could imagine the reactions of these young Dalcroze dancers, who must have dreamed only about graceful Greek dances. But to my further astonishment all passed very smoothly and regular work with them started. The result was that Madame de Salzmann offered Mr Gurdjieff a part of her demonstration to show his Sacred Gymnastics and Sacred Dances.

A flyer advertised:

An Evening Programme of the School of
Jeanne Matignon-Salzmann:
    Part I – Method of Jaques-Dalcroze
    Part II – System of G. I. Gurdjieff

Mr Gurdjieff's part of the programme read as follows:

1. Exercises of plastic gymnastics Nos. 3, 9, 12, 15, 17, 21, 23
2. Exercises from ancient sacred dances Nos. 23, 24, 25
3. Stop
4. Fragment of a round dance from the 3rd act of *The Struggle of the Magicians* by G. I. Gurdjieff.
5. Fragment of the mystery *Exile*, also by him.

After the great success of the first demonstration Mr Gurdjieff decided to give another. But this time he wished to give everyone a very different experience: it would be a new demonstration with none of the Dalcroze dances and nothing staged by Madame de Salzmann. The majority of the young girls were admirers of her and of Dalcroze and began to protest. In addition, since the girls were to take part in Mr Gurdjieff's Gymnastics, he told Madame de Salzmann to tell them they all would be paid a little. This was entirely too much for them. They all refused the money with disdain and began to protest seriously. It was a great worry to Madame de Salzmann. How easy it would have been for her to slip away from the great aim of Mr Gurdjieff's Work, in self-love and vanity. But here she was really wise: not a hint of offence was visible. With the whole force of her authority and the feeling of the rightness of Mr Gurdjieff's Work, she was able to persuade her pupils to take part in the new 'exercises', and the demonstration took place after intensive work.

The theatre was less than crowded. However, the aim was not to have many people, but rather to create conditions for a new experience, first of all, perhaps, for Madame de Salzmann herself. She was one of three principal dancers who had accompanied Dalcroze everywhere in Europe in all his model demonstrations. To work with Mr Gurdjieff she would have to sacrifice what she had worked for from youth, both for herself and for her girls.

*

At the beginning of May, during the preparations for the first demonstration, Mr Gurdjieff's brother had arrived unexpectedly. He had remained in Essentuki when we left for the trip through the mountains. It was in the basement of his house that we had hidden our trunks filled with the belongings we had brought with us from St Petersburg, because we feared they would be taken by the Bolsheviks. He now brought the news that the White Army had discovered the trunks though they were carefully concealed beneath piles of stove-wood. Thinking that they were stolen goods hidden by the Bolsheviks, the soldiers had confiscated them. The priceless antique porcelain had been smashed, the linen distributed to the hospitals and the furs divided among the officers. It was only when they came to a trunk containing my manuscript music with my name on it that the officer in command realized that the contents of the trunk actually belonged to a well-known composer and Guards officer. He ordered the remaining belongings to be taken to his own home. Unhappily, what was left consisted only of some furs, my manuscripts and a number of articles of little value. The officer told Mr Gurdjieff's brother that the owner could come and claim his property whenever he wished.

Mr Gurdjieff immediately decided that someone had to go to Essentuki to get what was left of our things and also to try to find the carpets he had stored there. A man could not go, because he would certainly be seized by either the White or the Red Army. It had to be one of our women, and Mr Gurdjieff decided that my wife was the only one who would be able to accomplish such a task. The following is an account of the trip in her own words.

When Mr Gurdjieff asked me to go, I was filled with terror because never in my life had I even walked in the street alone. Before my marriage, custom demanded that I always be accompanied by someone; afterwards, my husband was with me. Now I had to undertake, for these relatively insignificant things, a dangerous journey in absolutely unknown conditions. It was impossible to go directly to Essentuki through the Caucasus mountains, since the war had closed all roads. I had to take the train from Tiflis to Batum, then the boat to Novorossiisk, and finally the train to Essentuki. The return journey had to be made by the same route. What kind of accommodation, if any, would be available in wartime?

Preparations were made for my adventure. Friends gave me letters of introduction: one to their great friend, Levandovsky, in Batum, whose son was an officer in the regiment there, and a second to the manager of the best hotel. Mr Gurdjieff knew that paper money differed from district to district, so he gave me some gold coins, which I sewed inside my belt. In addition, he gave me a mysterious little box in which he said there was a special pill that I could take in case of extreme necessity; but he said he would be very pleased if I could bring it back to him untouched. The decision to accept this challenge was a very difficult one for my husband and me to make. I accepted it, but I confess that there was also a feeling of pride and vanity – not to show fear and to be able to rise to this challenge.

Next day I took the overnight train to Batum. Travel on the railway was terrible, women and men together in crowded compartments. I cried all night through, but luckily I couldn't even imagine what lay ahead.

I reached Batum the next morning and went at once to the hotel with my letter of introduction. The owner was not there; I spoke with his son, who said that he was very sorry, there were no rooms at all and that putting a bed in a sitting-room or dining-room was out of the question since they would all be filled with camp-beds for men. However, he suggested that I return later when his father would be in.

Leaving my little suitcase at the hotel, I went with my other letter of introduction to find the Levandovskys; but they had moved away without leaving any address. So here I was in a strange city, without a friend and without even knowing where I was going to sleep for the night.

I went to get information about boat passage to Novorossiisk *and found that the first possibility was a poor old boat that would sail in two days. The captain, an old man with a long beard, said there were no cabins and that he would not permit me to go down in the hold with the men, who were oriental tradesmen and salesmen. His only suggestion was that I sleep on a bench in the dining-room. Bravely, I bought my ticket — and then he told me I would need a visa . . .*

The English were occupying Batum at this time. When I went to get my visa for the trip to Novorossiisk and back again, the young officer said he could give me a visa only for the trip from Batum to Novorossiisk. Feeling uncertain, I did not wish to trust the young officer, and asked to speak to a senior one. After great discussion, I persuaded the commander of the English forces to give me a return permit, which he wrote on a small scrap of paper; paper was very scarce during wartime. I keep it still as a souvenir.

Happy to have succeeded with the visa, I went back to the hotel. The owner had not yet returned, and I again asked his son if some place couldn't be found for me. He gave me the same answer as before. I was in despair. Then an idea struck him, and he said that he and his friend lived in a little two-room cottage in his father's garden and that the two could share one room, leaving me the other. I accepted this arrangement at once with relief and naïveté, and we went to see the little cottage, which was very nice, deep in the garden, surrounded by beautiful trees. I was delighted. . . . We left my little suitcase there and I went to look for a place to eat.

On the street I unexpectedly met a singer and his wife whom my husband and I had known slightly in Tiflis. They were astonished to see me there alone and, having learned about my garden arrangement, thought it very unwise and asked me to stay with them in their hotel room, sleeping on their mattresses, which they proposed to put on the floor for me. However, I felt that the boys were quite nice and preferred to have a room to myself rather than to sleep on the floor and embarrass people whom I knew so slightly. So these friends said they would take me out for dinner

*and then take me to the cottage to show the boys that I was not
without friends in town.*

*We returned to the cottage early, and they left me saying they
would come to see me in the morning. I began to unpack and
install myself, and it was only then that I noticed that there was
no lock on the door. I wedged a heavy chair against it and slept
like a stone. In the morning I was awakened by a noise like a
locomotive going by, but found that it was the boys preparing
coffee on a Primus stove for me. They had already bought some
bread and a little milk. They were so nice and thoughtful that I
will never forget them.*

*I went back to town hoping to find a police station where I
could inquire about the Levandovskys. On the way I met an
officer, stopped him and asked where the regimental headquarters
were located. He in return asked me whom I was looking for in
the regiment, and when I replied, 'Lieutenant Levandovsky', he
answered: 'But I am Levandovsky!' It was too amazing . . . He at
once took me to his parents, with whom I stayed until my boat
left two days later.*

*All my new friends came to see me off, and I felt they were
very anxious about my journey. The boat sailed in the evening
and I sat on the deck. But soon the weather became very rough
and the captain said I should take his cabin, as I could not
remain on the deck. He assured me he would be outside on
watch all through the night, since a heavy storm was approaching. Feeling relieved and even happy at having a bed to sleep
on, I fell fast asleep. But in the middle of the night I awoke to
find the boat rolling alarmingly in the heavy sea; the captain's
coat hanging against the wall over my head was swinging like a
pendulum. I held in my hand the mysterious little box, thinking
that I would use the pill only if the ship went down. The tem-
pest was raging, there was terrible lightning and thunder, and it
was my first sea voyage alone . . . But, nevertheless, I finally fell
asleep and in the morning awoke to find the captain asleep at
the other end of the same couch. Later he told me that the
storm had been so severe he had been forced to steer a course*

for Trebizond, in Turkey, opposite to the direction of our destination, and that this meant we would be another night at sea.

I knew that the captain would be too tired to sit up another
night, so I decided on one of the benches in the dining-saloon,
where we took our meals. Unfortunately, a Greek passenger also
decided to sleep on one of the other benches and, during the
night, he woke me and wanted to start conversation. I quickly
jumped up and went to the captain's cabin and sat there near his
door, where I would be safe without awakening him. The Greek
followed me, but knowing that I would wake the captain if he
bothered me, he disappeared.

It was evening when we at last reached Novorossiisk and I
went at once to the house of Zhukov, who had remained in
touch with us. He was delighted to see me and at once arranged
his dining-room for me, putting his bed there. He had to sleep
on the floor in his bedroom. I told him why I had come and
we took the first train to Essentuki, as he did not wish me to
go alone.

In Essentuki I looked first of all for Mr and Madame Ouspensky
and, on entering their house, I saw Mr Ouspensky walking back
and forth carrying in his arms a little baby, who was crying
lustily. It was Lonya Savitsky, the son of Madame Ouspensky's
daughter. Then I went to see the commandant of the White
Army to ask about our belongings. He said he was very sorry
that almost everything had been taken before it was known that
they belonged to us. I told him that I regretted only the old
family miniatures, which were quite irreplaceable. He asked
what they were like and brought some miniatures from his
room, saying he had preserved them as they were so beautiful.
They were ours and I recovered them with great happiness. In
the trunks I found only valueless things, except for a good astrakhan coat and some manuscripts of my husband's music,
which were not so important because they had already been
printed. But among the pages there were eight beautiful old Persian miniatures, which were quite priceless. So, from everything
we had packed in the trunks, I collected just one bundle of

valuables. But a small suitcase, which I particularly hoped to find, was not there at all.

Then I went with Zhukov to look for Mr Gurdjieff's carpets at a special place where many were displayed for people to claim. I was able to identify two, one small, one large. The guard said that those were already claimed and if I wished to dispute it, I would have to bring another witness. Fortunately, Zhukov was there and he provided the required testimony. So I was able to bring back to Mr Gurdjieff two antique carpets.

Zhukov and I returned at once to Novorossiisk and I began to look for a ship to return to Batum. I was told that there hadn't been one for six months and that no visas were being given. I was frantic, since everybody said it was useless even to try. I found some sailors who said they would take me to Batum for a certain amount of money, but Zhukov forbade me this adventure ... However, I continued to search for a boat and two days later happened to see on the street a very small announcement that said that a transport company had a boat leaving the next day at six in the morning. I rushed to the indicated office and asked for passage. They told me that it was quite impossible, as one had to have a visa and the price of the ticket in gold. I said I had both. They would not believe me, saying that the English were giving permission to no one. I insisted that I would bring both the visa and the gold at once. They agreed to wait only ten minutes, no more, as they closed the office at noon. I went outside and, on a street corner, took off my belt, in which I had sewn the gold coins and the visa, and re-entered the office triumphantly. They sold me my ticket and I ran home to Zhukov full of joy.

Next morning at six, with my bundles in a hired, horse-drawn carriage, Zhukov and I arrived at the pier. There was a great crowd of black-bearded and dirty Greek and Armenian merchants; no women at all. Out in the Black Sea an English warship was visible and, to my astonishment, I discovered this was to be my boat. An English officer came to verify the visas and when he saw my visa and my passport, and found out that I was the wife of a Guards officer, he said that it was impossible for me to sail, since there were no cabins and no ladies could travel in the hold. I said I would be quite happy if they allowed me to stay on the deck, since I had to go no matter what. A little later the officer came back and told me in no case to go down in the hold, but to stay on deck near the smokestack with my baggage.

I said goodbye to Zhukov and went on board, taking my place on the deck. In a few minutes a smart English steward approached me, took my bags and led me to a cabin with four bunks. I asked, a little annoyed, who the other occupants were; he replied that the cabin was for me alone. He added that tea would be served at once and that in two hours he would bring me breakfast. There was even a bath in the cabin. At noon an officer came and brought me an invitation from the captain to have meals at his table. I enjoyed wonderful food in the company of the captain and twelve officers – this, after all my hardships ... In the evening after dinner we all sat in armchairs on the deck, the officers vying with each other to be entertaining and attentive. It was a beautiful, starry night, such a contrast to the trip from Batum, and I was even a little disappointed that the voyage was over so soon. In Batum I again met by chance my friends from Tiflis, and they could not believe that I was back from Essentuki within a week.

I took the first train to Tiflis and was quickly home, to the astonishment and delight of my husband, who was sitting on the balcony in the morning as I came in at the wicket-gate. He had not expected me to return for some time. I gave Mr Gurdjieff the two carpets and the little box with the pill in it. He was very pleased and said that the returned box was the best of all.

For Mr Gurdjieff, certainly, the carpets were not important, nor were our belongings to us. They were just a pretext to have me thrown alone into life, to see how I could manage in conditions far more difficult than anyone, even Mr Gurdjieff, could imagine in advance. And most important of all was to see whether we both could accept such a task and deal with it.

XIII
Musical Interlude

From the very beginning of our stay in Tiflis my wife and I had also been working very hard on our musical activities. We needed to become more widely known to attract more pupils and engagements. I had to prepare a repertoire for chamber music concerts and coach my wife in singing for her forthcoming performances.

I remember how, an hour and a half before one of these concerts, Mr Gurdjieff had a lesson with Madame de Salzmann's girls and I had to play for the Gymnastics – not quite the usual thing for a concert artist. I even had to demonstrate for the girls some difficult exercises that we had had in Essentuki: one was to put all the weight of the body on the hands while the feet made very strong rapid movements. And Mr Gurdjieff stopped the class only half an hour before my concert in the town hall.

The girls changed their dresses, and Mr Gurdjieff with Madame de Salzmann, taking all the girls along, went to the concert. The girls were much impressed by a man who could do difficult gymnastic movements and then almost at once play a concert. I knew Mr Gurdjieff wished to show how people working with him had to be able to function on different levels, so he made it as a kind of test for me: what kind of pianist was I?

Soon my wife also was tested when the time came for her to sing Micaela. It was very difficult because, although she had sung operatic arias occasionally in concerts, she was almost totally inexperienced in acting on the stage. On the eve of the performance she had quite a high temperature and was naturally nervous.

*

The dress rehearsal for Carmen went very well, and after it there was a meeting on the set. On one side of the stage sat the director, followed by Tcherepnin, Mr de Hartmann, Mr de Salzmann, the lead soprano (without whom the opera would not have taken place), and me. I was not considered an opera singer, only Mr de Hartmann's wife. The rest of the singers and opera members sat on the opposite side of the stage. I felt another kind of attitude towards me, a kind of jealousy from the other performers that had never occurred before during the rehearsals.

For the performance, Mr de Salzmann said he would come and help me put on my make-up. He told me to put on my costume and arrange my hair in two long braids, as the Bavarian mountain girls did. Tcherepnin was very nice to me and in all the rehearsals always reminded me not to pay attention to anything on stage, but only: 'Pay attention to my baton, to me, the conductor. There can always be mistakes on stage, so you have to attend to the orchestra and my baton.'

How thankful I was to him! During the performance Don José, in my scene with him, began to sing different words from those he had sung in rehearsal. I quickly looked at Tcherepnin, and he nodded and smiled, motioning to me with his hand to quietly continue, so I went on with my part as if Don José didn't exist. Since this was my first time in a real opera, I could very easily have been confused by someone singing the wrong words, and might have thought that I was the one who was making the mistakes.

In the intermission Tcherepnin came to see me and told me, 'Now in the last act you are alone in the mountains and do not have to worry about your partner. So only sing as you feel and I will follow you.'

When I entered the scene in the fourth act, I saw a black spot at the back of the hall. Since I knew that no one in the audience would be wearing a black hat, I knew it was Mr Gurdjieff who was there, and that probably helped me very much. He had told me once, 'If you are afraid, just look, and I will be there; sing and think about no one else in the hall.' I really sang my prayer of

Micaela quite wonderfully, dropping to my knees and taking the high C pianissimo, holding it for a long time, with feeling. I received an unexpected round of applause.

Later, I had to repeat Micaela a few times and I also began to learn Gilda from Rigoletto.

Nevertheless, I was not well and became weaker and weaker. Mr de Salzmann took me to a good doctor, whom he knew. The doctor told me I had something wrong with my lungs and that if I didn't leave at once for a sanatorium in the mountains, he could not answer for my health. Certainly we could not afford to go to the big sanatorium, which was in Austria, so I told all this to Mr Gurdjieff, asking his advice.

Mr Gurdjieff told me to eat bacon every morning and asked me to bring him a bottle of red wine, which he kept for several days. Then he told me to drink a little glass of it before eating any food. I had to lie in the open air on the terrace, although it was winter. Every day I lay there, covered with all the blankets we had, from twelve to one o'clock. I did everything that Mr Gurdjieff demanded, and in three weeks I went with Mr de Salzmann again to the same doctor. After he had examined me, he told me how glad he was that I had listened to him and gone to the sanatorium, as there was practically no trace of infection left in my lungs. I told him that I had never gone, but had taken another treatment and that I was very happy that he could give me such a result from his examination.

During this time Mr Gurdjieff found a big hall, and Gymnastics and conversations with him began. He did not allow me to do Gymnastics, because he was afraid for my health; so I had to be the cashier and take in money from people who came to do them.

My activities began to widen. I wrote for newspapers. My first article concerned an Armenian composer, Komitas Vardapet,*

* Vardapet is the honorific title of a senior priest in the Armenian Orthodox Church. On becoming a vardapet, Soghomon Soghomonian chose Komitas as his personal name, and is everywhere known as Komitas Vardapet.

about whom I wrote a biographical sketch and a critical analysis of his choral music and compositions for solo voices. Later, I gave lectures about him as an introduction to concerts of his music. My wife took part in these concerts. She even learned some of his songs in Armenian, as we had an Armenian pupil, Lili Galumian, who taught her how to pronounce the words. The Armenians themselves did not know what a wonderful composer they had and did not realize the place he held in their culture.

In addition to the Armenian music, the Georgians asked me to work on their music, which I did for two or three hours a day. Practically every evening we had supper with the director of the Opera House, Mr de Salzmann and a specialist in Georgian music. There was much conversation about the next season, when I was to conduct several performances, and our friendly relations with the director of the theatre were strengthened.

Soon Mr Gurdjieff found another task for both my wife and me. At the beginning of July we were to go to Erivan, the capital of Armenia, and give several concerts. Thanks to my reputation among the Armenians and to my articles about their composer Komitas, we were able to arrange this. We were aided in this project by Philippovich, the Polish engineer at whose home we had stopped near the end of the expedition and who had sung in our concerts in Sochi. His interest in Mr Gurdjieff and his Work had brought him to Tiflis to join our group not long after we had come ourselves. He, too, learned some songs of Komitas, and went with us to help organize the concerts and sing in some of them as well.

The trip by train presented many difficulties, as the war with the Turks had just ended. The railway passed through places badly devastated by the retreating armies, who had even destroyed most of the seats in the passenger coaches. We had to sprinkle the floor with disinfectant to avoid lice and vermin, which could have carried typhus.

As a result of the Turkish invasion, the Armenians were close to starvation. President Khatisov of the Armenian Republic told me that only a month before he himself had seen hundreds of people in the streets dying of starvation. However, by the time we arrived, American flour had come and there was no longer widespread famine. Even so, when we passed the market-place, we saw several people sitting like corpses, homeless and starving, awaiting death.

From the station to the town of Erivan was a walk of about two versts, since there was no transport. There were also no rooms to be had in the hotels. Here again the wonderful Eastern hospitality came to our rescue. People whom we hardly knew helped us to find an apartment, which had just been vacated by some officers. The only furniture was an iron bed covered with planks. It was early July and very hot. Again fearing vermin, we obtained kerosene and poured it over the bed planks and on the floor round each leg of the bed, so that the bugs could not get up on to the bed. I had to sleep on the floor and I drew a magic circle of kerosene around my place. My wife slept on the planks. In the morning when waking her, I discovered a bedbug on her face. In spite of the kerosene, the vermin had crawled up the walls to the ceiling and dropped upon their booty!

For Philippovich it was worse. Some officers invited him to use the apartment of one of their comrades who was away. When he turned back the blanket on the bed, he was astonished to find a *black sheet* – until he saw it was bedbugs . . .

After the night on the train and a night in conditions like these, we had to prepare for a concert – booking a hall, printing the programme, typing announcements, visiting prominent people and arranging all other details. But this was easy when we took it as a 'task' that had to be carried out as well as possible.

Three concerts were announced: the first of European and Russian music; the second consisting of a lecture by me about Komitas and a recital of his songs in Armenian by my wife; the third, a mixed programme. As Armenia was at that time occupied by English forces, an English officer attended the second concert and came backstage to see us afterwards. He asked how we had reached Erivan from Tiflis during such a time and said that if we could let him know when we were returning, he would arrange better accommodation for us.

On the last day we were invited to have tea and spend the evening with Archbishop Sarpazan Horen. His house was situated in the highest part of Erivan, from which there was an almost vertical drop to the Zanga River. Beyond green prairies, which stretched right to the horizon, there stood the two peaks of Mount Ararat, one very high, the other somewhat lower, illuminated by the rays of the setting sun. When night fell, a full moon shone through the warm southern air and Mount Ararat was wrapped in a shroud of mist: an unforgettable sight. To accompany this vision there was special Eastern music, because the archbishop had also invited a relative of his who was one of the best players in Armenia of the *tar* – a kind of stringed instrument.

Through this trip to Erivan Mr Gurdjieff gave us another opportunity of listening to real Eastern music and musicians, so that I could better understand how he wished his own music to be written and interpreted. To value such experiences it was necessary to live with Mr Gurdjieff so that one could develop the power of attention and take in these impressions strongly, without the distracting non-essential associations.

For our return, the English officer had a special car attached to the train, in which we travelled very comfortably back to Tiflis.

Soon afterwards we went to spend a few weeks in Borzhom, where the theatre from Tiflis had moved for the summer season. It was a mountain resort of unusual beauty, about ten hours by train from Tiflis, with famous springs of mineral waters like Vichy's. Mr Gurdjieff also came there. Our life was absorbed with concerts, which I conducted and at which my wife sometimes sang.

One day Mr Gurdjieff brought his overcoat to my wife, showing her that although the outside was badly worn and faded, the inside was fine. (At that time nothing could be bought in Russia.) Could she turn the coat inside out? My wife was quite uncertain, never having sewn anything and fearing that if she tried to do it, Mr Gurdjieff would have no coat at all. But he said it was very easy: 'One just takes white thread to mark the seams before undoing them. Then one rips it open, and irons as one goes along, ironing out the old folds and ironing in the new. The whole secret of good sewing is the careful following of the white thread and the ironing,' he insisted. And all this had to be done by hand and with an iron heated on a Primus stove ... With great difficulty my wife finally finished it and Mr Gurdjieff wore it for many, many years. He often said: 'If you know how to do one thing well, you can do everything.'

XIV

The New Institute

Everyone returned to Tiflis in the autumn. There, Mr Gurdjieff was preparing for a centre of the Work like that in Essentuki, but corresponding to the conditions of life in Tiflis. It began on the terrace of the house where we lived, because the weather was still hot. There were Dr Stjernvall, the two de Salzmanns, and we two. Mr Gurdjieff briefly explained the ideas of the new Institute he wished to organize there. He told about the aim and methods of work and the day when he hoped to open the Institute. Then he asked us: 'What name would you give our new Institute?' We tried to think of a name that would connect with all that Mr Gurdjieff had just told us. He rejected every suggestion. Finally, as if we had been squeezing our brains like a tube of toothpaste, the word 'harmonious' came out.

Afterwards it was clear to me that Mr Gurdjieff had decided on a name some time earlier, but instead of giving it to us ready-made, he forced us to look for it, pushed us, tried to bring us closer to the main thought, till this word emerged. Finally we had the name that Mr Gurdjieff wanted. It was: 'Institute for the Harmonious Development of Man'.

Representations were now made to the Georgian government to furnish us with a building for the Institute, and they promised to find us a suitable house. Meanwhile, Mr Gurdjieff began to work in a similar way on the text of a brochure about the Institute. Here, too, he woke up our brains and made us actively strive to describe exactly the programme he intended to establish there. In fact, he succeeded in writing the whole brochure through us.

When the brochure was finished and ready for the printer, the question arose about what should be on the cover. In the evening as we sat at the de Salzmanns', Mr Gurdjieff asked Mr de Salzmann to draw his portrait in an oval frame. We were all extremely interested in this and Alexandre set to work at once. Soon a good likeness appeared, but what was our horror and despair when, around the portrait, Mr Gurdjieff obliged him to draw an iron, a sewing-machine – particularly odious to us – and all sorts of other tools, seemingly to represent instruments of harmonious development. When all this was printed on thin yellow paper, the whole brochure had the appearance of an advertisement in bad taste for a provincial occultist. It drove a nail into my heart. I saw it as another stone set in our path by Mr Gurdjieff, which we would have to jump over. As it turned out, there was, in fact, no stone and nothing to jump over, because we still didn't have a place to enrol anyone wishing to join the Institute. The house promised by the Georgian government had not yet materialized.

During this same period Gymnastics had started again, in the biggest room in the de Salzmanns' apartment. Mr Gurdjieff bought a baby grand piano, old and in very poor condition. At my reaction he said, 'Every fool can play on a good piano. You must know how to play on a bad one!'

We began with the 'Obligatory' exercises, which I joined in when not needed at the piano. I 'knew' them well, having had them in Essentuki, but to do what I knew was never easy. The first one was especially difficult for me. Based on simple movements, it became increasingly complicated, with arms, legs and head having their own sequences, with repetitions at different tempos. When everything was put together, I found it utterly impossible. I was like an old, rusted, revolving machine, with no attention for the transitions from one pose to the next. Other exercises I found easier: 'Salute', 'Arms Forward' and the so-called 'Mazurka'. But I came to recognize that none of these exercises

Cover design for the prospectus of the Institute drawn by
Alexandre de Salzmann in Tiflis, 1919. The Russian text says:
(*top*) To Know – To Understand – To Be;
(*middle*) The Science of the Harmonious Development of Man, method of G. I. Gurdjie
(*bottom*) Western Section.

could ever be done with only theoretical knowledge. To do them properly demanded a lot of energy and concentrated attention. When I first began them, I had wondered, like a naïve child, when we would begin to have esoteric exercises from Tibetan monasteries and Hindu temples. I had to learn that the value of an exercise does not lie in the knowledge of its source, but in what one experiences in doing it with conscious work.

Soon the de Salzmanns' room became too small for Gymnastics, because more people joined us. One of the pupils arranged with her father, a dentist named Weller, to loan us a big hall in his house until the promised building was found. At the same time the director of the State Theatre placed at Mr Gurdjieff's disposal an office next to his own. Mr Gurdjieff wasted no time. In the mornings, sitting in that office, he dictated to L. the text of *The Struggle of the Magicians*. In the evenings, at Weller's, he began the first rehearsals for staging *The Struggle of the Magicians*, telling us that the State Theatre would present it in the spring. He started with the scenes in which the same dancers make the beautiful movements of the pupils of the White Magician as well as the ugly, deformed movements of the pupils of the Black Magician.

There came a need to create music for the dances of different peoples, and Mr Gurdjieff gave us the different modes of several nationalities, and not only the modes but also single details peculiar to the character of each nationality. These modes served, later on, for the creation of music for a variety of exercises, which he gave from time to time.

At this point Mr Gurdjieff said to me personally: 'Give up everything else, leave everything: theatre, conservatory, concerts, lessons . . . everything.' But I saw very clearly that I should not and could not fulfil this demand because it would leave me entirely without money. So I answered that whenever I was needed for the Work I would be available and nothing would interfere with that, but, as for the rest of my time, I would do whatever I considered necessary. Of course, my work in the theatre had to be given up since it would have occupied the whole day. By teaching in the conservatory and by private music lessons, which were over at seven o'clock – Mr Gurdjieff never needed me before eight – I could earn my living and at the same time maintain my position as a composer. We never knew what would happen later on. To have given up everything would not have been right. I remembered that Mr Gurdjieff had said to me, 'If I told you to masturbate, would you listen to me?' The future showed that I was right in my decision.

Work continued, but the house for the Institute, promised by the government, still remained no more than a promise. Mr Gurdjieff declared he would end his Work in Tiflis. Hearing that, Dr Stjernvall and Mr de Salzmann became very energetic. Stjernvall, an expert negotiator, undertook to speak to the higher government officials. De Salzmann, besides talking to any other authorities and city councillors he knew personally, drew a cartoon for the satirical Georgian magazine called *The Devil's Whip* and very soon the cartoon appeared on its pages. It showed the main square of Tiflis, called Erivan Place, with all kinds of furniture and dishes and pots and pans thrown together around an old stove, and in the middle Mr Gurdjieff surrounded by his pupils all bundled up in their coats. The caption underneath read: 'A voice from the window: "Somehow he found space for his Work."' This made such an impression on the city officials that they gave us a two-storey house across the river with a large ground-floor hall.

The next problem was to furnish the house. First we had to prepare the hall for Gymnastics. We had a piano, but we needed something for all the people to sit on. So several of us went to a lumber yard to get wood for benches. Somewhere Mr Gurdjieff found a hammer, a rasp and a saw, and the carpentry began. He worked on everything himself and proved to be an expert carpenter. Benches for fifty to sixty people were made and painted a very dark brown, washed over wildly with various colours. The ensemble had a marvellous effect when they were placed around the walls or arranged in rows for visitors when there were lectures.

Mr Gurdjieff moved into the house and insisted that Mr and Madame de Salzmann, with their new baby daughter, Boussik,

above Olga de Hartmann in St Petersburg days

below Thomas de Hartmann at military school in St Petersburg

above Thomas and Olga de Hartmann shortly after they were married

below Olga de Hartmann in her costume for *La Traviata* in December 1916

above Thomas and Olga de Hartmann (first and second from left) at Essentuki, 1918

below Thomas de Hartmann conducting his orchestra in Constantinople, 1920

above Olga de Hartmann, Constantinople, 1920   *below* Thomas de Hartmann, 1921

above Thomas and Olga de Hartmann, Berlin, 1921
below Gurdjieff with his dogs and cat in Olginka, autumn 1917

above Olga de Hartmann at the Prieuré, 1926
below Thomas de Hartmann with Boris Ferapontov at the Prieuré, 1923

above The Study House at the Prieuré, Dr Leonid Stjernvall at left
below 'The Initiation of the Priestess' (from the demonstration at the
Théâtre des Champs-Elysées, December 1923)

above Thomas de Hartmann at the piano in his home in New York, 1955
below Olga de Hartmann at the Prieuré, *c.* 1967

ინსტიტუტი ჰარმონიულ განვითარების.

ფანჯრიდან. როგორც იქნა დაჯაბნავე ეს სასარგებლო დაწესებულება...

De Salzmann's cartoon in *The Devil's Whip*, 14 December 1919. Recognizable, besides Gurdjieff, are Thomas de Hartmann seated at left, Dr Stjernvall with long beard, and the artist himself in the lower right corner. The Georgian text says: (*top*) Institute of Harmonious Development; (*bottom*) A voice from the window: 'Somehow he found space for his work.'

should occupy one of the rooms. It was the same demand he had made on us in Essentuki.

At eight o'clock every evening, except Saturday and Sunday, Gymnastics began. One hour earlier the samovar was heated so the pupils could have a cup of tea with sugar and a little sweet bread. We, however, could not permit ourselves this treat, since Mr Gurdjieff charged a very high price for it, the same price charged by the only remaining café in Tiflis. He did this to see who would permit himself such a luxury. But at the same time the money helped to support the Institute.

Work on the exercises began to go very intensively. A special women's class was formed of the most talented and inwardly devoted pupils. With them Mr Gurdjieff developed those women's dances that later were shown in the public demonstrations in Paris.

Several times the director of the State Theatre sent about fifty of his Georgian students to study our exercises. They were not of the intelligentsia, but were nice, simple young people, dreaming of work in the theatre. Mr Gurdjieff gave them special, uncomplicated exercises, for which Lili Galumian was always the instructor. In one of them, for example, to a slow rhythm of 'one . . . two . . .', she improvised an arm position on 'one', which they copied on 'two', and on each succeeding 'one' she added legs, head, trunk or changed some elements, all of which had to be repeated by the others on 'two'.

Revenue from our pupils did not cover expenses of the Institute and no one had the time to earn extra money, so Mr Gurdjieff himself had to find ways to get what was necessary. One day I had gone to his flat to speak about something when the doorbell rang. Mr Gurdjieff told me, 'That is someone who wishes to buy a carpet. Go into the dining-room and stay there. I will open the door myself.'

The door between the dining-room and the sitting-room had glass panels, so I could see everything that went on there. Mr Gurdjieff went away to open the door, but didn't come back.

Instead, there came in a stranger and, after him, a carpet seller. They began to bargain. I was really shocked when I finally realized that this carpet seller was Mr Gurdjieff himself, totally transformed. It made me afraid just to see him so.

The stranger bought two carpets, I think, and went away. When Mr Gurdjieff came into the dining-room, I was still so shocked that I couldn't face him directly.

'What's the matter with you?' he asked.

'I cannot even look at you,' I said.

'Why not?'

'I didn't recognize you when I looked through the door.'

'What do you wish?' he asked. 'That I speak philosophy with him as I do with the doctor? Would he then buy a carpet? And if I would speak with Dr Stjernvall as I spoke with this man, he would never follow me. So you must understand that I am with each one such as they need from me. Right now I wish to sell carpets, so I have to be a carpet seller and not a philosopher.'

On Christmas Eve Mr Gurdjieff invited the de Salzmanns and the two of us to spend the evening with him and his wife. He had arranged for the traditional rice porridge, made with honey and dried fruit, and a few other traditional Christmas things. This supper was thin and poor, and we had it in a cold, bare room. But since Mr Gurdjieff was with us, it was, as always, more than enough. We would not have exchanged this evening for another full of abundance and comfort.

Ever since early autumn I had been quite anxious about starting intensive work on *The Struggle of the Magicians*. All my stage experience indicated that it was necessary to work much faster than we were working if the performance was to be given in the spring. Mr Gurdjieff had said: 'Write the music as you wish for the first act', and so, naturally, I did. Returning one evening after supper, he finally, on my insistent request, began to whistle the music for the second act, which I tried feverishly to write in shorthand on music paper. Of course, I knew from experience that when Mr Gurdjieff would actually stage *The Struggle of the Magicians*, all this would probably be changed or even not be used at all.

One day Mr Gurdjieff brought in a dilapidated old grand piano. I was horrified to think that I would have to play on this ramshackle thing, but he soothingly said as he patted it, 'Lots of good things here', and he began to take it apart. All kinds of materials were needed for staging the ballet and at that time it was impossible to buy even a needle. And here appeared a pile of wires, screws, nails and wood: everything was useful.

At Mr Gurdjieff's request, Mr de Salzmann had designed a colourful stage set for Act I. The scene was filled with all kinds of figures, many of which were portraits of our people. Mr Gurdjieff himself was in it, and Dr Stjernvall, having his head shaved by a barber. De Salzmann even put himself and me in it. He also designed a setting for Act II.

For one of the scenes, Mr Gurdjieff himself made a doll of papier mâché with little lights inside that shone through tiny holes. The brilliance of the lights was controlled by a rheostat, also made by him. One evening he showed us his luminous doll and how the light dimmed or brightened at will. It was wonderfully effective.

Another evening, when the only pupils available were Madame de Salzmann, Lili Galumian, Nina Lavrova and a young girl of ten, Mr Gurdjieff worked on the scene where the elderly assistant of the White Magician arrives. One of the pupils asks him about the law of movement of the stars. Nina Lavrova had to play the part of the old man with a certain limping gait. The young girl portrayed the pupil's question with a convincing upward gesture to the heavens. The whole scene was mimed and their movements were quite originally conceived.

When Mr Gurdjieff began to organize a presentation of The Struggle of the Magicians, *we all made the decorations as well as we could with the help of the pupils. I, in particular, had to make a large urn, which was covered with tiny electric wires that were hidden from view, out of which was to come the spirit of the Black Magician.*

One morning I came to the hall and saw him with an axe, breaking all our decorations and the beautiful urn that I had made with such difficulty and ingenuity. I could not even enter the hall – I thought Mr Gurdjieff had gone mad. He saw me through the glass door and called to me to come in, then asked me, 'Why are you so astonished? We have done it, so we don't need it anymore. Now it can go to the dump.'

Only much later did I understand that this was one of the principles of Mr Gurdjieff's teaching: to make the pupils do something that is terribly difficult and demands all their attention and diligence, and then destroy it, because, for them, only the effort is necessary and not the thing itself.

When Mr Gurdjieff had announced that *The Struggle of the Magicians* would be performed in the State Theatre, it seemed to me like a joke, since we did not even have material for costumes. But if he had not said this, we would not have worked with the intensity he wanted. *The Struggle of the Magicians* was a disguise for real Work. We were probably not at that time advanced enough for work with Mr Gurdjieff to be our only aim; we still had to have an outer attraction, such as a public performance.

In the spring of 1920 the Institute gradually dissolved. It became clear that Mr Gurdjieff was finishing a period of his Work. In fact, he was thinking about another move. Whatever remained of the scenery and furnishings we had made for the ballet disappeared somewhere. Mr Gurdjieff said he had destroyed it all, but other information indicated it had been packed up in boxes to be sent on to Constantinople, but got lost in the upheavals in Georgia.

He began to act coldly towards me and it seemed that he didn't like my work with the Moscow Art Theatre. I had just finished the music commissioned by them for Knut Hamsun's play *In the*

Grip of Life, which had three performances in May, and also the music for Rabindranath Tagore's play *The King of the Dark Chamber*, which took place at the beginning of June. He said that this theatre did not understand the right methods, that, in fact, it contradicted the idea of a real theatre. 'In theatre as we know it,' he said, 'there is always contradiction between type and physical form.' Nevertheless, in order to stay with Mr Gurdjieff, I had to earn money. My music for the two plays was very well received, especially by the artists in the theatre, and this success was the reward for my perseverance.

One night in June near the Tiflis theatre I met Mr Gurdjieff and he advised me, without giving any reason, to make immediate preparations to move to Constantinople. But how would we find the means to go and live there? I had received a very large sum of money in advance from Meliton Balanchivadze, one of the composers in the theatre, for orchestrating his music. (His son became a very famous choreographer in Paris, and later in New York, under the name George Balanchine.) Now I had to repay him this money, as I would not have time to finish the work. Fortunately, my wife had not given to Mr Gurdjieff her astrakhan coat, which he had once wished to cut up to make little Caucasian hats. Instead, she had sold this coat for a very good sum and had kept the money hidden, not only from Mr Gurdjieff but also from me.

Our friends T. and M., knowing we planned to leave Tiflis, decided to have a farewell concert of my compositions in a hall belonging to a well-known Persian and built by a Persian architect. The hall had many slender columns decorated with tiny mirrors, and our two friends, understanding this kind of art, would not allow electricity to be used, but instead brought tall candles. The myriad reflections in the tiny mirrors gave a very beautiful effect. The piano was covered by a magnificent Persian shawl. The music was illuminated by two huge candles entwined with Persian flowers. Instead of chairs, there were benches covered with Persian rugs. My wife and Zalipsky, a very good tenor of the Imperial Theatre of Tiflis, sang and I was at the piano. Mr Gurdjieff was there and was satisfied, although the whole staff of the Moscow Art Theatre was also there.

Some days later he told me, to my great relief, that he was going with us to Constantinople. The money my wife got for the coat paid for our tickets and a part of Mr Gurdjieff's.

XV
Constantinople

In a week we went to Batum, *en route* to Constantinople. When our Armenian friends heard of this trip, they asked us to give a concert of Komitas's music in Batum. This took place on 2 July, and also brought us money.

In Batum I had a quite unexpected joy; my wife went to buy our tickets for Constantinople and, as they had to be ordered, she gave our names and our address. After she returned home, a messenger from the ticket office came asking our Christian names and five minutes later, to my great surprise, my sister Olga appeared. She was earning her living as manager of the ticket office in Batum. The head of the company was also a Russian friend of ours. The last day he asked us to take a large sum of money to Constantinople for him, as it could not be legally transferred or taken out of the country. My wife at once agreed to do it, put the money in her bodice and fixed her dress so that no one would see she was carrying anything.

Some days later the ship sailed and we left Russia, not suspecting that it would be for ever. But Mr Gurdjieff was with us. The Bolsheviks had already begun to enter the Caucasus, so we left just in time. The sea was calm, so different from our trip from Sochi to Poti.

At the beginning of the voyage all of us had to sleep on the deck, since we could not afford staterooms. Later, the captain gave Mr Gurdjieff some screens for privacy and let my wife and me have his working cabin at night because we gave a concert on the ship. So we were quite comfortable for three nights. But when we learned that we would probably have to be searched in quarantine on another ship before landing at Constantinople, we became greatly worried about the large sum of money we were carrying. My wife was horrified, because she would have to undress for the medical inspection and they would find it. She told the captain about the money and we escaped quarantine completely by remaining locked in the captain's cabin while all the other passengers, including Mr Gurdjieff, underwent the quarantine inspection. The money was saved, and my wife was glad that she could soon put it in the bank and be rid of it.

On a sunny morning early in July we sailed into the harbour of the most beautiful city in the world – Constantinople! The captain said his ship would stay in port for three days and that we could live there while we looked for a room. On our arrival we had only eight Turkish lire in our pockets. We would need to sell some jewellery to have some spending money, and we decided on a pearl pin my wife had given to me when she was my bride. But first we had to find a place to live.

We went to Pera, the European part of the city, by funicular. All seemed wonderful after the stringent life in Tiflis. Here the markets were full of all kinds of food – for those who could afford it – and we were impressed by the rich life of the Turks and the occupation forces. Walking through the streets we saw a sign for a small room for rent. We found it was owned by a nice Belgian widow and her son. When we told her we had only eight lire to pay on account, but that we would sell some jewels the next day to pay for the rest, she told us to try to find work first, thus, perhaps, avoiding the sale of the jewels. We were lucky again. The room was small but very clean and in the centre of Pera.

How can you live on eight lire? Well, in one lira there are a hundred piastres. A large loaf of excellent bread cost two and half piastres. The water of Constantinople, famous for centuries for purity of taste, was free. Living only on such bread and water, it

would be impossible to die of hunger. But we were not limited to
bread and water, thanks to Mr Gurdjieff. On our first day he
introduced to us the poor man's stew made from the celebrated
fat-tailed sheep. These sheep by nature have a very large tail,
where their fat accumulates; sometimes a well-fattened sheep grew
a tail so heavy that they had to support it on a little wagon that
trailed after it everywhere. Enough meat cost no more than
twenty-five piastres. Vegetables were very cheap in the market. A
large fireproof pot was filled with the cut-up meat, mixed with
eggplant, cabbage, green beans and onions, with water to fill up
the spaces, then carried to a baker's shop, put in his oven for one
or two piastres, and at noon the delicious dinner was ready for us
all.

On the second day Mr Gurdjieff invited us to supper where he
was staying, telling us to bring some sheep's heads, which could
be bought cheaply, already roasted in an oven and broken in
pieces, brains and all, ready for eating. Mr Gurdjieff was very
fond of sheep's head. To go with it he had sent for *zhalondkov*
soup, having a peculiar flavour but unusually nourishing. And he
had *douziko*, a strong anise-flavoured Greek vodka, which he
diluted with water. Altogether a celebration!

And we had something to celebrate. That very morning we had
discovered that Mr and Madame Ouspensky were living in Prinkipo, half an hour by boat from the city. With them were
Lenochka and her baby son, Lonya. They had survived the difficult Bolshevik occupation of Essentuki, during which many of
those who remained had contracted typhus. When the White
Army took it back, Ouspensky, with his excellent command of
English, obtained work in Ekaterinodar, from where he could
escape abroad. So when the White Army had to abandon Ekaterinodar, he and all his family sailed safely to Constantinople.
The city was full of Russians, for in the meantime General
Kolchak had been defeated and General Wrangel had evacuated
the remaining White Russian army from the Crimea to
Constantinople.

Ouspensky could freely correspond again with his English

friends. In the city itself he was going daily to the Russian YMCA, called there the *Mayak* or 'Lighthouse', where he had organized lectures concerning the spiritual development of man, which had attracted a large audience. Mr Ouspensky had, in fact, prepared a group of pupils, which he now offered to Mr Gurdjieff for his Institute, but the opening of the Institute did not take place until autumn. Meanwhile Mr Gurdjieff treated psychologically ill people who were brought to him, people who, at the hospitals, had been pronounced hopeless.

Work started again on *The Struggle of the Magicians*, and I remember very vividly the evening when Mr Gurdjieff dictated the song of the dervish for the first act; Ouspensky describes this in his book *In Search of the Miraculous*.

Three or four days later we had another surprise. This time we found that my wife's older sister, Nina, was there in Constantinople with her family, having escaped from Russia. We had had no news of them since leaving St Petersburg two years earlier.

I became acquainted with the head of the Lighthouse, a very nice American, and his Russian assistant, and they proposed that I give a daily lecture on music for five lire. Soon concerts began at which my wife sang and these also brought in money; life became secure again.

At the Lighthouse I later met the stage director of the Imperial Theatre in St Petersburg. As my wife knew the leading soprano part of Violetta in *La Traviata*, we considered giving the opera. At this time in Constantinople there were many musicians who had escaped from St Petersburg. But there was no orchestral music, so it had to be played from piano scores, and almost by heart. I played the piano and conducted at the same time. Not long before, the Lighthouse had received a quantity of dark green cloth for clothing the poor. Before it was cut up we used it as curtains for the stage. The costumes were contemporary; before the war we had seen *La Traviata* staged this way in Italy with Toscanini during the Verdi centennial festival.

By the last day all tickets had been sold. However, my wife was

developing a high fever and everyone was anxious for the production. At the dress rehearsal, when the 'father', the baritone,
made his entrance and saw her in a white evening dress, he was
stupefied, thinking another singer had taken her place. He had
never seen her before in anything but her ordinary everyday
working clothes. Fortunately, her voice held, and all went without a hitch, including the improvised orchestra under my baton.
Half of the box-office receipts went to the YMCA and half to
the musicians. Our share of the performance was 300 lire. We
were delighted.

The following day Mr Gurdjieff advised us to use this money to
go to live in Prinkipo, since my wife's health was not very good
and she needed sun and rest. The *pension* there was the residence
of a former pasha, and our room, in spite of its smallness, had a
piano, a bed and kitchen facilities. Soon Mr Gurdjieff also
came to live there.

We had built up the performance of *La Traviata* from nothing to
the point where it permitted me to have a good orchestra of sixty
musicians, with which I began to give concerts every two weeks. As
Turkish women could not attend the public concerts, we gave a
special performance each time for them. My repertoire consisted of
works of the best Russian and French composers, as well as of
Beethoven and Wagner, because I had the great luck to find all
the necessary orchestral scores and parts in the attic of the French
consulate.

Some time later two French generals came to our room. They
invited me and my orchestra to give a concert of French music on
Armistice Day, with my wife as soloist. We certainly agreed, but
refused any remuneration for ourselves in view of the reason for
the occasion. Afterwards, they kindly sent us gifts: for my wife, a
mirror in a silver frame; for me, a flower vase.

Mr Gurdjieff began to plan the opening of the Institute, as
Madame de Salzmann, with Lili and others of her pupils, had
followed him from Tiflis. A house was soon found. On the first
floor there was a large hall with benches; on the second, living

rooms for Mr Gurdjieff; and on the third, rooms for some of his pupils, including the de Salzmanns and their daughter.

A good upright piano was rented. Ouspensky provided a masculine element. He sent a group of tall young men, who, with great enthusiasm, began to come every evening for Gymnastics. I saw that, as in Essentuki, our work was always on strengthening attention.

Mr Gurdjieff continued the exercises he had given in Tiflis, but at the same time he added new ones. I will describe the beginning of one of them. First he demonstrated a movement of the foot and leg, very sketchily. Then steps and turns. We had to learn these. Then movements of the arms and head. Learn these as well. Then combine with the leg movements. I observed all this from the piano. At first it seemed to be evolving into exercises he had already given in Essentuki, schematic and rather dry. He gave me the tempo of the exercise and a melody he himself had written on paper, from which I was expected to improvise the music on the spot. But then he gave me also a separately written upper voice, which was meant to sound as if played on sonorous little bells. It was now impossible to play everything with two hands, so he told Madame de Salzmann to play the lower part and me the upper part. I struggled feverishly to get it all down on paper and we began to play. When he added the movements already given, in an instant everything was suddenly transformed into a dance of the dervishes. The more the pupils entered into the dance, the more exciting and beautiful it became, full of a magical force characteristic of all orders of dervishes.

Copying and editing the music of the dance was very interesting. Everything had to be done then and there, according to his instructions. The main melody was now in my left hand with the added voice above it. He told Madame de Salzmann to double the main melody one sixth lower with her right hand, and play the rhythm with her left. It was amazing how the accompaniment, the little high voice, and the two main voices a sixth apart, blended together like parts of a single machine.

Soon after that Mr Gurdjieff brought me another piece of

music paper, with an unusual combination of flats in the key signature – the notes of an Eastern scale. The melody, with a monotonous beat in the bass, was music for another big dervish dance, for which he began to show the positions. Later, in Paris, when this dance was being orchestrated for the demonstration at the Théâtre des Champs-Elysées, Mr Gurdjieff asked for some changes in the orchestration. To the fundamental melody he told me to add, in pianissimo, sub-voices, also constructed on the same scale. These supporting voices were to represent dervishes who were not active in the dance, but who, in low, muffled voices, were chanting their prayers. At the orchestra rehearsal Mr Gurdjieff told the musicians to pay particular attention to the pianissimo in the performance of these sub-voices. The sonority proved strikingly effective.

In the autumn of 1920 Mr Gurdjieff opened for public enrolment a 'Constantinople branch' of his Institute for the Harmonious Development of Man. By December we were offering:

1. Lectures in philosophy, history of religion and psychology
2. Harmonious Rhythms and Plastic Gymnastics
3. Ancient Oriental Dances
4. Medical Gymnastics

Instructors were announced as follows:

Madame Jeanne Matignon – Harmonious Rhythm
Madame J. O. Ostrovsky – Plastic Gymnastics and Ancient Oriental Dances
Professor Th. A. de Hartmann – Music
Doctor L. R. Stjernvall – Medical Gymnastics

It was added that the lectures would begin at 6 a.m. and would be read in Russian, Greek, Turkish or Armenian, according to the advance enrolment. Moneys received would go in their entirety to indigent pupils of the Institute.

*

156

Some time later a pasha in his red fez met me and very politely told me that the Turkish press was badly in need of money – could I help by giving a concert with my orchestra? At once I promised to do all that I could, without pay, since I was a guest in Turkey. I told Mr Gurdjieff about this and he proposed a demonstration of Eastern dances together with the music. As this demonstration was a success, it was repeated several times in Constantinople as well as in other places nearby.

The pasha often came to our concerts, and one day he asked my husband if he wished to see the whirling dervishes in the mosque of Pera, where each Friday they performed their ritual turning. He said that they belonged to the Mevlevi, a monastic dervish order that permitted marriage, and that he himself belonged to the same order. Mr de Hartmann certainly was very interested and asked if he could bring his wife and a friend. The pasha answered that he could bring his friend, but women were not allowed to sit with the men. He would introduce us to the sheikh of the mosque, but he could only permit me to watch the ceremony from a high balcony and through a grille. And so, the following Friday, we went with Mr Gurdjieff to see their ritual.

The dervishes came peacefully one after another into the hall where Mr de Hartmann and Mr Gurdjieff were sitting with the pasha and began to turn with arms outstretched. There were about fifteen to twenty dervishes, and in the centre stood an older man with a large stick. If the dervishes allowed their arms to fall below the horizontal, the old man would touch their shoulders with the stick. When the dervishes came much later to Montreal and New York to perform their turning for the public, it was not at all the same thing, it was more a spectacle than a religious ceremony. So I was happy that we had seen a real ceremony and not only a show.

After we had seen them turning several times, the pasha invited Mr Gurdjieff and me to an underground room of the mosque, where it was cool even on hot days, and there we sat on carpets drinking Turkish coffee while the musicians who had just played for the dervishes gave a concert of the best Turkish music with flute and drum. I wished to take notes, but was told I could only listen. So I paid close attention and as soon as I returned home wrote down everything I could remember. These finest musicians and experts of Turkish music all belonged to the same Mevlevi order. Their Turkish music was as beautiful as the mosque itself and left a profound impression.

As in Tiflis, so now in Constantinople: Mr Gurdjieff told me in December to give up my musical activities. In Tiflis he seemed glad that I did not actually do so, but this time conditions seemed to make it necessary. So I gave up my conducting activities, which took so much time. To maintain our living I gave only private lessons and private concerts. But, owing to this decision, I was sometimes without any money at all. My wife would have to wait until someone paid for a lesson so she could shop for food for dinner. One day a quite wealthy girl said that she had forgotten her purse and would pay next time. I said that was all right, but we certainly knew that we had to go without dinner that night.

I remember vividly one day when my wife was ill, money was needed and we had only a few small coins left. I decided to sell the vase given to me for the Armistice anniversary concert. The name of the shop and the price, twenty-five lire, were still on the vase. I thought, 'Why not take it back for half the price?' It was a cloudy day with dirty melting snow on the street. A man in a grey overcoat with a trombone was blowing a fanfare over and over as he walked down the middle of the street to advertise the opening of some new restaurant. I entered the shop, but the shopkeeper would not take it back for any amount. Suddenly a lady who was there said, 'For Professor de Hartmann, I offer two lire.' She had been to one of my symphony concerts. I was glad to give her the vase and buy what we urgently needed. I saw that 'fame is less than smoke', and for this realization I again thanked Mr Gurdjieff.

One day in January, when neither Mr Gurdjieff nor the rest of us had any money, we all came to the hall and discussed with Mr Gurdjieff what was to be done. My wife offered to cable her brother in New York to send some money, as he owed me a large sum, and in a few days 300 dollars arrived. We immediately brought it to Mr Gurdjieff, who was very glad that we thought first of all of paying the rent of the Institute. He gave us back enough to pay our own rent and to live on for a little while.

After that we never wanted: step by step things began to go better. With Mr Gurdjieff's blessing, I renewed my work with pupils, lessons, chamber concerts and the orchestra at the Lighthouse. And that was to last well into the summer.

In the spring Mr Gurdjieff made our hall into a sort of theatre so that Gymnastics could be performed on the stage. He also began to work on all kinds of supernatural phenomena: hypnotism, action at a distance, thought transference, etc. But he only started this programme here; it was developed later at the Prieuré in France. Now I will say only that it demanded from the pupils a maximum of attention and a quick comprehension, and had its fundamental purpose in Mr Gurdjieff's general Work of self-development.

Soon he began to think about leaving Constantinople and going to Berlin, because life in Constantinople had begun to deteriorate very rapidly. We began to collect visas from the delegations of Bulgaria, Serbia, Greece, Hungary and Czechoslovakia, as well as Germany, in order to travel through their regions. My wife and I also had to wind up our affairs and cancel some of the musical engagements previously planned. Two days before departure we gave a farewell concert, which brought in a good deal of money: enough for our tickets as well as for living in Berlin a whole year.

On the last day Mr Gurdjieff played a trick on me, which I must record. He said to me, 'Thoma, no money. You had a concert a day ago . . .' My wife, knowing the difference between the voice of Mr Gurdjieff when he really needed money and when he did not, would never have given him any; but I did. When we were about to board the freight car for Belgrade, a *hamal* (porter) brought a sack of bear meat to Mr Gurdjieff, who said: 'Thank you, Thoma. Owing to you I could buy this meat for our trip.' But then, smelling it, he threw it away . . .

I recall that once, in Essentuki, Petrov quoted something that Mr Gurdjieff had told him in Moscow: 'Today you are a fool for me, but tomorrow I will be a fool for you.' He further explained that 'Today you are a fool for me' signifies a stage of life where one is unable to be oneself, to act from one's real self. Through the work of self-development, a time would come when we begin to be able to 'act a part' freely from ourselves, even with our teacher. Once more I saw how the work of Mr Gurdjieff was a constant, beneficial playing with us to bring us to a right and active understanding.

XVI
Berlin

On 13 August 1921 we started off for Berlin with Mr Gurdjieff,
his wife, and my wife's sister, Nina, and her family. We rode in a
freight car and had to sit and sleep on the floor. When we arrived
at Sofia in Bulgaria the second evening, we spent the night in a
forest on the slope of a mountain near the railway tracks. The
next morning we continued on our way in the same freight car
and reached Belgrade in Serbia that evening.

Tired from the days in the freight car, we hoped to find a hotel.
Instead, when we wished to get out of the train the railway police
began shouting at us: 'Russians, go away! Entrance to Belgrade is
prohibited! Go elsewhere!' But a friend of ours, who was now the
Russian consul and to whom we had written, met us at the station
and solved our difficulties.

The next morning we were able to change to a second-class
German coach, as clean and comfortable as before the war. By
evening we reached Budapest, Hungary, and spent several days
there obtaining final visas for Germany.

The first morning Mr Gurdjieff again gave me a difficult time. I
naturally hoped that we would go into the centre of the town to
the famous Wiener Café and to the museum . . . but nothing of
the kind took place. Mr Gurdjieff strolled along the streets,
stopped near a shop and began to look at needles and bobbins on
display in the window. I was boiling inside, quite identified with
my own plans.

*

At the German frontier we were quite astonished when the customs officers, learning that we were Russians, were very pleasant and didn't even open our luggage. In the morning we arrived in Berlin, where we soon found a very nice apartment for ourselves. Mr Gurdjieff went to live with some old Russian friends of his, but he often came to see us and occasionally spent the night on the sofa in our sitting-room.

The first and greatest need, of course, was for funds to cover the living expenses of Mr Gurdjieff and his wife, and to organize the continuation of Gymnastics for those pupils who followed us from Constantinople. Many of them had no money of their own and needed to be supported while living in Berlin. My wife and I could generally support ourselves, but not much more. Dr Stjernvall had gone home to Finland to liquidate whatever property remained to him and his family there, and had promised to bring back money for Mr Gurdjieff's Work. For the moment, not much could be done, so we were free to occupy ourselves with more personal things.

Mr de Hartmann received a letter from his friend Count Wallwitz, who lived in Dresden, asking us to come and visit him. So we decided to go.

At the station we were met by an antiquated carriage with six horses in front, two coachmen in red court dress in the back of the carriage and two others in the front.

My husband and the Count had not seen each other since before the war, so they were very happy to meet again. The Count had with him his sister-in-law, Princess Gagarin, who was Mr de Hartmann's godmother. We told them where we were living, what we were doing and also everything about Mr Gurdjieff. They asked us to invite Mr Gurdjieff to come with us the next time we came to visit.

When we were on the train going home, we thought, 'What do we do now?' We certainly had to relay the invitation to Mr Gurdjieff, and perhaps he would accept; but ... when Mr Gurdjieff would see all the horses, carriages, uniforms and, during

*dinner, a footman standing behind each person's chair, perhaps he
would say, 'Why are these idiots standing behind us?'*

*Mr de Hartmann said, 'Well, we will in any case invite him.
How Georgivanch behaves is his business. If we lose our friends,
well, what can we do?'*

*Next week we again had an invitation to bring Mr Gurdjieff.
He came with us and, in spite of all the ceremony that greeted us,
Mr Gurdjieff behaved as if he had been born at court. The Count
and Princess Gagarin were charmed by him, especially the Princess,
who spoke Russian. Count Wallwitz himself spoke only German
and needed us to translate Mr Gurdjieff's words. After the dinner,
Mr Gurdjieff went home, but we stayed there for a week to rest.
The next day we received a letter from Mr Gurdjieff in which he
asked us not to stay long because he was tired and needed us to
return to manage things while he went away for a rest. He said,
'You can go rest when I come back.' Certainly the pupils could
not stay without either him or us.*

Dr Stjernvall had come back from Finland, bringing a considerable
sum of money for the Work. Before winter, Mr Gurdjieff rented a
big hall, where Lili Galumian worked on Gymnastics with all
those who came.

During the same period Mr Gurdjieff told us to learn English in
our spare moments, under the supervision of Boris Ferapontov.
For me, the task at first appeared quite impossible, since the
English language is not pronounced as it is spelled, but I
began to study it on my own.

Soon Mr Gurdjieff also began to study it. To check himself and
me, he would give me a list of Russian words to translate into
English; then he translated my list back into Russian. As my wife
spoke English and German from childhood, Mr Gurdjieff found it
useful to have her work with him at the café where he passed the
greater part of his day. He would sometimes practise speaking
English with her. He related words together by choosing a particular subject to talk about, such as sewing or another trade, or
ordinary conversational topics. My wife's knowledge of other

languages was also a help to Mr Gurdjieff at meetings with people who didn't speak Russian.

Once I had to accompany Mr Gurdjieff to a private dining-room in a hotel in Berlin, where he wished to speak to a German businessman who was interested in him. During the conversation the German said, 'Allow me to go for a moment to telephone Hamburg; they're waiting for me and I will be late.' Mr Gurdjieff said, 'Why? We will call a waiter and he can put your call through. Perhaps the line is busy, and you will go for nothing.' The waiter came and the man took a book from his pocket and told the waiter the number. The waiter left to make the call and when he returned, he said that the line was busy and he could not get through.

The conversation continued. I tried my best to translate exactly what Mr Gurdjieff answered to the man's questions. Perhaps half an hour later he again asked Mr Gurdjieff to excuse him so that he could telephone. Again we called the waiter, and when he arrived, the man began to take out his telephone book to tell him the number. But I at once told the waiter the number. The German was quite astonished and asked, 'How can you know my business number?' I answered, 'But you told the waiter the number half an hour ago.' He said, 'And you remembered?'

The waiter returned and said that the man should come because he had reached the party. When he left, Mr Gurdjieff told me, 'Well, you have probably earned me another zero on the cheque he wishes to write me.'

After that Mr Gurdjieff devised something very difficult for me personally. He rented a very nice little house by the sea and said that all the women had to go and live there for at least a week, maybe more. His wife, Madame de Salzmann, Madame Hinzenberg (later Mrs Frank Lloyd Wright), Madame Zhukov, Madame Lavrova, Madame Galumian and certainly I had to go.

All the men had to live in our apartment and Mr de Salzmann was put to work in the kitchen. You can imagine what an unhappy state I was in to leave my husband there and not even know how long it would be. I remember very well the first evening when I sat on the beach with Madame Hinzenberg and, quite sorrowfully, went to bed early.

Three or four days later, at eight o'clock in the morning when we were all still sleeping, someone knocked at the door. It was Mr Gurdjieff telling us all to get dressed and go home.

We wondered why Mr Gurdjieff had told us to study English, but soon the reason became clear. Mr Ouspensky, while still in Constantinople, had received the unexpected news that his book *Tertium Organum* had been translated into English and published with great success in both England and the United States. He was then able to go to London, where he at once organized a circle of people headed by A. R. Orage, the editor of *The New Age*, and began to give lectures dedicated to the exposition of Mr Gurdjieff's ideas. This circle had grown very quickly and those who attended these lectures now asked to be put in touch with Mr Gurdjieff personally. As a result, Mr Gurdjieff made a three-week trip to London in March, accompanied by my wife, as he could not yet speak English. It was later decided to organize an Institute in France, with funds coming from England.

When I think about our stay in Berlin, where we remained from August 1921 until July 1922, I see that it was, in fact, a preparation for the move to France, where Mr Gurdjieff finally realized his Institute for the Harmonious Development of Man on a large scale. I am sure that when we arrived in Berlin even Mr Gurdjieff did not know what would occur there and in which directions we would have to turn our efforts. He always waited for the right moment for the next step.

As soon as he returned to Berlin from London, he began to make a series of purchases that at first astonished me very much. I should mention that the German currency was very depreciated, so that having access to a foreign currency he could buy immeasurably more cheaply than elsewhere. Linen for sheets, blankets, table linen, every sort of household utensil, medical instruments, fine carpenters' and metal-workers' tools ... The list was endless. Apparently Mr Gurdjieff already had in his head a detailed plan for the organization of his Institute. We were still unable to picture it, but it was clearly as well thought out in detail beforehand as the Essentuki expedition through the mountains.

Every day, from springtime on, my wife was with Mr Gurdjieff all morning and again all evening after five o'clock. In making the household purchases, he had given her the task of finding samples of all the things he was looking for and bringing them to him for his approval. He trained her in his Work in general, and spoke with her much about his ideas and about inner work. It seemed that he was preparing her for greater responsibilities.

In Mr Gurdjieff's Work Berlin was a transitional period, mainly concerned with the training of responsible personnel, and with preparations for dealing with larger numbers of pupils.

All that year his work with Gymnastics in particular was uninterruptedly aimed at developing the class of specially gifted people he had chosen in Constantinople. He was still refining the form of the Sacred Dances, while training a class for demonstrating them and preparing instructors capable of teaching them to new pupils.

When all was ready, he left with us and some of the pupils by train for Paris. We arrived there on 14 July 1922 during the noisy and joyful celebration of the French national holiday.

XVII
Paris and Fontainebleau

The de Salzmanns met us at the Paris station and took Mr Gurdjieff and the other pupils to their various destinations. My wife and I were taken by my wife's cousin, a very wealthy Frenchman, to his villa in Neuilly. It was the last word in comfort. Two beautiful rooms, with baths, were prepared for us. We were entertained in the finest restaurants and theatres, and shown around Paris. Suddenly to have such comfort, after so many years of privations and restrictions, was extraordinary. It was as if Mr Gurdjieff himself had created this luxury and rest for us. After a few days, our hosts went away to their summer villa in Marly and we remained in their beautiful house, feeling absolutely free to enjoy it.

Very soon we were both given tasks by Mr Gurdjieff. My wife was told to find a property near Paris, with a very large house and grounds. I was given another task: to find Mr Gurdjieff a *pied-à-terre* in the centre of Paris – one room, with a kitchen and bathroom and a separate entrance.

After a long search I was finally told by an agency that they had a small apartment matching my description in the Rue de Miromesnil, but they would not give me the number unless I paid a deposit. I could not do this because I had no money. However, I already knew the street and had time to spare, so I decided to visit every building along the Rue de Miromesnil. At the tenth place the concierge told me that she had just the kind of apartment I was looking for. It even had a telephone.

I was overwhelmed with joy, because it was then practically

impossible to find any kind of room in Paris. I flew to Mr Gurdjieff and told him that I had found an apartment with everything he needed. He listened to me very indifferently and then asked: 'Is there a gas stove?' I had not thought to look. But how revolting of him, I thought, to ask about such a trifle instead of being thankful for my lucky find.

The lesson here was not to lose my head, even while feeling great satisfaction. The 'luck' would not have been diminished in any way if I had kept my attention and examined all other details. This reminder was Mr Gurdjieff's way of thanking me for having found the apartment.

People from London began to arrive and, in order to keep them together and have constant contact with them, Mr Gurdjieff rented a row of apartments on Rue Michel-Ange. In one building he located the women from Berlin and London; in another, the men. And we, too, were told to move into a third.

He told my wife to purchase all kinds of material, thread, needles, scissors, thimbles and a sewing-machine. Then he himself began cutting out the patterns for different types of men's costumes for *The Struggle of the Magicians*, and everyone who was able helped to make them. There were no philosophical talks, just sewing. For the English people, attracted through Ouspensky's lectures on Mr Gurdjieff's philosophical system, this sitting together around a common table in a community dwelling was something new, but everyone worked, even those who were not well acquainted with the ideas.

One of Mr Gurdjieff's pupils, Jessmin Howarth, a choreographer of the Paris Opéra who also gave lessons in the Dalcroze School, was able to arrange for us to have the general use of a room in the school. This made it possible to continue with Sacred Dances and Gymnastics, which we now began to call 'Movements' since in France 'Gymnastics' had a different meaning. We could also work there on costumes and on painting the material by hand or with a sprayer.

*

One day we learned that a beautifully furnished house, with every-thing we needed, had been found by my wife at Fontainebleau, forty-four miles from Paris. We did not believe it would be possible to purchase it, because the price was high. Mr Gurdjieff decided, nevertheless, to buy the property without even having seen it – the Prieuré d'Avon.

This property belonged to the widow of a famous lawyer, Fernand Labori, who had defended and liberated Dreyfus. As payment, the Dreyfus family had given the Prieuré to him. The house was a remodelled mansion of the seventeenth or eighteenth century that once had been a monastery for priors, so it was called the Prieuré. The rumour was that it had once been the residence of Madame de Maintenon.

Mr Gurdjieff gave my wife the task of arranging the terms with the owner. In Berlin he had begun to train her as his secretary and assistant. He had taught her how to keep attention alert, how to develop memory and how to try in all circumstances to remember herself. He now told her how to act with Madame Labori, the owner of the Prieuré – to hold in mind at all times what she wished to get from her and not for a single moment to lose this thought. Such advice from Mr Gurdjieff was like gold to those who really tried to work with him.

It was necessary to find a million francs to buy the Prieuré, so my wife had to try to persuade Madame Labori to rent it to us for a year with the option to buy. In the end she succeeded in getting this agreement, but Mr Gurdjieff wanted something more.

The windows looked out on a beautiful park with a fountain playing in a pond, beyond which was an avenue of lime trees and then a second pond with a fountain. In all we had about forty acres of beautiful pines.

Everything would have been wonderful except for Madame Labori's condition that her gardener should remain in the nice little garden house by the gate. Mr Gurdjieff wished the gardener to leave, so he asked me to go to her again and persuade her to send the gardener away. I was almost sure that she would not do that, as we had only just rented the house and it was filled with antique paintings and furniture of great value. Mr Gurdjieff told me, 'Even if you speak with her about the most trivial things, but have uppermost in your mind that the gardener has to leave, she will do it.' I took it as an exercise from Mr Gurdjieff and tried to do as he told me. To my great astonishment, after about a half-hour's conversation, she said, 'Yes, all right, I will send the gardener away. I trust you that nothing will be ruined in the house.' And I had not even suggested it to her!

We could not immediately move into the big house, since some of the staff were still in residence there. But a smaller house on the property, called 'Paradou', was cleared for us, and our Russian people moved in there. The English were housed in a hotel in Fontainebleau, but spent the whole day with us. My wife had the responsibility of organizing their work.

The very day after we moved in, wheelbarrows and shovels were brought and we began a task of earth removal. Already a future hall for Movements was envisioned and it was necessary to prepare a large, level space on which to build it. In this work we were indeed 'unskilled labourers'. The earth we removed had to be piled on one side. As the pile grew higher, wheelbarrows needed an ever stronger running start to reach the top of the cone, so the earth would increase the pile and not roll back on to the space we were clearing.

At the end of the day Mr Gurdjieff ordered 'combined food' for us — meat, vegetables, potatoes and beans, all cooked together and served in their cooking juices so that none of their nutritious properties was lost.

There was a piano in the dining-room. When supper was over, Mr Gurdjieff asked the young people to move the table out of the room and, with renewed energy, we began to do the series of Dervish Movements. Next came the Obligatories, and before we finished we had covered the entire programme of all the exercises we had done in Tiflis, Constantinople and Berlin.

*

Soon the big house was vacated and we were able to explore it at last. The first impression was of great elegance, but not of comfort; in the entire house there was only one bath-tub. But good water was connected and accessible everywhere, both the city water and our own private spring, one of the conditions on which my wife had firmly insisted.

On the ground floor there was a long hall, hung with paintings, and an elegant formal dining-room. On the right there was a reception room; further on, a library with bookcases in Jacobean style; and still further, a large drawing-room, with a Pleyel concert grand piano. This was no battered old Tiflis piano! Everything comes to him who knows how to wait, and with Mr Gurdjieff it was always so.

Beyond the drawing-room was the study of the former owner and next to it a room with a beautiful billiard table. We never had a chance to play on it, though, because Mr Gurdjieff very quickly ordered it sold. But then again, none of us even knew how to play billiards.

Mr Gurdjieff immediately christened the second floor 'The Ritz', the name of the most luxurious and expensive hotel in Paris. The first room on the left side, with a dressing-room attached, he took for his own. Beyond, along a spacious corridor, were several rooms decorated with exquisite French engravings. One of these was a beautiful bedroom with antique furniture and fine bronze fittings. It was in this room that Katherine Mansfield died a few months later.

On the third floor the rooms all opened on to the same corridor, which was painted dark brown and black. We called it the 'Monks' corridor' and here all the people who had come with Mr Gurdjieff had their own rooms. Over Mr Gurdjieff's was an empty room, which was seldom used, and then came our room, Madame Ostrovsky's and Madame Ouspensky's together, then Miss Merston's and Miss Gordon's, also together. And in the furthest rooms were Lili Galumian and the de Salzmanns. There was even an attic where additional people could stay.

At right angles to the main house was a large wing, with a big kitchen and dining-room on the ground floor, where we always had our meals. Its second floor was called the 'English corridor'. It contained an ironing-room with linen closets, and quarters for the rest of the English and Russian pupils, and for others who little by little came to the Prieuré.

In the back courtyard there were stables, a garage and a cowshed, which had a hayloft, where Mr Gurdjieff often liked to rest and breathe the air.

Our everyday life started. At six in the morning, when one of the pupils ran through the corridors with a little bell, we had to get up quickly, go down to the dining-room, hastily drink coffee with a small piece of bread and go straight to work. Mr Gurdjieff knew how to distribute work among people in such a way that not a moment was lost. Sometimes he would call everyone for a special task and say: 'Throw yourselves in with all your force', and a big job would be done in a few hours. Outdoor work continued from early morning until seven in the evening or until dark, with a break at noon for lunch. Mr Gurdjieff looked unfavourably on anyone who lingered in the dining-room smoking or talking. Then, when the big bell rang, everyone went to a dinner of meat with potatoes, beans or peas, coffee and bread.

After dinner, we had to change quickly from work clothes into city clothes – present-day gymnastic outfits were not then available – and be in the drawing-room by eight o'clock for the Movements. Mr Gurdjieff invented new, not very complicated exercises, all connected with developing attention. There were, for example, three different simultaneous movements for head, arms and legs, with counting. These marvellous combinations occupied the whole of one's attention and the mechanical flow of associations ceased to bother one.

The winter that year was unusually warm. The alley of lime trees in front of the big house was a marvel of French garden art. They were stout old trees with trunks eight feet high, whose thick branches had been trained like candelabra. Each branch ended in a cone, shaped like a pair of clasped hands. In the spring new shoots would sprout, so last year's shoots had to be removed in winter. Mr Gurdjieff bought pruning shears, and all young men and women who were not too heavily built were assigned to prune the old shoots.

There were two ladders, one big and high, the other smaller. Both from the outset became my close friends. The small one, a stepladder, was easy to move. The tall one refused to co-operate. But precisely through this work I found out I could move it by myself. If I stood under it, held the middle rungs in one hand and lifted straight up, by careful balancing I could move it from place to place. This and many other such discoveries were for me revelations, which, in my previous life, I never even suspected.

During this time we had warm, sunny days, wonderful air, and working was a joy.

One day there was a big emergency when soot in the kitchen stove-pipe caught fire and threatened to spread. Everybody quickly took part in putting it out with pitchers and basins of water. How fortunate that we had such excellent water sources!

That led me to be assigned to a number of repair and maintenance jobs, beginning with chimney-sweeping. I had no idea how to do this, but someone found long brushes and metal balls on chains that were specially made for the purpose. The biggest problem was getting safely on to the roof and sometimes having to reinforce the chimney before it could be 'swept'.

Another job I was given was to fix the lath and plaster where there was a hole in one of the ceilings. I first had to remove the loose plaster, repair the lathwork, then mix new plaster. Mr Gurdjieff wanted to spread the mixture himself, as I was not familiar with plastering techniques. By the time I was ready and went to tell him, he was in his dress suit ready to go to Paris. In spite of that he climbed up the ladder and skilfully covered the hole.

I graduated from plastering to masonry: I was asked to brick up some useless doorways. Plastering and masonry, when they really mattered, were two jobs Mr Gurdjieff did not assign to amateurs and nincompoops. So he had brought in a local expert, known as Père Fontaine, to repair a fine stone wall. Naturally I went to see how he and his assistant went about their work.

I watched attentively as they were mixing their plaster in the trough, taking it up in their trowels, throwing it smartly on the wall, and filling the spaces between the stones. Having noticed my interest, Père Fontaine invited me to try throwing some plaster with the trowel. I could see from the way they looked at each other that they were expecting something amusing connected with my inexperience, and they were right! When I threw the mixture at the wall, it all splashed back in my face. Of course there was an explosion of laughter. It seems the art of throwing plaster consists in not throwing it straight at the wall, but at an oblique angle and from above. Then the plaster, penetrating between the stones, flows downwards and covers the wall.

Mr Gurdjieff became very fond of Père Fontaine, as he was a most honest, energetic and hard-working craftsman, and loved to play jokes. In fact, for a certain period, both Metz and I were allotted to Père Fontaine's team as extra helpers to speed up the work on several other assignments. Exactly at 6 a.m. we had to be waiting for the two of them at the front gate. Père Fontaine was absolutely punctual. His day began with a cigarette and a sip of wine *'pour tuer le ver'*.* Then he went straight to work on whatever the job of the day was.

Materials were supplied by his assistant, an old man who was a good friend of Père Fontaine. The assistant's horse, also not young, was a clever and obedient animal named Caroline. She brought materials in the cart when called, and stood still when told to. Her owner invited Metz and me to sniff snuff – my début in this particular art. Many years later a renowned physician prescribed snuff for me 'to give rest to the brain'.

When it came to plastering the ceiling of the Prieuré, lathwork

---

* 'To kill the worm' – the custom of drinking a glass of spirits before breakfast.

was fitted cross-wise between the beams. Then, from underneath, wide planks were placed against the lathwork to support the pouring of the basic plaster coating. The job for Metz and me was to lift these heavy planks high over our heads and hold them tight against the lathwork till Père Fontaine could jam several poles underneath to secure them in place. This holding was increasingly tiring. All the time, while making jokes at our expense, Père Fontaine was running around to save us even a minute of pain. 'Is that better?' he would say as he put up the first pole, but we still had to press the panel tight with full force, till all the poles were in place.

We became fast friends with Père Fontaine. Afterwards I said to Mr Gurdjieff, 'Now I know the psychology of a working man.' He, with some annoyance, just waved his hand. I think he meant me to understand: 'It's not the psychology of a working man you have to study, but yourself.'

Mr Gurdjieff spoke to us quite often in the evenings, when we gathered in the drawing-room. He began to speak about the nature of our forthcoming work. His words were very condensed and when he pointed out something, it was as if a special weight was attached to the thought itself. In this way he told us, for instance, 'There will be work for the emotional centre.' Nobody seemed to understand what he meant, and to me and some others it seemed very strange. But the following day I understood, when, as a result of some awkwardness of mine, he shouted at me *'Balda!'* ('Blockhead!') This wounded me very deeply and the feeling did not pass for some time. But that same evening Mr Gurdjieff told me: 'So, Thoma, today you also received something.' I realized that work on feeling had begun and all my oppressive emotions vanished.

The word *balda* was carefully chosen for my character and state. It is the gentlest of such words – very tough-skinned people, or those who were considerably more advanced, he would call *svolotch!* – and the manner in which he spoke to me afterward absolutely melted away my unpleasant feelings. I saw again that if I began to boil with anger, my task was to struggle with it internally and not to manifest it.

In connection with this, Mr Gurdjieff once told me that one should never be resentful of such comments in the Work, but to consider them a healing medicine. With him it was always necessary to 'listen with all one's ears' and respond correctly to his 'chess moves'. However, the art with which he brought us this pain was so great, his mask so well assumed, that in spite of our having decided in advance not to react and to remember that it was being done to help us, when the experience took place we were quite sure that there stood before us a cold and even a cruel man. We were outraged and, against our will, protests exploded like gunshot. Mr Gurdjieff's face would at once begin to change. He resumed his usual expression, but looked very sad and would walk away without a single word. We were then consumed by a feeling of terrible dissatisfaction with ourselves. We had 'forgotten', not 'remembered', why we came here and had reacted in an unsuitable way.

Every activity in the Work showed clearly that the aim was never for outer results, but for the inner struggle. For example, Mr Gurdjieff once sent everyone to prepare the earth for the kitchen garden, but later the garden was abandoned. Very often he said that he was in a hurry to finish one or another job and that we had to do it as quickly as possible. I must say that this pressure to finish was always a stimulant, but this very stimulant provoked in us a kind of unconscious identification. I remember Mr Gurdjieff saying: 'Identification, identification!' – the Russian word is literally 'merging' – meaning that we had become completely absorbed in the task. At other times he showed us that when we really work we have to 'identify' while leaving a little bit of attention with which to observe ourselves.

On the other hand, Mr Gurdjieff watched closely how we worked and never permitted us to overdo. Once when I was doing something very strenuous, which was probably too much for my heart, he said unexpectedly: 'Thoma, now go and burn some leaves.'

One day by chance I saw the following list that Mr Gurdjieff put up:

List of the Responsible Members of the Institute of G. Gurdjieff.

In the Capacity of Instructors:
1. Julia Ostrovsky
2. Olga de Hartmann
3. Dr Leonid Stjernvall
4. Thoma de Hartmann
5. Pyotr Ouspensky
6. Alexandre de Salzmann

In the Capacity of Assistant Instructors:
1. Sophia Ouspensky
2. Jeanne de Salzmann
3. Olga Hinzenberg
4. Elisaveta Galumian
5. Boris Ferapontov
6. Dr Konstantin Kiselev

I asked Mr Gurdjieff why he had listed me as a 'responsible member' when I didn't at all know what to do. He answered, 'That is why I listed your name – so that you will learn.'

XVIII
English Interest Grows

On the terrace of the Prieuré Mr Gurdjieff spoke for the first time with Orage, who had just come from London. I had to translate for them, as Mr Gurdjieff still spoke little French or English. Orage stayed with us. As a job for him to do, Mr Gurdjieff told him to dig a ditch not far from the kitchen garden, because, he said, the rain from the little hill always made too much water collect. He showed him the place, and the length and width of the ditch. Orage had never had a spade in his hands before, but he began the project with great zeal.

Every morning when Mr Gurdjieff went to the kitchen garden to look at how the work was going, he would tell him, 'Well, well, very good, Orage!' But the third or fourth day he told him, 'Look, the edges of the ditch are not equal. You must take a little piece of string and measure across so that the edges will be quite equal.' Orage did this and the next day, when Mr Gurdjieff passed, he stopped and said, 'Orage, it is very good. Now put the earth back in it, we don't need this ditch any more.'

Mr Gurdjieff had done the same thing to us when he destroyed all the decorations we had made for The Struggle of the Magicians.

During the next year the English people sent money and, with an extra sum from my wealthy cousin, we were able to buy the Prieuré with a mortgage.

Soon more English people, sent by Ouspensky, came from London. At the same time Katherine Mansfield also arrived. The

English asked Mr Gurdjieff some questions. It is interesting to see which questions concerned them most at that time. Orage and I interpreted for Mr Gurdjieff and recorded the questions and answers as follows:

Question 1 Has Mr Gurdjieff's educational system produced an example of the type of man that he wishes to develop?

Answer With regard to the results achieved by pupils here during this short period of time, first of all we can note:

1. Improvement in their health. That means that there was established a basis to improve their future health from the chronic diseases that they had. The following can serve as examples: improvement from obesity, the strengthening of their weak memories and bringing in order their disordered nerves.

2. The second result is the enlargement of their horizons. In general, people have a very narrow outlook on life; it is as if they wear blinkers which prevent them from seeing more. Here, thanks to a great variety of new conditions of work, and thanks to many other things, this field of view is enlarged, as if a new horizon is acquired.

3. A new interest has been created. The majority of people who came here had quite lost any interest in, and for, life. This is also because they had such a narrow outlook on life. Here, a new interest is born for them. (This result had to be stressed as the *most* important, Mr Gurdjieff said.)

It is possible to list a thousand examples of results acquired by people from being here, but most of the results would come from these three fundamental ones; that is why it is not important to list them.

Since the Institute has been in existence for a very short time, it is only recently that some pupils have emerged who measure up to the results I expected. But generally speaking there are no limits for self-perfecting, and so each attainment is only a temporary state. People in their outer life are not tied to the Institute. They can play any social role, fulfil any job, have any occupation that occurs in life. Many people live their own independent life and Work at the same time. The difference lies only in that if, before, someone was a good shoemaker, by becoming a pupil of the Institute and continuing to learn, he will become a different shoemaker; if someone was a priest, he will become a different priest.

Question 2 How do you explain the despair that some pupils of the Institute fall into in the beginning?

Answer There exists a principle in the Institute about which I will tell you at once, and then this period of despair will begin to be quite clear to you.

A man generally lives with a 'foreign' mind. He has not his own opinion and is under the influence of everything that others tell him. (The example was given of a man who thinks badly of another person only because someone else has said bad things about that person.) In the Institute you have to learn how to live with your own mind, how to be active, to develop your own individuality. Here in the Institute many people come only on account of their 'foreign' mind; they have no interest of their own in the Work at all.

That is why when a man arrives at the Institute, difficult conditions are created and all sorts of traps laid for him intentionally, so that he himself can find out whether he came because of his own interest or only because he heard about the interest of others. Can he, disregarding the outside difficulties that are made for him, continue to work for the main aim? And does this aim exist within him? When the need for these artificial difficulties is over, then they are no longer created for him.

The periods of despair in life are the result of the same cause. The man lives with a 'foreign' mind and his interest arises accidentally, owing to some outside influence. As

long as the influence continues, the man seems quite satisfied. But when, for some reason or other, the outside influence ceases, his interest loses all meaning and he falls into
despair.

What is his own, and cannot be taken away from him
and is always his – this does not yet exist. Only when this
begins to exist, is it possible for these periods of despair to
disappear.

Question 3 Does Mr Gurdjieff view the Institute as something experimental? That is, is one of Mr Gurdjieff's aims
the acquiring of some knowledge through the Institute? Or
is it the putting into practice of a system that he has already
completed during his life?

Answer The putting into practice of a system I completed
during my life, but at the same time there are also other
aims.

Question 4 Why does Mr Gurdjieff put so much emphasis
on physical work? Is it temporary or permanent?

Answer Temporary. For most of the people now gathered
in the Institute, the physical work is indispensable, but it is
only a period of the whole plan of the Work.

Question 5 Is the attainment of any kind of occult possibilities one of the subjects of this 'education'?

Answer Truth is one. It existed always and is as old as the
world itself.

In distant times there existed a real knowledge, but owing
to all kinds of life circumstances, political and economic, it
was lost and only fragments of it remain. These remains I
collected with other people. We learned of them and found
them through people, monuments, customs, literature, our
own experiments, comparisons and so on.

Question 6 What is the origin of this system? Has Mr Gurdjieff personally acquired it? Or has it been transmitted to him?

Here, Mr Gurdjieff did not answer. *(I wish to say that Mr Gurdjieff's silence was not meant to avoid the question. It was obvious that he felt that the question had already been answered in other words.)*

Question 7 What does Mr Gurdjieff hope to do in Europe? What is his opinion about the value of Western science? Why has Mr Gurdjieff chosen Paris?

Answer I chose Paris because it is a centre of Europe and I have thought for a long time that an Institute was necessary here. It is only political circumstances that have held that up for two years.

From the West I wished to take the knowledge that the East could not give me. From the East I took theory; from the West, practice. That which is in the East did not exist in the West and vice versa. That is why each alone has no value. Together they complete each other.

Question 8 What made Mr Gurdjieff choose his pupils? Did he think he would produce teachers from some of them? Can they begin to be as he is?

Answer Each pupil is a teacher to the one who stands lower than he. Everybody can become like me only if they wish to suffer and work as I did.

Question 9 Is Mr Gurdjieff alone in this undertaking, or is he a part of an already existing group?

Answer Alone. All of my doings are personal. Those who came before are scattered around the world and I have lost contact with them.

Question 10 Does the teaching of Mr Gurdjieff form part of some historical school still in existence? Was the knowledge that he possesses ever the property of a ruling caste? And was there any kind of civilization founded on it? For example, was there in India a government in the hands of people who wished to put into practice the ideas of Mr Gurdjieff?

Answer Tibet is an example where, ten years ago, all government was in the hands of the monks. But they couldn't put my ideas into practice, because my teaching was not known to them. My teaching is my own. It combines all the evidence of ancient truth that I collected in my travels with all the knowledge that I have acquired through my own personal work.

Question 11 What is Mr Gurdjieff's doctrine about Necessity, Free Will and Death? Can people in general become immortal or only some of them? For those who have not acquired immortality, what will happen to them? Does there exist for them something like reincarnation or eternal recurrence?

Answer Yes and no. Those people who have a soul are immortal, but not everyone has a soul. A man is born without a soul, with only the possibility of acquiring one, and he has to earn it during his lifetime.

For those who have not acquired a soul, nothing happens to them. They live and they die. Individuals die, but the atoms live because in the world nothing ceases to live.

But even immortal souls exist in different stages. Full immortality is quite unique.

In general, in his discussions with us Mr Gurdjieff never used the word 'soul'. He referred only to a 'something'. However, in his discussion with these new people, it was necessary for him to use words that they would understand and for that reason he used the word 'soul'.

XIX
Construction

When we first moved into the Prieuré property, it was immediately evident that for Movements a bigger hall was necessary. The largest salon was too small. The day after we arrived we had begun to prepare the ground for a new Movements Hall, which Mr Gurdjieff began to refer to as a 'Study House'. He had chosen a site to one side of the long garden alley, so that the beautiful view of the fountains and rows of trees would not be spoiled. But at that time we had no idea at all how it was going to develop.

Now it appeared that the skeleton of the future Study House was already prepared for us. As Mr Gurdjieff said, 'There are no chance events in the world.' Mr de Salzmann had discovered that the French military department was selling an old wooden air force hangar for virtually nothing. He arranged to bring over two sections of it, enough for our whole building.

So into the orchard one morning came two big trucks loaded with the dismantled parts of these two sections, and the necessary nuts, bolts and iron rods to put them together and anchor them into the earth. When all this was unloaded into one big pile, we had to figure out which parts went together – a real puzzle for such inexperienced people – and then carry them over to the lawn next to the building site. It took three of us to carry the big upper triangular part of each truss on our shoulders. To my surprise I found myself being strong.

Mr Gurdjieff gave me the job of putting together the parts of each frame into one. These frames were like cross-sections of the structure, with a vertical post to support the wall on each side of the building, and a triangular truss across the top between them to support the roof. Beginning at one end, these frames had to be positioned vertically and then connected horizontally with one another by means of boards. They were brought and put up in one piece by collective effort. Both men and women took part in these manipulations. Lifting them was dangerous. After a frame was raised by ropes and pulleys, it had to be held exactly vertical from both sides while two people standing on tall ladders connected it to the previous frame. In this way the structure of the whole building took shape.

One team began to fill in the roof with planks and cover them with tar paper, while others were making the walls. Planks were nailed on both sides of the posts about an inch apart. The space between the planks was stuffed with dry leaves by the women.

Dr Maurice Nicoll and I were then assigned as plasterers. We began to cover the outsides of the planks with a smooth thickness of clay, the very clay that had been removed from the slope to make level the space for the new building. In this way nothing was wasted.

Now I can give an example of intensity in personal work. Nicoll and I had almost finished our coat of clay on all the walls when Mr Gurdjieff looked at them and said the clay should have been squeezed between the planks into the dry leaves behind them; then the external coating of clay would have a direct connection to the inside of the wall and grip it tight. This would prevent the clay facing from just falling off the wall. Of course we now saw that this was true. So Nicoll and I began all over again to scrape the clay and push it through the cracks to the inside.

The weather was nasty. It was drizzling all the time. The nights were expected to get colder and the frosts would begin. Somehow the exterior had to be completed before winter, so we were hurrying in every possible way to finish the job. Dusk was closing in . . . It became pitch dark, but we still kept on scraping, 'by heart', as you might say. Light was almost unnecessary. We reached

the south-west corner, at the far end of the Study House. To work
on that corner we would have to slog through mud . . .

Suddenly we heard the voice of Mr Gurdjieff. 'Now then, stop
your work and come with me.'

'But Georgivanch, there may be frost tonight and we won't
have it finished!'

'No matter. Come with me.'

He brought us to the kitchen. Both of us were given a shot of
vodka with an appetizer. Then he took us to the cowshed, and up
into the gallery, where there was hay covered with rugs and a
blanket. It was warm there, with the healthy smell of manure. He
laid the blanket over us and we fell into a deep sleep, that kind of
sleep in which, according to him, our centres lose all connections
with one another and one reaches a state of energizing rest. For
one hour in that warmth we completely relaxed, then went to
dinner. After dinner we went to Movements.

When we began building, Mr Gurdjieff had given orders to leave
a definite space between the separate frames of the hangar, and
now we began to see why. In one part of the garden were big
hothouses, at one time provided with steam heating. But
this was not functioning any more; the pipes were all rusted and
the system was no longer serviceable. Mr Gurdjieff told us to
carry the glass panels to the Study House. In the spaces he had
indicated between the hangar sections, precisely one or two glass
panels would fit as windows. When the windows were in place,
the walls and roof completed and doors installed on both sides of
the end nearest the château, we at last had a primitive hall shielded
from the weather.

Inside it seemed like a military barracks or a covered market-
place. There was no floor, of course. You entered into a rectangular
space, at the far end of which was a section where the earth had
been left a foot and a half higher than the rest of the ground when
we first were digging there. This now appeared as the future
stage, big enough for any needs of the Movements.

Three big iron heating stoves with chimney-pipes were installed, thanks to which we were able to continue the work there when the colder weather set in. It was not long before linoleum was laid on the stage, and we were able to begin to use the Study House for the Movements.

When the building of the Study House began, Katherine Mansfield went away on the advice of Mr Gurdjieff, because he was afraid her consumption was too advanced and that she could give it to some of us. But she was very unhappy and transmitted this message to Mr Gurdjieff through Orage. She was permitted to come back and, as she was quite ill, was given the middle room in the Ritz corridor. One of the young women was assigned to look after her. I asked the young woman who always brought her lunch to give it to her as elegantly as possible in her room. In the daytime she went to the gallery in the hayloft of the cowshed. Mr Gurdjieff told her to lie there and inhale the air, which was beneficial for her lungs; the heat from the cows was very healthy during the winter. On the ceiling above her resting place, Mr de Salzmann painted beautiful designs and caricatures to amuse her.

Every evening before supper she came to our room and we had a very good and simple relationship with her. We learned from her that she was unhappy that her husband never wished to come to the Prieuré to see her, but preferred to remain in London. One day early in January 1923 she received a letter from him saying that he would come to visit her, and it was touching to see how happy she was.

When her husband came, she took him to see the progress of the building of the Study House. As it was not yet ready, in the evenings we always met in the salon. Mr Gurdjieff asked me to invite her to come with her husband to the salon, where we would all speak and Mr de Hartmann would play music. She was very happy and began to come down the staircase with her husband and me. On the stairs she fell and blood flowed from her mouth. I left her husband holding her and ran for the doctors, who came and took her back to her room. In fifteen minutes she was dead.

*

Work on the interior of the Study House was carried on sporadically all through the following year, but before I describe its completion, I wish to mention something that still seems to me as if it could never have happened – the building of the Turkish bath at the same time as the construction of the Study House up to this point.

In Essentuki and Tiflis Mr Gurdjieff had introduced us to traditional steam baths. In the baths of Constantinople there was an additional attraction, a marvellous clay that, when spread on the body, removed all hair and left the skin elastic and soft. That is why it was said that the Turks never had lice. Not surprisingly, Mr Gurdjieff's plans for the Prieuré included construction of a bathhouse.

In the park, at the edge of the forest, was a big shed intended for storing garden equipment. At the back of it, built into an abrupt rise in the ground, was a large root cellar, consisting of two rooms, a smaller one at the entrance and a more spacious oval room inside.

First we were to widen this larger room. Against the back wall of it we would then construct the housing for a water tank on one side, and on the other side a place for the steam room. For that we had to dig out a large amount of earth, a volume about half as big again as the existing room, using pickaxes, shovels, hoes and wheelbarrows.

In the beginning the earth was soft, but small rocks began to appear. Finally we hit almost solid rock, which, despite all our strivings, could not be removed without dynamite. At this point we had not the resources to finish the bathhouse in the structure and style that later became famous, so Mr Gurdjieff began to adapt a temporary one from the room that already existed.

We began to work there nearly every evening, still without electricity. I clearly remember a characteristic moment when Mr Gurdjieff, with bricks and clay, was building a small stove to enclose the hot-water boiler. Around him stood ladies with lanterns, handing him more clay and bricks. Outside, men were mixing cement for the big room, to make a floor with water channels, drains and so on, and benches around the walls. They carried it in wheelbarrows down a difficult descent and poured it into prepared wooden forms.

We had few proper tools and worked practically with bare hands. I had to work a lot with cement and it never entered my mind that it might ruin the skin. Later, when I had to play the piano, it felt as though I was playing on needles. Mr Gurdjieff had a good laugh over that.

Naturally after that I could feel for one young man who completely wore out his good city shoes working there. What to do? There were no galoshes or wooden shoes to be found. Some of the men had used primitive clogs with wooden soles, and later tossed them away on the dump when the soles completely disintegrated. Then I remembered that in the woodworking shop I had seen some new wooden soles waiting to be made into clogs, but they had no straps. So I searched in the dump and found an old pair, removed the leather straps, hammered them to make the leather soft and nailed them to a pair of wooden soles. My makeshift cobbling turned out well and served the young man satisfactorily, and others afterwards.

In the presence of Mr Gurdjieff intensity of tempo and heightened attention often enabled us to find better means to make the work go faster. For example, we needed square stakes for the cement forms when making the benches in the bathhouse. But ready-made stakes were unobtainable, so we had to saw them out of one-inch boards. Fastening the board in the vice of a carpenter's bench and cutting strips off with a handsaw took much too long. We wanted to devise a way to do it faster. In one of the greenhouses we had found a big two-handled forestry saw for cutting logs; I wondered if it would be possible for one person to use it alone. But such a big saw needs a thicker and heavier piece of wood to bite into; while cutting a one-inch board the saw would dance about wildly, damaging with its teeth ... Solution! Clamp several boards together, tighten them at a convenient angle in the vice, climb on the carpenter's bench and saw away! The test run was successful.

Generally, when given personal tasks, the attempt to think and invent while working always helped me very much. Mr Gurdjieff often said, 'First and foremost a donkey works.' But we are not donkeys. Before beginning a task we need to think about how to fulfil the goal in the most intelligent way, spending the least possible force for the greatest possible result. We should not forget that the same goal can be reached in various ways. And sometimes there are shorter ways, which, at the same time, give greater profit.

In all these works was the characteristic trait of Mr Gurdjieff — everything done by hand, made from available materials, without modern sophistication and with the help of people who had never experienced anything similar. In spite of all that, what came out of these people was something completely satisfactory, which served its purpose.

Only in the case of the bathhouse, at our first attempt, did we fail to obtain the desired result. The stoves for the main hot-water tank were insufficient to heat the premises when everyone was bathing. So Mr Gurdjieff added two more iron stoves. When these were red-hot, water poured over them produced hot steam, as in a true Turkish bath.

The following year the bathhouse was rebuilt. A full-size water container was put into the steam room and equipment installed to heat the steam up to any desired degree.

At one point it was necessary to make an iron ring to surround a pipe inserted in the roof. The ring had not to be flat, but slightly bent in, in order to hug the roof tightly, which at that point was somewhat convex. The making of this ring demanded blacksmith work. And blacksmith work demands superlative skill.

In one of the outbuildings we had found a small portable furnace with an anvil and the necessary hammers and tongs. When we got the furnace heated and in working order, Mr Gurdjieff himself came. He took up the ring with the big tongs in one hand and, after heating it white-hot, he took it to the anvil and began to hit it with the hammer in his other hand.

And just then, I will never forget, suddenly in front of me stood a genuine blacksmith. From early childhood I used to visit the smithy on our estate to watch how Nikita, our blacksmith, did his work. This image of a genuine blacksmith was indelibly in my memory.

The legs of Mr Gurdjieff somehow became bent in the typical posture of blacksmiths in order to be at the right level with the anvil. The strokes of the hammer, the handling of the tongs, the way he replaced the chunk of cooling iron back inside the furnace – here was a true blacksmith.

In such instances Mr Gurdjieff would say, 'I spent ten years doing that work.' To that Dr Stjernvall would reply, 'If we add up all these "ten years" when you were busy with cooking, tailoring, carpentry, blacksmithing and so forth, then you must be well over 100 years old!' Whatever the truth was, Mr Gurdjieff always had this uncanny ability to assume the mask of a person whom he wished to portray.

In any case, when finished, the remodelled bath worked perfectly. The old entrance room became the dressing-room.

Every Saturday from Paris arrived the 'fans of the steam bath'. Afternoon hours from four to six were assigned to the ladies. The men joined the others in the Study House from eight to nine, then went for their own bath, followed by a sumptuous dinner, after which we all went into the big drawing-room, where I played music.

At the Prieuré all these constantly changing works engulfed the whole person. Life outside somehow ceased to exist. Reclusiveness of life in the Prieuré was totally unlike that of a monastery, where external life is rejected and there is concentration on prayer, abstinence and elevation of thought. In the Prieuré the life of a person, like a ball, was thrown from one situation into another. Our prayer was the Work, which concentrated together all spiritual and physical forces. The variety and constant change of tasks continually reawakened us. We were given minimal hours of sleep, just enough to give strength for the following day. Instead of abstinence, there was spending of forces to the utmost, attentive work renewing energies as they were spent, in the manner of a rhythmic fly-wheel. There was no rejection of life within the Prieuré. On the contrary, life was expanded to the utmost intensity and spirituality.

XX
Kitchen

Generally, work continued every day from the time we got up at
six in the morning till suppertime, and then at eight in the evening
there were Movements in the Study House. The old Pleyel piano,
which had belonged to Madame Labori, was now replaced by an
excellent Bechstein, which stood to the left of the stage on a small
platform for greater volume of sound.

Easter was approaching; there would be a feast. Besides all
those living and working at the Prieuré, many guests were invited.
And so, added to everything else, there was concentration on
making *kulich* and *paskha*.

Two people had to knead the *kulich* dough by hand in a huge
container. We took turns because this muscular work was very
fatiguing. When the dough had been worked into a smooth round
lump about two and a half feet across and half that in height, it
was placed on the kitchen table, where we continued to knead it
some more, still without adding any raisins or candied peel. Just
then Mr Gurdjieff appeared: 'What's the matter? Is this the way
to knead dough? You have to use your feet! Take off your boots!
Climb on the table!'

It was already getting on towards evening. We had been working
the entire day outside. You can well imagine that our feet were
not of the first cleanliness. With heavy hearts we began to unlace
our boots . . .

The situation was saved by my wife's initiative. As soon as the
subject was raised about the unproductive kneading of dough, she

had immediately grasped what Mr Gurdjieff had in mind. She slipped away unnoticed, dashed to the second-floor linen closet and brought back clean socks. We put them on, climbed on to the table and began to dance on the dough.

Next morning, after the dough had risen, the kitchen team was wondering where they could bake so many *kuliches*. Mr Gurdjieff suggested using the ovens in the steam bath. This was Good Friday, and some of us were working on the lawn in front of the château. I can still see in memory Madame Ostrovsky and her helpers, with *kuliches* in metal containers, coming in cheerful procession past us to the bathhouse . . .

Several hours later, the same procession came slowly back, with sad faces. I asked, 'How are the *kuliches*?'

'Burnt to cinders. We should have tried *one* first. We put them *all* in.'

These two stories, of the socks and the baking, show how one should never listen to the words of Mr Gurdjieff uncritically, in blind subservience. What was needed was a conscious execution of the task assigned, by the best possible means. For that we had to reason, to think. Orders of this kind were given in the tone of a strict boss or army general and always exuded a certain convincing flavour, against which one also had to struggle. These were difficult moments. When met with disobedience, Mr Gurdjieff was able, with utmost anger, to yell at you, '*Svolotch!*' At the same time there was a demand not to answer back, either by raised tone of voice or show of hurt feelings, and never to hold a grudge.

Every evening after supper, we all went to the Study House. Mr Gurdjieff walked up and down the little path in the middle of the hall and once, quite unexpectedly, said in a very loud angry voice, 'Now I see where my millions go . . . to people who do not use the precious vegetables from the kitchen garden and let them go bad! The ones who did it have to go on the stage and stay there with their arms outstretched for half an hour!'

Can you imagine, those people were his wife and Madame Ouspensky! They had not used the vegetables that the two English ladies who looked after the kitchen garden brought to be cooked, because we Russians never eat these vegetables, and only give them to cows. One of these English ladies had been quite appalled and had gone to Mr Gurdjieff and told him that it was really terrible that such wonderful vegetables should be left to spoil.

When she saw Madame Ostrovsky and Madame Ouspensky go and stand on the stage with arms outstretched, she came to me, begging me to please ask Mr Gurdjieff to let her stand in their place. She was profoundly unhappy.

That is an example of how Mr Gurdjieff dealt with a person who reported to him about somebody else. He never permitted that.

In the summer of 1923 among the works that Mr Gurdjieff organized was forestry in the north-eastern corner of the park. This part of the property was completely wild, essentially a forest of century-old pine trees. Under them were dense, thorny bushes; it was a long time since anyone had cleared the undergrowth, as was done in the rest of the park.

Mr Gurdjieff had decided on this place as the site for a future permanent Study House, this time of huge size and built of brick. We cleared the area of thorn bushes and then began to cut down some of the pines, which, with other kinds of trees, would be used as material for the new house. Everybody took part, men and women alike. We learned how to make trees fall in a predetermined direction; how to work with a lumberjack's long-handled axe; how to cut through the trunk of the tree in pairs with a cross-cut saw; and how at the last moment when the tree begins to lean, it is necessary to jump clear, remembering that the lower part of the tree can jump up again. Sometimes inexperienced people came too close and unexpectedly received a strong blow from the trunk bouncing up.

While some were felling trees, others were cutting the branches off the trunks. These were gathered into piles for winter fuel. The trunks were cut into logs, which were then stacked up.

The logs were always carried by two men. I soon acquired a

certain skill in lifting the logs to my shoulder and then walking with them. Once my partner in this process was an Englishman, Dr James Young. The trick was to lift up the log and toss it on our shoulders, and then walk in rhythm to our destination. I was facing the end of the log in order to toss it as always on to my right shoulder. But when I did so I suddenly noticed a look of anticipation on Mr Gurdjieff's face as if he expected something funny. And there was a reason why: at the same time my partner, facing his end of the log, had tossed it on to his left shoulder. So we were back to back, and when we walked away, the log slipped from our shoulders and fell to the ground behind us. Everyone laughed. Mr Gurdjieff never said a word, but I know it was murmured among the others, 'Where was our attention?'

In the middle of summer, it seems that the overseers of the kitchen, Madame Ostrovsky and Madame Ouspensky, had become tired and needed a rest. Mr Gurdjieff seized upon a complaint someone had made and in the Study House one evening said that these two cooks were no good at all and he had decided to pass the responsibility of the kitchen to – of all people – me!

I wish to share my sufferings in connection with this.

First of all, I had to get up at five o'clock, so that by six hot coffee would be ready for everyone. The first part was simple. There was bread to slice and milk to warm up, which could be done easily on the gas stove. But the second step, preparation of the breakfast itself, was considerably more difficult since it was necessary to heat the oven. One must say that the oven in the Prieuré could shake hands with the samovar in Essentuki, which also never wanted to get hot. The prepared kindling would burn, but the coal would not catch. And on those occasions Mr Gurdjieff was particularly impatient and merciless. 'Andreyich,' he would say, 'it would be a good idea to have the samo*var*' – the last word was said in a voice with a higher pitch and more accent on the last syllable.

And so now. The kindling burns, but the coal refuses. At last the coal catches and I have to add more. I add, but I smother the flame; the fire is out again. And time is running ... It is six o'clock and now the stove is needed. This is not so difficult. Everyone comes at once, each with his own cup. By 6.30 they've all had their coffee and have gone to work. It seems a good time to start heating the oven again.

But it doesn't work out that way. Particularly in summer, many English and Americans come to the Prieuré for short visits. They are quartered in the Ritz corridor on the second floor in beautiful, sumptuous rooms. In the kitchen we call them 'guests'. It is necessary to prepare coffee for each guest individually. One wishes it now; in half an hour, another; some time later, a third ... It seems like a treadmill. And all the time it is necessary to clean vegetables, and soon to put the soup on the stove to be simmered and ready by noon.

Everybody would have a bowl of soup for lunch with a piece of boiled meat. But the English people didn't like this boiled meat and often left it uneaten. An idea popped into my head. When the soup and meat were fully cooked, I took the meat out, sliced it into pieces and put it through the meat grinder. After that I added salt, pepper and other seasonings, rolled it into a long cylinder on a wooden board and sprinkled some finely chopped fresh parsley on top.

Here at once a problem appeared: how to divide it equally between thirty or forty people? Of course there was no ruler. Necessity brought a practical solution to my hands. I divided it in half, then each half in halves, and further into smaller divisions of two or three, until I had the right number of portions. All was ready for lunch ...

I received the highest possible award for my invention: Englishmen, coming with plates for soup, were asking, 'May I have this on my bread?'

This success gave me wings and my culinary fantasy prompted me to ever newer inventions. The following day I discovered that on yesterday's cold soup a thick layer of solid fat had formed, and above that there was a considerable quantity of boiled cabbage. In the kitchen was a big frying-pan. Knowing that the English are not squeamish about fresh meat fat, I smeared the frying-pan with this fat, put the cabbage on it and topped it with breadcrumbs. (Parmesan cheese was not allowed in the Prieuré.) By this means I added to the meat and vegetables.

When lunch together was over, a queue came to the kitchen-boy and me, asking for more. First in line was Dr Young, with whom I so 'successfully' shouldered that log. He asked for a second helping of vegetables. 'So very juicy,' he said.

I was terribly pleased. On the following day there was an opportunity to make meat patties out of the soup material. The only people I could not please were *mothers*. They said to me, 'The soup is good, but the second course is too fat and not appropriate for children.' I tried to explain that it was all only the same old soup with a piece of boiled meat, and everything additional was only the 'fruit of my fantasy', so to say; how could it not be fit for children of tender age? But they did not *wish* to understand.

The crowning glory came when, besides leftover vegetables of two days, there was also *kasha* porridge left over from the previous day's casserole. The resulting creation acquired the nickname of 'three-storey-factory'. The mothers recognized the porridge in it and complained to Madame Ostrovsky ... But I did not have to stand that evening in the Study House for half an hour with my arms held out. Instead, that casserole came into general use in the Prieuré's menu, and that brought me a certain moral satisfaction.

I write these lines laughing now at how I was trying to convert myself into a cook for thirty or forty people. From five in the morning I was the whole time on my feet, with no possibility to take a break. As soon as I had finished serving lunch, a piano was brought out into the alley under the lime trees and I had to play endlessly 'The Fall of the Priestess', a Movement just recently shown to the pupils by Mr Gurdjieff.

One day I was playing and playing like that when I suddenly stopped. My head fell on my hands. Evidently my centres lost their connections all at once and I fell into a deep sleep. Just as suddenly I woke up. It appeared that while the Movements were going on Major Pinder's little daughter, Yvonne, fell into the pond at the end of the alley. My sleep interrupted the Movements and provided the opportunity to see what had happened. The pond was not deep, and mother and child escaped with only a scare.

I was not the only one who had reason to be tired. There was Ivanov, who was in charge of our cows and had to get up every day at 4 a.m. to start work. Like everyone else he worked through the evening hours in the Study House till Mr Gurdjieff made his pronouncement: 'Who wish, may go sleep; who wish, may stay.' This always provoked annoyance in anyone who terribly wanted to sleep, which was what he was trying to achieve. Of course we had to stay – and oh, how we wanted to sleep! But one night Ivanov completely openly got up and went off to bed.

In order to wake up in time for his chores, he had his own system, which was called 'Ivanov's system'. If you had to get up at four o'clock, you drank four glasses of water before going to bed. If you had to wake at three o'clock, you drank five glasses of water. At the appointed hour, something better than an alarm clock wakened you.

Why do I mention this in connection with the kitchen? Because at ten o'clock each morning I had absolutely to remember to give Ivanov coffee and substantial, well-deserved sandwiches to sustain his energies. During the rest of the day Ivanov had no sleep, until Mr Gurdjieff's next announcement, 'Who wish, may go sleep; who wish, may stay.'

One day while I was preparing supper Mr Gurdjieff returned from Paris and dropped into the kitchen. He pretended he was sniffing the air and with a sweet, artificial voice said: 'Something tasty!' He asked for a piece of meat and cut it into thin slices. Then, putting it all together, he very skilfully began to scrape the surface vertically with a knife blade until the meat acquired a particular texture. *Skoblionka* he called it, which means 'scrapings' – and it is usually served with lots of appetizers.

The following day I decided to do something similar for everybody; of course, I did not scrape the meat but put it through a meat grinder. The obligatory sour-cream sauce was easy to replace with a sauce made out of milk, adding a bit of flour. Mr Gurdjieff again dropped into the kitchen and asked, 'What do you have for supper?' Stupidly, I called it *skoblionka*. He was very angry: in the first place, I had no right to prepare a dish in imitation of one he himself had made yesterday – that was an exquisite dish for himself alone and under no circumstances a dish for the working classes . . .

Of course I had not made *skoblionka*. I had not scraped the meat. It was well received and well eaten, and I hadn't wasted my time. But in that moment I learned how important it is to be accurate in what I say – even when joking – a lesson that I am trying to remember now as I write.

On my last day in the kitchen Madame Ouspensky, who all the time was in the background supervising and directing the life of the kitchen, decided for my last supper that I should make 'Tsar's Pilaff' – rice with meat. She had to show me how to boil rice, mix it with chopped meat, put it in the cast-iron pot with handles, then poke holes in the rice with a stick to let the steam escape.

Just here the stove became capricious. For a long time I wasn't able to get a fire started at all and then all of a sudden it burst into flames. It was already almost time to serve the pilaff. In order to heat it quicker, I put it in the hottest place . . .

Now rice, when it is burnt, smells particularly bad and the flavour penetrates the entire dish. Madame Ouspensky was horrified when she came in again to have a look. What to do? Usually, in such situations, one puts charcoal, wrapped in cloth, into the dish and that draws out the odour. But this time nothing seemed to help.

We transferred the contents into another pot and decided to serve it for supper. And for the second course we offered clotted milk . . .

After supper, Maria Andreyevna was passing through the

kitchen. Madame Ouspensky asked her how she liked the pilaff. 'Well, that was good,' she said, 'but the clotted milk had a smoky taste.' Madame Ouspensky and I roared with laughter.

That evening, after playing music in the Study House, I went to bed. The following morning I could sleep as much as I wanted, and woke up only for breakfast – breakfast in bed, for Madame Ouspensky brought my breakfast to my bedside: a most tasty ragout – the final chord of my existence as a cook.

XXI

Demonstrations

All summer evenings were devoted not only to Movements but to the study of the difference between real inner phenomena, such as telepathic sight, thought-reading and so forth, and what Mr Gurdjieff called 'tricks' and 'half-tricks' by which these phenomena could be simulated. I will say more about this when I speak of the demonstrations in America. For the time being I will content myself with describing one of the exercises given in preparation for them.

During the summer and autumn of 1923 our work by day was physical labour in the open air, but something more was added. We were given long lists of words to memorize. Mr Gurdjieff insisted that we should not set aside special time for it, but do it while working in the garden.

In the course of trying this I made one very important discovery. Usually when one observes oneself during physical labour, particularly work consisting of repetitive movements like digging and scything, one's thoughts wander freely in directions that have nothing to do with the labour. Associations flow, following one another in complete disorder, without goal and without result.

Now that Mr Gurdjieff had added these memory exercises during just such work, there was no room for leaks of wandering associations. At times it was necessary to stir oneself and direct attention to the digging itself, which at other times became almost unconscious. But the characteristic feature in all this was complete collectedness. Not a single bit of consciousness wandered away beyond the limits of the person. Everything was concentrated inside. This is one example of the many varieties of the Work, which always has as its ultimate goal the development of the person's being.

When I described the first big push of our work on the Study House, only the outside had been finished. Inside it was empty and cold. As soon as the three big stoves had been added, just before the onset of winter, we were able to transfer some of the evening sessions from the château to the Study House. Then, when electricity was connected, we continued to complete the most necessary parts of it by day while using it for its intended purpose in the evenings.

Mr Gurdjieff had told us that he was planning big Movements demonstrations, to take place in Paris in mid-December. During the summer, therefore, I had been orchestrating and copying the parts for much of the music, but much more remained to be done, depending on Mr Gurdjieff's choice of Movements. So one morning I went to the Study House to try to find out what to begin next. When Mr Gurdjieff saw me standing there, he shouted at me, 'Why are you loafing? Go up in the gallery and fix the cracks in the wall.' I worked some days at this, but then decided that I had better go on with orchestrating the rest of the music I had, as cracks could be fixed by anyone.

By this time the inner arrangement of the Study House was basically complete. The stage for Movements was at the south end of the building, covered with linoleum. Along the side walls we had built high benches with footrests. These were places for guests and visitors, who would soon be permitted to come on Saturdays to watch the Movements. In front of the benches was a wide passageway covered with matting, beyond which was a low ornamental wooden fence, which enclosed the central working space of the hall.

Inside the north entrance, underneath a balcony, was a kind of *loge* as in a theatre. That was Mr Gurdjieff's place. Three sides of it were draped with curtains, the open side faced the pupils and the stage. The floor of his *loge* was raised twenty-eight inches above the main floor, so that when he was working with the pupils he could conveniently sit down and watch.

On both sides, along the inside of the ornamental fence, mats were placed. These marked the places where the individual pupils sat, separated from one another by colourful bolsters. The places on Mr Gurdjieff's right were for men, those on his left for women.

The Study House acquired its final appearance only in December 1923, when it was necessary to complete the décor, as Mr Gurdjieff said, '*on time*', for the Paris demonstrations. At such moments he commanded absolutely everybody, except the cooks, to work together till done.

We painted the walls, fences and windows with Eastern-style ornamentation. All the inner space was covered with oriental carpets, and some of the finest ones were hung on the walls as well.

To conceal the structural woodwork of the ceiling, a huge canopy was made of white calico. All the women worked on it. They first transferred the design to the material spread out on the floor, then Mr Gurdjieff showed them exactly where he wanted the many aphorisms inserted, and they painted and embroidered them in a special cipher script that he had taught us.

When the canopy was ready, its centre was raised up to the ceiling by means of a sturdy pole, which temporarily had to support the canopy's whole weight. Once the centre of it was securely fastened, one by one the four corners were raised and fixed in place, and everything fitted exactly, though it had all been worked on upside down.

Now came a dangerous moment. The centre pole that supported all this added weight had to be taken away. Mr Gurdjieff told my wife to stand outside and not let anyone else in. The danger was that, when the pole was removed, the strain on the roof might bring everything crashing down . . . But all stood firm!

Over the passageways at intervals hung small electric lamps with translucent red shades. And two mechanical fountains

with changeable lighting were installed not far from the stage.
Mr Gurdjieff occasionally scented them with Eastern spices and
perfume. Then their functioning made the air fragrant and
aromatic.

When the main lights were switched off, the entire hall was
submerged in semi-darkness, and all the oriental rugs and Eastern
ornaments, bathed in the dim red glow of the lamps and reflecting
the changing multicoloured light from the fountains, became even
more beautiful and expressive. Mr Gurdjieff often asked me to
play the Essentuki Prayer, and when the pupils, led by my wife,
began to hum it, the combination of music with the magnificence
of the scene created a very deep and unforgettable impression . . .

During the final push we worked without relief. We had begun as
always at six o'clock in the morning and worked all through the
day, but there was still an enormous amount to do if we were to
finish on time. Night was falling and the tempo of work continued
without a break. On and on. At four in the morning Mr Gurdjieff
sent a message to the kitchen to bring everybody coffee with milk
and white bread. With this we strengthened ourselves and continued on.

The time came for morning coffee. It was also brought to the
Study House.

At noon appeared bread and big pieces of meat. But the intensity
of work did not diminish by one iota.

Finally, I remember, the last nail was hammered in at seven
in the evening. We had dinner and went to bed. The following
day we did *not* have to get up at six o'clock. We were allowed to
sleep as long as we wished . . .

During all this time Mr Gurdjieff had also been creating new
exercises, and more and more music had to be composed and
orchestrated. My difficulty was increased because I had only 35
musicians instead of 100, the usual number for orchestral performances in the Théâtre des Champs-Elysées. I could not use trumpets
because, masking my few strings, they would have sounded blatant.

Eight performances of our programme were scheduled between 13 December and Christmas Day. The last three nights before the dress rehearsal I did not sleep at all. What sleep I had was snatched during travel between Fontainebleau and Paris.

My composer-friend Tcherepnin came along to a late rehearsal to see our work and listen to my music. Of course it was just then that Mr Gurdjieff told me that the Mazurka music sounded 'limp'. I didn't know what to do. In desperation I decided to leave the music as it was, but I added another melody above it. I really had a feeling of satisfaction when, after the rehearsal was over, Tcherepnin told me how wonderful it all sounded.

The night before the dress rehearsal, all rugs, goatskins, mattresses and even the fountains from the Study House were brought to the theatre. The foyer became an oriental palace. For the public there were all kinds of Eastern delicacies and the fountains were filled with champagne instead of water. Pupils who did not take part in the demonstration, among them an English diplomat, stood at the entrance, dressed in the costumes we had made for *The Struggle of the Magicians*. The Movements were much appreciated, but the greatest reaction was to the women who walked in a circle around the stage with outstretched arms. The audience began to shout 'Enough! Enough!' because they could not understand how it was possible to maintain it for so long.

According to accounts that reached me, there was one person who was very displeased with the demonstration. This was Emile Jaques-Dalcroze. Perhaps it was because everything that he saw contradicted his own system of movement, which had been widely accepted. Here everything was based on quite another principle of anti-mechanical movement, simultaneously developing physical work with consciousness and even prayer, as in the Dervish Movements.

When the demonstration ended I asked Mr Gurdjieff, 'How did everything go?' He looked at me, smiling, but said nothing. That gave me a strong inner experience, and from it I realized that in work of this kind we do not seek words of praise or encouragement. We have to fulfil the task as best we can and there should be no consideration for whether one is praised or not: that is the aim. Mr Gurdjieff so often said: 'Never think of results, just do.'

At one of the later performances Mr Gurdjieff sat in the front row. During one of the Movements he took the baton from me and himself conducted the whole Movement from the floor.

At another performance, when at the very end Mr Gurdjieff shouted, 'Stop!', the pupils on the stage held their postures and held them quite long. Then Mr Gurdjieff had the curtain brought down without saying that the 'stop' was finished. One of the pupils did not continue to hold the 'stop' once the curtain was down and Mr Gurdjieff scolded her very strongly. He said that the 'stop' had nothing to do with the audience or the curtain . . . that it is Work and cannot be finished until the teacher says so, that it has to be held even if a fire should break out in the theatre.

After the last demonstration all the carpets, fountains and other things were taken back to the Prieuré. That year we celebrated Christmas on New Year's Eve. Beforehand Mr Gurdjieff went to Paris to buy rich presents for all the children. Dinner was in the Study House itself. There were entire roasted lambs, suckling pigs, oriental meat dishes and Eastern sweets. To this feast many French guests were invited, among them painters. One of them – I believe it was Soutine – was simply destroyed with exaltation. I remember asking him whether he wished to taste anything else and he simply threw up his hands, saying he couldn't find any words to express his delight.

XXII

America

When everything was back in place at the Prieuré, Movements continued just as strongly. The demonstrations were, in part, preparation for a possible trip to New York. I say 'possible' because until the last moment we did not know whether the money for the tickets and living expenses would materialize.

Mr Gurdjieff had sent Orage and Dr Stjernvall to New York in advance to make this trip possible. It was difficult to believe that it could take place, because almost everyone who took part in Paris was to go. We had to prepare 'as if'.

The time of departure was fixed for the first week of January and Mr Gurdjieff put my wife in charge of passports and clothing for all the pupils. Among the pupils going to America were not only Russian citizens with old Russian passports, but also Lithuanians, Armenians and Poles. All their passports had to be registered and renewed at Melun near Fontainebleau, and none of us at that time had a car, except Mr Gurdjieff.

Everyone had to be taken to Paris and outfitted, in some cases literally from head to foot. Of course, it was not possible to consider individual taste or desire but only to choose what was suitable for the purpose of the trip.

Finally the cheque from America arrived and the tickets were bought at once. Movements went on until the very last evening. We left a good number of people in the Prieuré, with one person in charge during our absence. There had been no time for my wife to buy a hat and coat for herself, so Mr Gurdjieff took her to

Paris in his car the morning of the day of departure. In fact, the last of the necessary formalities was completed only half an hour before our train left for Le Havre.

As we arrived at the dockside, there stood the huge French liner *Paris* just across the platform – 40,000 tons! Only the English liner *Majestic* was bigger. Most of us, particularly the Russians, had never seen anything remotely like it.

As we were boarding at the gangplank, where we had to present our passports, one of the young women suddenly said to my wife, 'Olga Arkadievna, I don't have mine with me!'

'How not? Where is it? They won't let you on the steamer!'

'I hid it in my trunk!'

And the trunks were already loaded on the ship! Happily, with the captain's permission, the young lady and my wife were escorted on board, went down into the hold and successfully extracted the passport.

We were all very happy to be going to America. Everyone, myself included, dreamed of triumphal demonstrations and the large profits so indispensable to Mr Gurdjieff for carrying out his future plans. But, in fact, the reality was to become so mixed with difficulties that our American trip began to seem like another 'crossing of the mountains'. As always with Mr Gurdjieff, the goal was not a triumphal tour, but work and effort on ourselves every day in other circumstances – the simplest and humblest of living conditions and food in an environment of the most luxuriously tempting possibilities.

In Essentuki Mr Gurdjieff had begun to give us exercises for this purpose, including some for the concentration of thought and some quite complicated ones with regard to breathing. I do not think I should describe them and, besides, it could not be useful to just read about them. Mr Gurdjieff often warned us that exercises connected with breathing could even be harmful if they were not done in the proper way. For the same reason he said not to repeat to others his personal talks with individuals, especially talks about breathing and sex energy.

One feature that all the exercises have in common is that they require all our attention and so avoid the flow of uncontrolled associations that waste our life energy through very stupid, sometimes very painful, sometimes fantastic, sometimes erotic thoughts, feelings and sensations, which we all more or less experience. Mr Gurdjieff frequently said that 'conscious labour' and 'intentional suffering', by reducing this unconscious flow of associations, could prolong life. For those who work on attention and use it in the struggle with associations, who do not forget to 'remember themselves' – for those people attention begins to be not only the centre of life, but also the factor that lengthens it.

Mr Gurdjieff had a first-class cabin. The rest of us had very comfortable second-class cabins and excellent food. As we had promised to give a demonstration of Movements as a benefit for the crew, the ship's purser allowed us to use freely the first-class public rooms, except at mealtimes. But all the trip was not to be as smooth as the start. Soon the sea began to be very rough and by seven o'clock the first night most of the passengers, including our pupils, did not appear for dinner. My wife and I were not feeling very well either, but as we wished to stay with Mr Gurdjieff, we struggled not to give in but to overcome the nausea. Later, during this and other trips, we stood stormy weather very well. It was one of the worst crossings the *Paris* had ever had; even the big mirror in the *grand salon* was cracked.

The following days were spent in visiting all our sick people who were not able to enjoy the ship's advantages and could swallow nothing but orange juice.

The day before our arrival, however, the weather changed and the sun came out. Mr Gurdjieff ordered everyone to rehearse Movements because the demonstration was to take place in the evening. After so many days lying in bed, it was necessary to limber up the muscles.

When I went on deck I saw a crowd of people watching something with eager curiosity: it was our pupils practising Movements under the direction of Ferapontov. During the day we had a full rehearsal in one of the lounges and after dinner we gave the demonstration before all the passengers, dressed in our white costumes, silk for the ladies and cotton duck for the men. The programme began with one of the pupils explaining in a few words the aim of the Movements. Then my wife sang the 'Bell Song' from *Lakmé*, which Mr Gurdjieff particularly liked. The Movements performed were nearly all those that had been given in the Théâtre des Champs-Elysées in Paris. At the end Mr Gurdjieff, who sat in the first row, shouted 'Stop!' The audience was amazed to see the pupils achieve this in spite of the ship's rolling, which was so extreme at one point that the piano slowly, but steadily, slid from one side of the stage to the other, myself following it on my stool.

The following morning we arrived in New York. The personnel of the ship had been very attentive to all Mr Gurdjieff's pupils when they were so ill, but no one had any money for tips. However, when Orage appeared with some reporters and a photographer, he quickly resolved this problem.

The photographer took pictures of Mr Gurdjieff, including one when he was saluting America with his astrakhan hat in hand. This photo, in which the face of Mr Gurdjieff has a profoundly inner expression, exists. I like especially another photo of him taken in Olginka in the Caucasus, sitting with his dogs and his cat. All his kindness and tenderness, particularly towards animals, shows clearly. We saw him like this very often in those far-away times . . .

When all landing formalities were over, Orage brought Mr Gurdjieff, my wife and me to the Hotel Ansonia, while some of his friends took the rest of the pupils to another hotel, with Madame Ostrovsky to look after them. Having settled in our rooms, my wife looked in the phone book and quickly found her brother's number. At first he refused to believe that his own sister was speaking from New York. Of course this was again an unexpected joy.

Orage brought an American journalist to meet Mr Gurdjieff and we all lunched together in the hotel restaurant, a very expensive one. The roast beef had an odd bluish shade. It was surely from frozen meat, which Mr Gurdjieff refused to eat. Afterwards we always bought chickens or meat from Jewish butchers, because they didn't deal in frozen meat.

When he was paying the bill, Mr Gurdjieff took out his very beautiful leather wallet. The journalist admired its many-coloured oriental design and inquired where it came from. Mr Gurdjieff asked, 'Do you like it?' 'Oh, of course!' was the answer. Then Mr Gurdjieff took out his money and papers and handed the wallet to the journalist, explaining that in the Orient if a guest expresses his admiration for something in the house of his host, the host always presents it to the guest. The journalist was stunned.

The next day the question was raised of determining a place and date for our demonstration, and at once difficulties arose because not a single theatre was free. The pupils had to rehearse, sometimes twice a day, but where? Neither private halls nor dance studios like those in Paris were to be had. Finally, we found something appropriate and inexpensive, called Leslie Hall, on the west side of Broadway, not far from where the pupils were staying. It was a longish two-storey building. Each floor had a hall along its length, but on the ground floor there was only a small stage and a meeting room, which was not appropriate. The upper hall had plenty of space but no stage from which the Movements would be visible. So Mr Gurdjieff had one quickly built by the pupils to the design and direction of Mr de Salzmann.

We could perhaps have had much better conditions, because the Moscow Art Theatre was just then visiting New York and the artists and manager were very well known to me, as I had written music for them during our year in Tiflis. Mr Gurdjieff knew all this, but for one reason or another he did not wish to change from Leslie Hall.

The date of the first New York demonstration was set. The piano was carried up from the ground floor. Two days before the performance Mr Gurdjieff summoned me and said, 'Would it not be possible to arrange the music for an orchestra of about five musicians?' It had to be done of course. After the sound of the orchestra at the Théâtre des Champs-Elysées, although even there we had had only thirty-five musicians, this seemed a quite pitiful number. To tell the truth such an 'orchestra' was not necessary at all; the piano would have been quite enough.

At the rehearsal in the afternoon we had five good Russian musicians with whom Mr Gurdjieff could communicate. In the middle of the rehearsal he particularly wanted to interest them. So he ordered all the pupils to go to the far end of the hall, asked the musicians to choose a word and whisper it to him. Then he told them to play a foxtrot and himself took up the tambourine from the percussionist and began very skilfully to strike an interesting rhythm. In a minute or two the word was loudly pronounced by the pupils from the other end of the hall. The musicians were quite astonished.

In fact, the violin, cello, double-bass, clarinet and percussion played wonderfully together. It was agreeable afterwards to be told by the cellist, Bukinik, who came from Moscow and was a connoisseur of oriental music, that all the music pleased him very much, especially the melody that we called 'Geese'.

On the evening of the demonstration the hall was filled with very elegant Americans. There were journalists and writers invited by Orage. Even the celebrated conductor Walter Damrosch came. The whole programme of Champs-Elysées was given. At the end of this very long performance, when the public began to leave, I wanted to speak with some of them. But I could not, because Mr Gurdjieff told me to play the music for 'The Fall of the Priestess' and he told the pupils to perform it, not on the stage but on the floor of the hall, where it continued until all the public had left. That spoiled the evening for me and I never understood the purpose.

We gave only one performance in Leslie Hall. Afterwards, we had to take apart the stage. As it turned out, soon after our departure from New York, the building was demolished and a multi-storey building took its place. But for the time being fate had assigned it to us.

Later we had several demonstrations in the Neighborhood Playhouse on Grand Street. The Lewisohn sisters, who had founded this theatre, were patrons of experimental arts and provided the space to Mr Gurdjieff free of charge. In the same theatre an amateur group was rehearsing Prokofiev's opera *The Buffoon*. There was also one evening dedicated to American Indians and their music. Mr Gurdjieff sent me specially to observe and listen, and write down their melodies. These notes I have still.

As time passed, there were fewer and fewer people in our audience and we had no further prospects. Our food ration diminished day by day. Madame Ostrovsky had to be extraordinarily inventive to feed us all cheaply, tastily and satisfyingly. I remember particularly the *kisel* jelly she made, which I had not tasted since my typhoid days, though where she found the particular kind of cranberries I cannot guess.

Finally, Mr Gurdjieff decided that there was nothing else to do than repeat what he had done in Sochi in 1918 after crossing the mountains. He told us he had no more money, that we were now responsible for our own livelihood and each of us should look for work. We all decided to go to an employment agency in the morning, list our professions and then wait for calls.

At the agency I offered myself as a musician, but only cooks were really in great demand. There was also a request for someone who could restore paintings. I gave them the name and address of Mr de Salzmann, who was particularly in a difficult situation. He had just received news of the death of his mother, whom he adored. I tried in vain to console him in his grief. 'After all,' he said, 'you cannot feel what a wonderful person she was.'

Hardly had I returned home from the agency when our phone rang and a familiar voice spoke in Russian. I said, 'Bolm, is that you?'

'Yes, it is really I.' Adolph Bolm was a former *premier danseur* and one of the most eminent persons in the Imperial Ballet in St Petersburg. Having had great success with the Diaghilev ballet troupe, he had stayed in Chicago and opened a successful ballet studio there. He found me through the Moscow Art Theatre. He was looking for me, thinking that the music of a small ballet, *Tanzlegendchen*, was my composition. Actually, it was by a pupil of Richard Strauss, whose name was Hermann Bischoff. Confusion of Hermann and Hartmann had perhaps caused the misunderstanding, but his mistake led to a total change in our fortunes.

I told him what I was doing and spoke about Mr Gurdjieff. He was very interested and asked to be introduced. As a result, Bolm invited us to come to Chicago, and not only offered his studio for our rehearsals, but also said he would help us organize a demonstration in a major theatre there. Mr Gurdjieff accepted his invitation and decided we should all go to Chicago. So conditions changed once more, from very bad to very good.

One of the important parts of our programme in America presented examples of both real and simulated psychic phenomena, such as 'transmission of thought' at a distance. A word would be whispered by a person in the audience to one of the pupils, usually Madame Ostrovsky, who moved about the hall, and the pupils on the stage had to guess the word. They also identified objects hidden in people's pockets. And if someone chose to think of the name of an opera, music from that opera would be played on the stage. Before all these experiments it was announced that some would be real and others would be tricks. The public was invited to say which were which. This interested young people and students tremendously, but they were never able to understand how we did it.

Perhaps this all stemmed from a time in Essentuki when Dr Stjernvall was at our little house. There was a knock on the door and Mr Gurdjieff entered wearing Mandzavino's tall silk hat. Laughing, he asked us whom he resembled. The doctor said, 'A circus director!' And indeed his black moustache that day was particularly curled.

The very next evening my wife and I had gone to Kislovodsk to attend a seance of a famous hypnotist, whose posters we had seen. On the stage several doctors were present to try to determine whether the person in the hypnotic trance was a partner of the hypnotist, who walked about among the audience asking repeatedly, 'So-and-so, are you asleep?' His voice was somehow nasal, not a normal voice. The hypnotized person, blindfolded, was able to locate and identify objects hidden by the public, among them a needle.

The following day I told Mr Gurdjieff about the seance, and he said, 'I know how they do it.' He added that in his early years he and his friends decided to check on the nature of hypnotic seances performed for audiences, as well as telepathic sight, reading of thoughts and so forth. Having devoted a definite time to this, they had succeeded in demonstrating publicly all of these phenomena. Whether that was really so or not, what Mr Gurdjieff began to talk about in Essentuki he finally translated into reality in the United States.

Before going west, Mr Gurdjieff arranged demonstrations in Philadelphia and Boston to give us more practice. In Boston, before the performance, Mr Gurdjieff did not miss an opportunity to give me an emotional experience. In the orchestra pit where I was to play on the piano, there were some folding chairs, which he wanted put away or moved somewhere. There was something that I 'failed to understand'. He made a comment that hurt me and provoked a turmoil of inner complaint: 'Everything connected with the music depends entirely on me and here I am being picked on for a trifle.' In half an hour the demonstration was to begin and I had to be able to concentrate all my attention. In the intensity of the moment I looked to see what was missing, and finally realized that if the music needed know-how, there must also be know-how for the chairs. In other words, I should not be lopsided, and at that moment it was more necessary to pay attention to the chairs than to my inner complaints over this painful stroke. That realization cleared my mind and the demonstration passed successfully. The very same evening we returned to New York.

We had to find the cheapest way to get to Chicago. I began my inquiries with the big railway companies in Grand Central and Philadelphia stations, but my researches finally led me to a little agency across the river in Hoboken. Having learned what my business was, the agent first offered me a cigar and then proposed a price for all the participants that was considerably lower than all the other offers, but the trip would take longer.

When I told this to Mr Gurdjieff, he consented to this plan and told me to leave for Chicago the next morning with all the other pupils under my guardianship. He himself, with my wife and Orage, would take a direct train, not leaving until 6 p.m. the same day as ours, but arriving in Chicago early the following morning. Our train would not get there till 5 p.m., so they would have time to prepare everything for our arrival and make the necessary contacts, interest the press, visit Bolm's studio and so on.

My trip with the pupils was not without difficulties. One episode makes me shiver whenever I think about it. Our route was through Niagara, and the pupils found out that our tickets gave us the right to stop over to visit the Falls, then continue three hours later on the following train. Every Russian from childhood had seen pictures of Niagara Falls in illustrated magazines, so all of them were delighted at this possibility. I had a queer presentiment that we should not take time for this, although certainly Mr Gurdjieff would not need us the day we arrived. I had great difficulty in persuading everyone to continue the trip and give up Niagara, but they accepted it as part of the Work.

When my wife met us at the Chicago station, she told us we would have to perform for the French consul in two hours. Mr Gurdjieff had accepted his request that we give an advance preview for his friends to speed up publicity. Everyone saw how right it had been not to interrupt the trip.

The demonstration for the consul went well and as a result a concert hall was engaged, as big as Carnegie Hall and with a stage as large as in Paris. Many people were at the performance and both the Movements and our 'tricks' were well received.

Returning from Chicago to New York, we gave a last demonstration in Carnegie Hall at the beginning of April.

*

There were a lot of people. My husband and Ferapontov translated
what Mr Gurdjieff said in Russian, and Orage relayed it to the audi-
ence.

After the demonstration I said to Mr Gurdjieff, 'I looked out at
the audience and saw that half the people were not even interested
and seemed quite asleep. Why do you allow all these people?
Wouldn't it be better to have fewer people, who are interested?'
Mr Gurdjieff answered me, this time even a little angrily, 'How
can you judge? Perhaps for those who seem asleep today, in
twenty years something will be awakened in them, and those who
now seem so eager will forget in ten days. We have to let everyone
hear. The result does not belong to us.'

The day of our departure for France approached. Mr Gurdjieff
told my wife on the last day that he needed me to stay with him in
New York. As her presence was indispensable at the Prieuré, she
was to go back with the pupils. My wife could not agree to this
and asked Mr Gurdjieff to decide which he needed more: her
presence in the Prieuré or mine in New York. Mr Gurdjieff was
very displeased with her refusal, but in such a situation my wife
could not be moved and he knew it. During supper he told her
that he preferred her in the Prieuré and that he would keep
Madame Galumian with him. So I could also return to France.
Some hours before the departure my wife found that there was
not a single dollar left once the tickets had been bought. She went
in haste to pawn one of her rings. It was the very one she once
told Mr Gurdjieff she would never part with because it was my
mother's wedding ring. She asked Madame Galumian to find her
brother, who was temporarily out of the city, and ask him to
redeem it. Madame Galumian could bring it with her when she
returned to the Prieuré.

We sailed back on a very nice ship, the *George Washington*.
The weather was splendid and this time all our pupils were able
to enjoy the good meals. Some of the youngest, after several years
of simple Institute meals, discovered they could have second helpings of anything. Once they asked for and received six helpings of

ice cream. All this did not upset their healthy stomachs, even at sea. Plainly they were able to enjoy the rewards of their efforts for Mr Gurdjieff in the United States. One of his principles was: 'If something is given, then take!' – and make full use of it. He knew how to give, generously and at just the right time, and the use of his gifts always brought joy and new force.

We arrived back at the Prieuré in the morning. Madame Ouspensky, who had remained there with several others, prepared for us a simple meal, and after that I changed into my work clothes. Then Ivanov and I took shovels and went to the far kitchen garden to dig . . .

When Mr Gurdjieff came back, we learned that he had kept Madame Galumian with him in New York in order to dictate to her some recollections of his youth in the Caucasus, concerning his 'Universal Workshop'.* He scraped together enough money to rent two small, cheap rooms, where they began as energetic a work as only Mr Gurdjieff knew how to create – dictation, transcription, typing, revision, again dictation . . . For a while they literally starved, not having the wherewithal to buy food, but the work had to go on, and it did. And when it was finished, money appeared, from lectures by Orage and Movements classes for Americans given by Madame Galumian. They returned at the beginning of June in first-class cabins.

Some of us met them at the station in Paris. Then everyone except my wife went back to the Prieuré by train; Mr Gurdjieff asked her to wait and go with him by car. When they were in the car, he took out the ring I mentioned earlier and handed it to her. He said: 'You should not have done it without telling me. Your brother might have forgotten or not redeemed it in time, and the ring would have been lost.' She was very happy and was touched by his words.

*

* The 'Universal Workshop' is contained in 'The Material Question' in *Meetings with Remarkable Men*, Harmondsworth, Arkana, 1985.

When Mr Gurdjieff entered the Prieuré gate we were working in the courtyard. He got out of his car and looked at us with a very serious expression – we did not know then what awaited us.

XXIII
Catastrophe

Regular work at the Prieuré began again when Mr Gurdjieff returned from New York. As a result of the American visit it was necessary to solve certain equipment problems at the Institute, since about eighty more people had asked to come to the Prieuré at the beginning of the summer.

At the same time Mr Gurdjieff began again his weekly custom, which he had started over a year before, of driving to Paris for an evening and staying the night in his apartment at 9 Rue du Commandant-Marchand. The following morning my wife would meet him at the Café de la Paix for her secretarial duties, which included acting as translator for new people who came to talk with him, attending to his correspondence and going to the bank with the cheques he received in the mail. Whatever the morning programme was, Mr Gurdjieff left Paris at three in the afternoon to drive to the Prieuré, invariably taking my wife with him. Although during these trips he was generally silent, there were some occasions when she could speak with him and he would give her directives for the work at the Prieuré or for herself.

My wife had to deal with wholesale houses in order to get the best prices on the new equipment for rooms, laundry and kitchen. And as Mr Gurdjieff wished to change his apartment at the end of June, she had to look for a new one.

It was also during this period that Mr Gurdjieff told her that it was an unnecessary inconvenience for him to have to sign cheques, sometimes interrupting his talks with people. He therefore put all the money of the Prieuré in a bank account in her name. This worried her greatly and she asked the director of the bank, whom she knew, to accept a letter in which she stated that the money in her name actually belonged to Mr Gurdjieff. This she did without telling him, of course. The money question was always a great problem to her. When cheques arrived, she had many accumulated bills to pay. There were also taxes, insurance and the mortgage to think of. She knew that sometimes Mr Gurdjieff expected her to bring him some of the money, but often, after having paid the indispensable bills, there was nothing left over. I remember once Mr Gurdjieff planned to take a trip as soon as some money arrived. It arrived, but after she had paid the bills, only 100 francs remained. What can you do with 100 francs? Most of the time Mr Gurdjieff accepted it indifferently and was not at all annoyed. Sometimes he pretended to blame her for paying the bills instead of thinking of his need for money, but she always had the feeling that she had to pay all the debts of the Prieuré first and only afterwards dispose of the rest of the money. It was always a hard task for her.

On Tuesday, 8 July 1924, Mr Gurdjieff was expected at the Prieuré at about five o'clock as always. I waited for him because he liked to work with me on music upon his return from Paris. I happened to be passing near the front gate when the bell sounded. A gendarme entered, asking if this was the house of Gurdjieff. On hearing that it was, he informed me that Mr Gurdjieff had had an automobile accident and had been taken by ambulance, unconscious, to the hospital in Fontainebleau. The ground opened under my feet. All dreams, all hopes of further Work collapsed. I went to the hospital immediately with Dr Stjernvall; we stayed until the next morning, when we brought Mr Gurdjieff home, still quite unconscious. What had happened my wife will describe in her own words.

That morning, instead of going to the Café de la Paix, I went to the new apartment I had found for him on the Boulevard Pereire.

Mr Gurdjieff had planned to go outside the city to look at a quantity of equipment I was preparing to buy for the Prieuré. To my astonishment he was not ready. And when I reminded him that we had to start immediately, he said, 'Oh, telephone that we will come tomorrow.' This surprised me even more, knowing how considerate and gentle Mr Gurdjieff was when it concerned people outside the Work, though certainly not with us.

I told him the store manager would be very annoyed, but he was quite firm and told me to phone him that we would come tomorrow. Then Mr Gurdjieff said to write at once to my parents in Leningrad, telling them to sell everything of ours and theirs and come to the Prieuré, because soon there would be a serious famine.

Later, he and I went to his garage and he asked me to tell the mechanic to check his Citroën thoroughly, especially the steering-wheel. He told me he would be having lunch at an Armenian restaurant to do some personal business, after which he would take the car and drive directly to the Prieuré. I was to return to his new apartment to make an inventory and then take the train back to the Prieuré alone. I was again astonished and, of course, disappointed, because Mr Gurdjieff always took me back in the car. I liked that very much because then I could ask him many questions, and sometimes we stopped in the forest and sat still, which was my greatest pleasure. It was July and very hot, and I would have a lot of packages to take back to the Prieuré. I didn't know why he couldn't come and fetch me before going to Fontainebleau.

I returned to the apartment and finished my inventory about three o'clock. I telephoned the garage to see if Mr Gurdjieff's car was still there, so I could put my packages in it. They told me he had just left.

My train was not due to leave until five o'clock and, as I was feeling very tired, I sat down in an armchair in front of the window, which was on the ground floor, and fell asleep. Then suddenly I heard the voice of Mr Gurdjieff calling me: 'Olga Arkadievna! Are you there? Let us go.' I jumped up and looked out the window, thinking that he had changed his mind and come to get me, but neither Mr Gurdjieff nor his car was there. I thought perhaps he had called and, as I did not answer, he had just gone away. I asked the concierge: 'Did Mr Gurdjieff pass by?' She said she had not seen him although she had been sitting by the entrance for some time. I looked at my watch: it was four-thirty – just time for me to take a taxi and catch my train.

One of our pupils met me at the station at Fontainebleau. From his face I saw at once that something had happened and asked, 'What is it? Is Mr Gurdjieff back already?' He said, 'Yes, he is back.' But I saw that there was something he did not tell me. I insisted, so he said that Mr Gurdjieff had had an accident on the highway and was now in the hospital. I ran up the steps from the station to the street, stopped a truck and persuaded the driver to take me to the hospital.

There I found my husband and Dr Stjernvall, who took me into a private room where Mr Gurdjieff was. It was terrible to see him lying unconscious with his head and hands all bandaged.

There was no opportunity to ask my husband what had happened, but a pupil told me that quite by chance a gendarme on a bicycle had seen a car smashed against a tree, with the steering-wheel broken. He found Mr Gurdjieff lying unconscious on the ground, his head upon a double cushion that had been taken out of the automobile. Who could have taken out this cushion and laid Mr Gurdjieff's head on it? Nobody was around.

Shortly afterwards, an ambulance passed by, which stopped and took Mr Gurdjieff to the hospital. He was identified by a card found in his pocket. In the hospital was a very good surgeon, Dr Martry, who at once did all the bandaging necessary. Later, we thought that perhaps somebody had caused the accident and robbed Mr Gurdjieff, but I looked in his pocket, where I knew he had a diamond that he had just bought, and everything was in place.

Now I began to understand all my apprehensions since the morning, which I had tried to overcome and do what I had to do. Now I really experienced for myself the sense and meaning of life with Mr Gurdjieff and understood the significance of his per-

sonality for all of us. I felt as if, without him, the forces of life would stop, and that if he died, all that lives would die. I felt that his whole life's Work would be undone. Such fright overcame me at this idea that, at the same time, another feeling rose up and I told myself: 'If God exists, it cannot happen. If God exists, Mr Gurdjieff lives, so he will not die. Perhaps there will be weeks or months of incapacity, but he will live, because he has to live.' I repeated all the time within myself, 'If God exists . . .' Now, as awful as it was, in my heart I had this faith that Mr Gurdjieff would live and the only thing left to do was to act.

We decided that our two Russian doctors in Paris, both well known, one a surgeon and the other a general practitioner, should be summoned at once. I went to find the doctor who had admitted Mr Gurdjieff to the hospital to ask for his permission to have our Russian doctors come, and for the actual facts of Mr Gurdjieff's condition. After much difficulty, I finally located him at a dinner party.

He was quite willing to have our doctors come to see Mr Gurdjieff and told me that his condition was quite critical; there were severe head injuries and lacerations of the hands, but, as far as he could tell, no fractures. The only thing he was afraid of was that Mr Gurdjieff had had a major concussion.

I was happy to know that Mr Gurdjieff was under the care of a nice man who was a good surgeon and that his life did not seem to be in immediate danger. Only then, when I heard that, could I cry for the first time. That same evening I tried to write about the main experiences that we had had during our stay in the Institute, now that we saw all the old aims and questions in quite a new light. At the same time, this writing would perhaps serve to inform those who were not at the Institute during this period. The accident and the time following it brought such serious results for the whole life of the Institute that each little detail, even if only from the point of view of my personal understanding, would be very interesting. Mr Gurdjieff's teaching now began to be understood in a different way.

*

Dr Stjernvall went to the scene of the accident to see if he could find some sign of what had happened. Mr Gurdjieff was quite a good driver and the road was wide enough for a car to pass. Even if he had to drive off the road through the grass, it was not necessary to hit a tree. Perhaps the steering-wheel broke before the accident. All kinds of thoughts entered everyone's head. I must say that, at this time, I was interested as to why or how the accident happened only if it could help the doctors in one way or another.

At six o'clock in the morning our two Russian doctors, Aleksinsky and Sirotinin, arrived from Paris to see Mr Gurdjieff. They confirmed the diagnosis that no bones were broken and that, although the concussion appeared to be very severe, the actual condition would be known only after several days. They thought it was quite possible that he had had only a haemorrhage, because when his eyes were opened, they reacted to light, though they were very dull. Perhaps at this moment I understood how in reality the eyes of Mr Gurdjieff reflected his whole being, and it seemed to me that if his eyes would open, everything would be as before.

The doctors decided that the best thing to do would be to take Mr Gurdjieff back to the Prieuré. They moved him very carefully on to a stretcher and brought him there in an ambulance. When they put him in his bed, he opened his eyes for a second and even made some little movements with his right hand, but again fell into an unconscious state.

The time that followed seemed to be divided into definite periods. During the first period, when he was unconscious all the time, one had the feeling that not he himself was ill, but only his body, and that he looked from somewhere on himself, examining, trying to move, but unable to say anything. That was why we were so afraid of doing something that would perhaps hinder him from doing what was necessary for himself. From another point of view, we understood very well that there were really necessary physical things that had to be done.

Madame Ostrovsky, of course, had all the worry and responsibility for taking care of him. My wife and I offered to share shifts with her at his bedside, which she accepted. I took on myself the night shift.

During those first few nights Mr Gurdjieff lay motionless, completely quiet and without any signs of consciousness. On one of these occasions I was very tired and, in spite of all efforts to keep awake, at one moment my head involuntarily sank in deep sleep on my chest, as had happened once before during Movements in the lime-tree alley. Suddenly, I heard a voice – not at all a physical voice coming from the lips of Mr Gurdjieff, but some kind of very real voice inside me – that said clearly, 'Keep your head straight!' I was wide awake at once and did not fall asleep again.

From the first, we could distinguish when he really slept from when he was not asleep but only lay without movement and with eyes closed. We could tell what was necessary to do and what he wished, because we had a feeling that he helped us. If he wished to drink, he made a very slight movement with his hand when we asked him; but if he didn't wish to drink, he pushed our hands away, sometimes with force, and turned his head away from us.

The first two days it was not even possible for him to drink; we only wet his lips with a damp cloth. He began to be restless again and the French doctor wished to give him an injection of morphine, but Mr Gurdjieff made indications that he didn't wish it, and we all decided against it.

After the third or fourth day, the doctors said that there was no danger to his life. But they could not tell how long it would take for the normal state of his brain to return. They said that there had to be a great stillness around him, that nothing should waken him artificially. So we waited patiently for the happy day when he would awaken by himself.

On the third day, when the French doctor replaced the bandages, he told me to hold Mr Gurdjieff's hand so that he would not instinctively try to pull them off. I tried to take his hand, but he put his fingers in a fist and would not move them. When the doctor said, 'Au revoir', Mr Gurdjieff bent his head. There were other

*moments when he said something, but they were only moments
and then he would fall asleep again.*

*Finally, on the sixth day he opened his eyes. He called his wife
and asked her, 'Where am I?' When my husband entered the next
room, he asked, 'Who is there?' When he was told it was my
husband, he said, 'Oh, let him come in.'*

That afternoon, after I had had my sleep, I dropped into Mr
Gurdjieff's room to see how he was, and to my inexpressible joy I
saw again his former self freshly awakened, his eyes luminous
with kindness. I could not restrain myself from expressing my
happiness . . .

I was not needed just then, so I went to the dining-room to
have some breakfast. Afterwards, when I returned to his room I
was astounded by the change in Mr Gurdjieff's face. It was not
at all the same Mr Gurdjieff I had seen before my breakfast, but
the face of an abnormal man. His attention was drawn to the
big painting by Styka of Arabs praying in the desert. His wife
had to perform their ritual gestures several times before he quieted
down.

*Once again, for two days, he slept and slept. Then – it was a
Wednesday – for the first time he began to eat, apparently even
with pleasure. There were very peaceful days, but there were also
days when he was extremely restless.*

*He began to ask us in a very serious tone to give him one
cigarette after another, saying that he needed them. We had to be
aware of when it really was necessary and at the same time learn
how to keep him from smoking all the time. It was very difficult
to understand what to do in each case. For example, one day Mr
Gurdjieff told me: 'Take down the second picture from the wall.'
But there was only one picture, which I took down. Later, we
understood that, owing to the concussion, he must have seen two
things instead of one.*

*Suddenly one day Mr Gurdjieff said that he wished to get
dressed, and to our horror he actually went into the garden,*

*ordering someone to follow him with an armchair. He went out
near the chicken coop, where in general he never went, and told
us to bring an axe, chop down a tree, cut it into logs and make a
fire. Then he returned to his room.*

*Mr Gurdjieff did not seem to remember the accident at all. He
questioned us several times about what had happened, but each
time it was clear that he was picturing it differently. When he
asked me where he had been before setting out for the Prieuré and
I told him he had lunched 'chez Simonian' he did not seem to
remember even that.*

*He decided he wanted to see for himself the scene of the acci-
dent. He told me, 'Let the old car be brought and let us go
together and see where the accident took place.' I spontaneously
said, 'Mr Gurdjieff, you cannot drive the car and I do not know
how to drive.' But he insisted and began to be agitated, as he was
still quite ill. I knew that if I refused, he would ask someone else
to go with him. I decided it was better to tell him, 'All right, Mr
Gurdjieff, I will only go upstairs first and then they will bring
your car.' I called someone and asked him to bring the car to the
door while I put on my hat. When I came back, the man was
standing beside the car. I asked him to go and get Mr Gurdjieff,
and tell him that the car was at the front door and that I
was ready. As soon as he went away, I bent down in the car and,
with a pair of scissors that I had taken from my room, I cut the
accelerator wire.*

*Mr Gurdjieff came down, sat in his place and I sat in my seat,
as peaceful as a saint. He began to pump the accelerator with his
foot and nothing happened. He was quite annoyed and said,
'What is wrong? What is that?' The man who brought the car
said, 'When I brought it, it worked very well.' Then I added, 'The
car has stood in the garage for weeks. It is damp and rusted.
When he first began to run it out of the garage, it worked, but
then it broke. We will send it to the garage for repairs and go
tomorrow.' Mr Gurdjieff went to his room and forgot about his
idea of seeing where the accident took place.*

Months later, when he was quite himself again, I asked him, 'Do you remember that you could not go and see where the accident took place when you once wished it?' He said, 'Yes, something was broken in the car.' I asked him if he knew how it got broken, and he said, 'No.' I told him very peacefully that I had done it. Mr Gurdjieff became as red as a tomato with anger and said, 'Only you would permit yourself to play me such a trick.' But then, in a second, he turned and, with quite a different face, said, 'Fortunately, you dared to do it, because I understand now that if I had driven then, you and I would both be dead.'

In those weeks immediately after the accident we never knew what to expect. One day Mr Gurdjieff went to the Study House. As he was walking in, Madame de Salzmann whispered to me, 'Already he is acting.' He did not take his usual place, but went inside the fence and sat down on the cushions on the left side near the piano. He summoned several pupils to stand on the rugs in front of him and showed them a new Movement, beginning with leg movements: steps backward, to the right, to the left, forward, again back, and so on in a very complicated combination, and when the Movement ended it came out that all were back in their original starting positions.

For me it is inconceivable to think that a man out of his mind could invent such a complicated combination. On the contrary, I think that even a 'normal' man is hardly likely to be able to do so.

Later, when Mr Gurdjieff began to walk more and, on some days, to try to give orders about everything, it was really a nightmare. We felt that he did it all from excited nerves and that nothing could stop him. At the same time we knew it could be harmful for him.

He began to come to the Study House in the evenings. We were all very worried that it would make too strong an impression on him and that we would not be able to get him home. As always, he asked those who led the Movements and showed the positions, 'Jeanne, Lili, Nina, what are the pupils working on?' And he asked my husband to play the music. The first time it happened we decided to go away at ten o'clock so that even if Mr Gurdjieff wished to stay longer, he would see that everybody had gone and so would leave too. But later we could not even do that anymore. He ordered everything himself as before.

It was not long before Mr Gurdjieff insisted anew on going to the scene of the accident. That was quite an event. We rented a car with a driver, and my husband and I accompanied Mr Gurdjieff to the fateful place, all of us for the first time. It was at a crossroads near the hamlet of Chailly, on the main road from Paris to Fontainebleau.

Mr Gurdjieff got out and inspected everything around the area. He began to make suppositions and draw conclusions, finally settling on what seemed the only possible version: he was travelling at high speed along this stretch, for the road was in good condition and straight as an arrow, when suddenly a car came out of the side road in front of him, blocking his way. To avoid an inevitable collision, he swerved off the road to the right around a signpost at the corner and headed for a grassy space between some trees. Here a second obstruction faced him. To reach the grass the car had to get over a low stone embankment. Consequently, he had to hold the steering-wheel very tightly. From the shock of hitting and lurching over this obstacle, the steering-wheel itself snapped, its wooden ring falling to the floor, where it was found later. The wheel could not have broken before this point, since the tracks left by the car before mounting the embankment were perfectly straight.

From the spot where the steering-wheel broke to the tree where they found the crushed vehicle was not a great distance. All the evidence showed that during those few seconds before the automobile hit the tree, Mr Gurdjieff was working with the brake while trying to manoeuvre the car by holding on to the stump of the steering-column with the help of his hat, before opening the door to jump out of the car himself. His car was a Citroën 'dix chevaux' whose door closed so tightly that he would have had to give it a very strong push to open it.

We don't know exactly what happened after that. Seeing that he was bleeding badly, he somehow managed to get a seat cushion out of the car to lie down on, after which he lost consciousness. When they found him, he was covered with mud and blood, and by the stains on his clothing they concluded that he had been trying to reach his pocket handkerchief.

In a word, it is clear that Mr Gurdjieff was not in the car when it struck the tree, and that the breaking of the steering-wheel made the accident much more extreme.

When Mr Gurdjieff grew stronger and was able to walk further afield with the help of his wife or one of us, he returned to the idea of making fires. He told some of the men to go with us into the park near the far vegetable garden where tall old poplar trees were growing. One after another he had them cut down and made into big bonfires. Fire evidently pleased Mr Gurdjieff. He told us that he drew force from it. But as none of these pupils knew much about cutting trees, the trunks were falling in every direction. We could never understand why Mr Gurdjieff wanted such large fires, since they were so dangerous with these inexperienced people.

The period of convalescence was really a great trial for all of us. Mr Gurdjieff's strange behaviour lasted a long time. I think Madame de Salzmann was right in saying that, although the accident was real, his continued strangeness was mainly 'acting'. If he had seemed fully himself, we would have reverted to our old ways, always asking him what we should do about everything. Throughout his illness we were on our own and had to depend on ourselves for every decision. Even when we consulted with the doctors, we were careful to check their advice against our own instinctive feelings, so as not to do anything harmful.

It gradually became obvious that, though his body had been

gravely affected, inside 'Georgivanch' remained 'Georgivanch'. His acting had been in part to test how far we were capable of carrying on his Work without him. We felt that now, inside at least, he could do everything and that he knew everything, and that it was ridiculous to try, so to speak, to tell him what to do.

And at the same time, my wife and I, and Mr Gurdjieff's wife also, saw very clearly that in his body he was not well, that he was not the same as before, that something had not yet come back to him. Even his sight was impaired. We felt we had to protect him, though we might be wrong. We did not know his real condition. How could we? But to let him do everything like a healthy person was not possible. We felt obliged to stop him, and to try to do it in such a way that no one could notice it and that he himself would not realize our intention if he really were still not quite recovered.

We were not prepared for what happened next. On 26 August 1924 Mr Gurdjieff dictated to me a whole speech, which he wished to give in the evening. He called everyone after dinner to come to the salon. He did not wish to speak after two phrases and told me to read what he had dictated earlier:

I was very ill. Now, thank God, I feel better and continue to be better. What happened to me, how it happened, I do not know. I remember nothing. I went to the place where it happened and imagined how it happened. There are not many people who could speak with you like this after such an accident. In principle, I had to die, but accidentally I stayed alive.

Now I am healthy, only my memory is weak. At first, I had no memory at all, then it was weak. When I walked and spoke with you in the beginning, I forgot everything. That is why, if, during this time, I have done something disagreeable, if I have offended some of you, I ask you to forgive me. Only a few days ago I began to live as before. My memory came back and I can live as before, not as an animal. So, I repeat, to whomever I said something disagreeable, you have to forget it. I had also forgotten everything that I did and only three or four days ago I began to remember.

When I came back to myself, my first thought was, 'Did I die or not? How will everything be now? And what about the Institute?' I saw that I was alive, and I decided to close the Institute for many reasons.

First of all, there are very few people who understand. I gave all my life for my Work, but the result from other people in general was not good and that is why I think it is not necessary for those few to sacrifice their lives here. And I don't wish to continue as I have done until now. All my life I gave up all my money to other people, but now I have decided to close the Institute. Forgive me. I wish now to live for myself and tell everyone that the Institute is closed.

I will liquidate this house. There are many people here; they can live here as guests. I always received guests for two weeks, and now my house is also open for two weeks, but later I will ask everyone to leave. All the same, I cannot throw away all my Work.

Now everyone has to think. Does he wish to go away tomorrow or in two weeks? I always helped people and now I will also help them to arrange their affairs.

In the meantime those who stay here will be only guests, but they will have to fulfil all the rules that existed; even new people will have to do that. Those who don't do that will have to leave at once.

In two weeks I will begin a new work. The names of those who may stay will be posted. Others will have to leave.

But even now life will continue and duties will be carried out by those whom I ask. Others, if they wish to work, can work in the garden, in the kitchen garden and in the woods; but they have to ask me and live as guests.

Before, I could look after everything myself. Now I cannot do it any more and cannot oversee everything. This way everything will be written out in advance. When I am here I will look after it all myself. But my assistants will be Madame de Hartmann and, in the household, Madame Ostrovsky. Tomorrow I will say who will be on duty. Meanwhile it will be Dr Stjernvall and Mr de Hartmann and some others.

Each one has to ask himself: does he wish to stay or not? But I hope that now it will be better than before.

Again, I repeat that the Institute is closed. I died. The reason is that I was disenchanted with people after all that I have done for them and I have seen how 'well' they have paid me for it. Now, inside of me everything is empty.

That is my first reason. The second reason is that I wish to live for myself. I have to rest and use all the time for myself. I don't wish to continue as before, and my new principle is – everything for myself. From today the Institute will be nothing. My Work will be different and those who are not invited cannot come to this Work. Tomorrow you will tell me who wishes to stay, but for now it is enough . . .

XXIV
New Directions

Remaining in the Prieuré after the closure were Madame Ostrovsky, Dr and Madame Stjernvall with their son Nikolai, the de Salzmanns with Boussik and Michel, Miss Merston, Miss Gordon, Lili Galumian, Nina Lavrova, Bernard Metz, Rakhmilevich, and the two of us, along with members of Mr Gurdjieff's family: his mother, his sister Sophia with her husband, his nephew Valya and his niece Lucie. The rest soon dispersed. There remained only those few of us, and at the same time there remained the same pile of work required to maintain a huge estate.

In September Mr Gurdjieff summoned us all to Paradou. He told us to bring picks, shovels, wheelbarrows and the big pull-cart, and set us to work. In two months his brother, Dmitri, with his wife and three daughters, would arrive and live there. He wanted us to landscape an unfinished area between Paradou and the alley to the Study House. It was very heavy work: earth to dig up, big stones to split and then to reshape the surroundings. We laid out a garden with a flower-bed and paths through it to Paradou, all of which was ready when the family arrived.

Mr Gurdjieff's money was again reaching rock-bottom. We had to eat, but all of us were moneyless. Meals were reduced to fresh white bread and soup with pieces of beef. How happy we all were on those days when lentil soup was served. But no matter how poor our soups were, they were always tasty.

The difficult times did not continue for long. News came from

Orage that a lady well-wisher of Mr Gurdjieff had heard about his accident and was sending $10,000 to help his Work. Our food now became richly varied. To taste life fully was one of Mr Gurdjieff's principles. During our life with him we tried every sort of Eastern dish, some extremely exotic. He told us that in the East they have always paid particular attention to the refinement of food elements. During festivals they sometimes serve meals of more than fifty dishes. The aim of such feasts is not so much to gorge oneself under the table, but rather to sample, in tiny portions, all kinds of variation of taste experiences.

The number of people at the Prieuré gradually grew again, but never on the former scale. Although to outside appearances life continued as before the accident, it was not the same and caused us great concern. The health of Mr Gurdjieff himself did not improve as fast as we expected, and Madame Ostrovsky also was not well. Another very great strain, for us personally, was the arrival in November of my parents and my younger sister, Zoya. I said before that they came because Mr Gurdjieff insisted, on the morning of his accident, that I write and tell them to come without delay. Surely, he had a premonition of what was to happen in Leningrad. Rooms were prepared for my parents next to us in the Monks' corridor, and for my sister next to Nina Lavrova.

My parents stayed until 1929. They were too old to take part in our activities, and that annoyed them. What was most difficult for them and made them suffer was the ruthless manner in which Mr Gurdjieff very often spoke with all of us, his pupils. We also suffered from it, but we knew we were there for a reason, so we accepted it.

One morning I saw Mr Gurdjieff and my father sitting on a bench in the garden. I had to ask Mr Gurdjieff a quite simple question; in answer he shouted at me in a terrible way and I saw that my poor father was ready to leave. But Mr Gurdjieff turned to him and said: 'You see, father, what you make me do? You never shouted at your daughter, so she has not had this experience, and all sorts of impressions are necessary for people. So now I am obliged to do it in your place . . .' My father's attitude changed, and I could see from the expression on his face that he understood how everything Mr Gurdjieff did for us was to give us new experiences.

During his recovery Mr Gurdjieff could not sleep very well at night, whether he was at the Prieuré or at his apartment in Paris, and often wakened one of us to bring him coffee and stay with him. And even when he was practically well, Mr de Salzmann and my husband often came to sit with him before he fell asleep. Since very little money was coming in and since the only ones who had any money of their own – Dr Stjernvall and my husband – had already given it to Mr Gurdjieff, Mr de Salzmann and my husband had to go to Paris by day to earn money for the Prieuré: de Salzmann painted café walls with murals, and my husband composed music for films.

On one occasion when I took Mr Gurdjieff coffee at night, he asked me, 'Could you write what I will dictate to you? Are you too sleepy?'

I said, 'I can, I am not sleepy.'

'Then bring your notebook.'

He began to dictate in Russian a kind of melodrama where brothers killed each other and so on and so on. I wrote practically three pages before Mr Gurdjieff stopped and asked, 'Does it please you?' With my usual directness, I told him in all sincerity that I felt it was awful, and revolting, and that I'd like to throw it away.

Mr Gurdjieff very quietly told me, 'All right. Throw it in the waste-paper basket. We will write something else. Perhaps it will please you better.' With great pleasure, I tore out the three pages and threw them away.

Mr Gurdjieff began to dictate again: 'It happened in the 123rd year after the creation of the World. Through space flew the ship Karnak ...' He did not stop dictating till I had written three pages, and I sat there quite transported to another sphere.

He asked, 'Does it please you now? Do you wish to continue?' I *could not even utter a word, but he understood from my face how happy I was.*

This took place on 16 December 1924 at 47 Boulevard Pereire. On that night Mr Gurdjieff called his talk 'The Conversation of the Old Devil with the Young One'. The manuscript began without any preface.

It happened in the 123rd year after the creation of the World.

Through space flew the ship *Karnak*.

It was on its way from Sirius, via the Milky Way, to the planet Karatas.

On the ship was Beelzebub, travelling with his kinsmen and his household. He was returning to his home after quite extraordinary events, and at the request of his old friends he had consented to, and taken part in, a conference about these events.

Although he was already old, and such a long journey with all its unavoidable hardships was not an easy task at his age, nevertheless, in remembrance of his long-standing friendships, he had decided to accept this invitation.

Only a few months before this trip he had returned to his native land, after having spent many years far away in very difficult conditions, and this long and extraordinary life under such inexorable terms had left a deep imprint on his health.

Time itself had aged him and the unusual conditions of life had brought him to an exceptional old age – him who in former times had had an uncommonly strong, fiery and handsome youth.

Long, long before, when he still lived in the Solar System Absolute among others like himself, he was among the attendants of His Endlessness, our Lord God.

At that time Beelzebub – due to his boiling and turbulent Reason, which, because of his youth, was not yet fully formed, and due to his inexperience, his unrestrained and stormy thought, and the narrowness of his understanding, peculiar to every young mind – having perceived in the way the World was run something that, according to his understanding, was illogical, and having found support among other young minds like his own, mixed himself up in what was none of his business.

His interference, due to his tempestuous and vigorous nature, captivated the minds of many and brought this great kingdom to the brink of revolution.

Having learned of this, His Endlessness, in spite of His All-embracing Love, was obliged to send him away into exile to a remote slum, the system Ors, whose inhabitants call it 'the Solar System', and decreed that the place of his existence should be on one of the planets of this particular system, which they call 'Mars'.

This exile of Beelzebub was shared by many of his kinsmen and servants, and also by many of his sympathizers.

They arrived at this remote place with all of their families and households and, in the course of years, a colony was established on this planet, encountering all the inevitable events that occur in such cases.

Little by little, the population accustomed itself to its new world, and even found occupations both on this planet as well as on those nearby – little islands, lost in the big universe, on which nature was poorly endowed – and the people lived there for many long years, which the inhabitants there call 'centuries'.

So Beelzebub* *was born, and on the first draft, from the beginning to the last page, Mr Gurdjieff worked only with me. Once he had begun to write* Beelzebub, *he continued almost without stopping, day and night – at the café in Fontainebleau, the Café de la Paix in Paris, which was his 'headquarters', and during his trips. He*

* *Beelzebub*: informal title for the book later published as *Beelzebub's Tales to His Grandson*, first series of *All and Everything*, New York, Harcourt Brace, 1950; London, Routledge & Kegan Paul, 1950.

wrote himself or dictated to me. Then I had to type it. He corrected and I had to retype again, sometimes as often as ten times.

When Mr Gurdjieff found that the Russian text had taken the form he wished, my husband would make an interlinear translation into 'English', word by word with a dictionary. Next it passed to Metz, who arranged the words in normal English grammatical order. Then it went to Orage, who put it into real English idiom and style. Finally, Orage and I checked this translation against the Russian text and after that we read it to Mr Gurdjieff. I remember very well that several times Mr Gurdjieff, who still did not speak much English, stopped Orage and said that the English did not at all correspond to his original idea. I had to translate again for Orage, trying to help him understand what Mr Gurdjieff wished, although I myself was certain that Orage's translation was very exact. Finally, after many attempts, Mr Gurdjieff was satisfied.

Later, I understood that Mr Gurdjieff knew very well that people accepted the first thought that came into their heads, but, after thinking it over two or three times, they would notice some particular aspect that they had totally missed when they said something at once. It was not so important to him whether it was good or bad; he only wished to press us until we ourselves understood more fully the meaning and were very exact with our language.

When finally Mr Gurdjieff approved the English translation, someone read it aloud in the evening to several people and he watched the expressions on their faces. These readings continued late into the night. Sometimes even visitors were allowed to attend.

When Mr Gurdjieff was considerably improved, towards the spring of 1925, he decided to acquire a good new car. This was a blue Citroën with adjustable seats. It was brought to the Prieuré one Sunday after breakfast and Mr Gurdjieff immediately wanted to try it out. As we all felt sure that he still didn't see very well or have the speed and agility of movement that he formerly had, everyone began to object. He was angry and told my wife to go with him. They found some others willing to go along. Mr Gurdjieff then circled around the village of Fontainebleau and everything finished without a hitch.

This was the beginning of many excursions, sometimes almost every day, criss-crossing France in all directions in winter cold and summer heat, with all kinds of difficulties, adventures and breakdowns. He never travelled alone, but took with him, in turn, pupils to whom he wished to give new impressions and trials of attention and quickness of wit, and not only adults but also children, sometimes very small ones. On such trips the places were divided up as follows: three in the back seat, three more on the two folding seats in the middle and one sitting beside Mr Gurdjieff, who always drove. On all these trips my wife went along and can better describe them.

I went with Mr Gurdjieff to arrange his driver's permit after his accident. The chief examiner was very nice and there was no difficulty in renewing it. In fact, during lunch with us, the examiner asked me if I wished to have one too. I said, 'But I don't know how to drive yet.' He told me, 'If you give me your word that you will not drive before an examiner says, "Now you can have a licence", I will give you one today.' And so he did. But I never seemed to have time to learn.

I always had to go with Mr Gurdjieff to find rooms, arrange everything and translate for him. One terribly hot day we arrived in Vichy. Mr Gurdjieff was quite tired and asked me to take the car to the garage to make sure that everything was in order so that we could continue travelling the next day. As I still did not know how to drive a car, he asked Mrs Orage to go with me. The car was big and, I don't know how, Mrs Orage hit a peasant cart. Although there was no damage, we stopped at once and a crowd appeared. They sent for the police.

We had to sit and wait for the arrival of the policeman and I told her to prepare her driver's licence and papers so that things could go quickly. She answered that she had left her licence in

America. This was very bad, because at that time if someone drove without one, they could be sent to gaol.

Since I had my driver's licence (even though I had never driven a car), I told her, 'Let us quickly change our places before the policeman comes.' I had to listen to a great discourse by the gendarme about how awful I was and how could I drive such a big car without knowing how to drive properly. And, of course, I had to suffer on my own head all the bad feelings of the crowd. Having made his report, the gendarme told me I could go home. But now, how could I go? I didn't know how to drive.

I told the policeman, 'Well, I am so nervous about everything that has happened that I really do not want to drive, so will you permit my friend to drive? She knows how to drive very well, but has left her permit at home.' So he said, 'All right.' Mrs Orage took the car safely to the garage and we peacefully went home to lunch, not telling a single word to Mr Gurdjieff.

These trips, though often to holiday places, were nothing like conventional holidays. They continued to be learning experiences for everyone, often in most unexpected ways. A task given to one person might seem like nothing at all to the others, but cause much inner suffering to the one who had to find the strength to perform it. And on the contrary, a task that might seem cruel to everyone else could bring an experience of growth and understanding to the one who received it.

One incident will perhaps illustrate how well Mr Gurdjieff understood the inner life of people and how he could sense it even at a distance. We were coming back from a trip late one winter evening. I felt that Mr Gurdjieff was driving too fast and recklessly. My nervousness was aggravated by the fact that my husband was also in the car. Mr Gurdjieff realized it very well, so when I could not stand it and asked him to drive more carefully, he scolded me roughly, saying that I was not to interfere in what he was doing. I did not take this well, feeling that I was right; and I answered him, quite unaware at that moment of what I was doing, in a tone I should not have used with my teacher. Mr Gurdjieff stopped the *car. I got out and my husband followed me. Mr Gurdjieff went on. It was a cold winter's night and neither of us was wearing a warm coat. We thought of asking a passing car to drive us home, but Mr Gurdjieff himself came back to get us. We drove to the Prieuré in heavy silence. The following days I tried to avoid him, because I was still trembling with anger. Two days passed and then I began to think: 'How could I behave so towards my teacher?' A kind of remorse arose in me. I went to a room in the Ritz corridor where almost nobody but I had the right to go, and I sat there beginning to think deeply about myself in an absolutely new way. Just at that moment the door of the room opened and I saw Mr Gurdjieff enter. In a voice and a manner in which there was no reproach, nothing to remind me of what had happened, he said: 'I was looking for you. I have a lot to be typed. Come quickly . . .'*

XXV
Music

When he was at the Prieuré, Mr Gurdjieff worked with me a great deal on music, but not for Movements. The exercises he showed in August 1924 were the last new Movements he ever gave at the Prieuré. Beginning in July 1925 he began to create another kind of music, which flowed richly from him during the next two years.

I had a very difficult and trying time with this music. Mr Gurdjieff sometimes whistled or played on the piano with one finger a very complicated sort of melody – as are all Eastern melodies, although they seem at first to be monotonous. To grasp this melody, to transcribe it in European notation, required a *tour de force*.

How it was written down is very interesting in itself. It usually happened in the evening, either in the big salon of the château or in the Study House. From my room I usually heard when Mr Gurdjieff began to play and, taking my music paper, I had to rush downstairs. All the people came soon and the music dictation was always in front of everybody.

It was not easy to notate. While listening to him play, I had to scribble down at feverish speed the tortuous shifts and turns of the melody, sometimes a repetition of just two notes. But in what rhythm? How to mark the accentuation? There was no hint of conventional Western metres and tuning. Here was some sort of rhythm of a different nature, other divisions of the flow of melody, which could not be interrupted or divided by bar-lines. And the harmony – the Eastern tonality on which the melody was con-structed – could only gradually be guessed.

It is true that Mr Gurdjieff would repeat several sections, but often – to vex me, I think – he would begin to repeat the melody before I had finished writing it, and usually with subtle differences and added embellishments, which drove me to despair. Of course, it must be remembered that this was not only a means of recording his music for posterity, but equally a personal exercise for me to 'catch' and 'grasp' the essential character, the very *noyau*, or kernel, of the music. And, I might add, this 'catching the essence' applied not only to music. For me it was a constant difficulty, a never-ending test.

When the melody was written, Mr Gurdjieff would tap on the lid of the piano a rhythm on which to build the accompaniment, which in the East would be played on some kind of percussion instrument. The entire melody, as given, would somehow have to blend with the background of this rhythm, but without ever being changed or adjusted to fit the accompaniment. And then I had to perform at once what had been given, improvising the harmony as I went.

When I began the work of harmonizing the melodies, I very soon came to understand that no free harmonization was possible. The genuine true character of the music is so typical, so 'itself', that any alterations would only destroy the absolutely individual inside of every melody.

Once Mr Gurdjieff said to me very sharply, 'It must be done so that every idiot could play it.' But God saved me from taking these words literally and from harmonizing the music as pieces are done for everybody's use. Here at last is one of the examples of his ability to 'entangle' people and to make them find the right way themselves by simultaneous work – in my case, notation of music and at the same time an exercise for catching and collecting everything that would be very easy to lose.

It gradually became Mr Gurdjieff's custom, when he returned from Paris, to work with me on new music notation. After supper, when everyone was gathered together, the most recently harmonized music was played, then the latest text of *Beelzebub* was read, after which music was played again.

Mr Gurdjieff's music had great variety. The most deeply moving was that which he remembered hearing in remote temples during his Asian travels. Listening to this music one was touched to the depth of his being . . .

Here, unexpectedly, Thomas de Hartmann's writing stopped. He died so suddenly that he had not even read what he had written.

The evening before, he had played with tremendous force his Second Sonata for Piano, dedicated to P. D. Ouspensky's idea of the fourth dimension, for a group of musical friends who would not be able to attend the concert that was to take place in two weeks.

So I was left with an unfinished manuscript, which my husband felt to be very important – as can be seen from his Introduction. In the first chapters he described in detail a period of Mr Gurdjieff's Work from which only I am alive. I felt that my husband's writing should not be left unfinished, but I can continue it only by describing my own experiences.

To be impartial, not too personal and as sincere as possible is a very serious task for me. It has to be an account of our last years with Mr Gurdjieff as seen through the eyes of one of his pupils. I hope Mr Gurdjieff himself will help me to be unconcerned with other people's judgement of what I write. My veneration of him and of his teaching is profound. So I feel free to say what I judge to be true, subjective as it may be.

XXVI
Conclusion

During these years Mr Gurdjieff's mother died. Soon afterwards the state of Madame Ostrovsky's health became alarming. There was no longer any doubt that she had cancer. Surgery and treatment were useless, so Mr Gurdjieff, on the advice of her doctors, took her back to the Prieuré. He stayed much of the time in her room at the end of the Ritz corridor. It was a beautiful, large room and everything was done for her comfort. An upright piano was brought in because she loved music and often she asked Mr de Hartmann to play for her. When Mr Gurdjieff was in Paris one day, she asked him: 'Since Georgivanch is not here, would you play Chopin for me?'

We knew that her days were numbered and surely she was aware of it herself, because she asked my husband to find a Polish priest who spoke Russian. (She was of Polish birth.) He went at once to Paris and found one. I will not forget her happy face when I told her that the priest had come.

Two of the younger pupils looked after her, but we were in and out of her room constantly.

I remember vividly the day when Mr Gurdjieff, sitting in an armchair near the window in Madame Ostrovsky's room, asked for half a glass of water. He did not drink it, but held it in his hands for about five minutes, and then told me to give it to Madame Ostrovsky to drink; although I told him that she would not be able to take even water, he insisted it be given to her. Madame Ostrovsky did swallow it without pain and then was able to take some liquid food for several days.

This improvement could not last for ever, of course. Some days later she fell into a coma and at four in the morning Dr Stjernvall told all of us who were in her room or in the long corridor that she had died.

We who had known Madame Ostrovsky since Essentuki had lost an essential link in the Work, although she was, so to say, at the same time unnoticeable and yet always there. She liked the long conversations with my husband in Russian, when she told him about her life, of which we knew so little. Together they would recollect all we had lived through since we met. I was aware that her life had been full of suffering, but we all were witnesses to an extraordinary change in her during her last years.

At the same time the work indispensable to the maintenance of the house went on. Movements classes, the composition of music, talks by Mr Gurdjieff in the Study House and individual work with pupils − all this continued as before. And nothing, but nothing, was done at the Prieuré that was not intended to give experiences to one or another of us, most of the time quite un- expected by the person for whom it was given and quite unnoticed or not understood by others whom it did not concern.

One gorgeous morning when, as always, we were up early, I went out towards the beautiful avenue of lime trees and was filled with such a feeling of the beauty of Nature and with such happi- ness that I lifted my arms high in the air.

'What are you doing?' It was the voice of Mr Gurdjieff behind me. 'This is the gesture of a priest before making Holy Commu- nion, to bring the higher forces down. The priests have now surely forgotten what this gesture means and perform it quite mechani- cally, but it is really a gesture that can bring higher forces down, because our fingers are a kind of antenna.' And he added: 'Don't do it without understanding what you are doing.'

While all of us were in the Study House only one person would stay in the château and he had the task of being doorman. One evening the doorman came to Mr Gurdjieff and told him something. Mr Gurdjieff called me and told me to go back to the house and answer a phone call from Mr Ouspensky, who was at the station, and to remind Mr Ouspensky that he had already told him he did not wish him to come to the Prieuré. I was terribly worried because I did not know how I, a young woman, could tell this to Mr Ouspensky, an older man, even if the message came from Mr Gurdjieff himself. So I did not go to the house by the direct way, but went around through the cowsheds, hoping during this time to prepare what I would say.

When I reached the house, nobody was there and nobody was on the phone. I ran back to the Study House, very happy that I did not have to tell Mr Ouspensky anything. And can you imagine, I immediately saw Mr Gurdjieff sitting with Mr Ouspensky, in a very good mood, looking at me and twisting his moustache. I could certainly say nothing and went to sit down. Later I asked Mr Gurdjieff why he gave me such a difficult thing to do. He only said, 'That is my business.' But I understood that he wished to see how I would behave.

On another occasion Mr Gurdjieff received news that Madame Ouspensky had come to Fontainebleau and was staying in the Hôtel de la Forêt, which was not far from the Prieuré. I don't know why, but Mr Gurdjieff told me to tell the doorman that that evening he should let no one pass without his permission. Generally, after ten o'clock we all could do as we wished, except the five young boys, who did not have the right to go out.

Mr de Hartmann and I wished very much to visit Madame Ouspensky, whom we had known since 1917, so, after ten, we went for a walk in the forest of the Prieuré. Far away from the house we climbed over a wall and went to see her. We did not stay long and came back the same way.

Soon after we returned, someone knocked on our door and told us that Mr Gurdjieff asked that I should go to him. Although it was very late, I went. Mr Gurdjieff told me with great reproach, 'How can it be, when I ask that the doorman should let no one pass, that you and your husband went out and thereby made the doorman break the rules?' I told him that we never made the *doorman break the rules. Mr Gurdjieff asked me, 'Where were you and your husband this evening when no one could find you?' I told him we had gone to see Madame Ouspensky and explained to him which way we had left. Mr Gurdjieff began to laugh . . .*

One day I was waiting for Mr Gurdjieff to finish writing something he wished me to retype. A fly came and flew around the big table in the sitting-room. I tried to chase it and kill it, but did not succeed. I asked Mr Gurdjieff, 'Is it true that in the Islamic religion insects cannot be killed? If it is true, will there be any place for people?' Mr Gurdjieff told me: 'It is true that in the Koran it is written that no one can destroy a fly if they are not able to replace it. Think about it and when you understand, come and tell me.'

I really could not see what it meant, but having translated many conversations between Mr Gurdjieff and different people, I quite suddenly saw that I could perhaps understand it if I accepted that the whole story about the fly was an allegory or a symbol. But of what, I did not see yet. After thinking about it in quite a different way, I finally felt that perhaps it meant that we can destroy nothing, even a belief in something, if we cannot replace it with something else. I asked Mr Gurdjieff, 'Could it be that?' He was very glad that I could understand it.

In November 1927, when Mr Gurdjieff finished dictating Beelzebub to me, we were sitting at a little round table in the Café de la Paix. I must confess that I was so emotional by the last words of Beelzebub that I could hardly write. He noticed it and told me, 'We have a whole other book to write, so be peaceful.' Almost that very day he began to dictate to me about his father, about his first teacher, Father Borsh, and other remarkable people he met during his travels when he was young.

Soon again I had to write, type and retype. But it was much easier than Beelzebub, in which there were many things I could not understand.

When he came to the part about Father Giovanni, he dictated to me something and then told me, 'Leave it, it will come later.'

I kept the page, but the 'later' never came. So now I have this page about Father Giovanni, which I cherish very much:

I would be happy if you could know what I am thinking and how I am thinking at this moment; just what I am thinking, but not what I am saying.

One cannot say what one thinks. But it is not because one does not wish to say it – no, even if one wishes to, very much, one cannot say it. Our language, which is the only means to express our understanding, is so limited and so badly adapted to it, that even a thousandth part of our subjective understanding we cannot transmit to others by our talk.

Understanding is not our thoughts; understanding is the essence that we receive from the material we possess. It is necessary to have certain material, to have a certain essence. So if we wish another person to have an exact understanding, we have to transmit to him all our material from which this essence is built – transmit the taste of it – and that we cannot do. Much time would be necessary, as much time as it took us to collect this essence.

That is why I have said that I wish my old friend Father Giovanni could know not what I say but what I think. If he could know, he would be very happy and at the same time very astonished. He would be happy that I now, finally, understand what I did not understand then, thirty years ago, when he told me this – and astonished that I have actually reached this point, the impossibility of which he many times argued during our conversations.

In 1929 Mr Gurdjieff undertook another trip to New York at Orage's insistence. But this time he did not wish to show the Sacred Dances. He planned to make known his writings and to let people hear some of his new music. Consequently, only Mr de Hartmann and I accompanied him. This voyage was much more interesting and restful for us than the first one in 1924 with all the twenty-two pupils. We again sailed on the Paris.

From the first day out Mr Gurdjieff began to talk to Mr de Hartmann about how the time had arrived for him to organize his life in Paris independently of the Prieuré and to devote himself to composition. My husband had already begun the previous year to write music for films, under a pseudonym. It had been necessary to earn money for the Prieuré as well as for us personally.

In New York, with the assistance of Orage, talks and readings began at once. One or more chapters were read each time, either from Beelzebub or from Remarkable Men.* Sometimes music was played the same evening, while other occasions were devoted entirely to music.

All this activity was partly connected with the formation of groups. There were many new people who wished to meet Mr Gurdjieff, and they generally met him at a Child's Restaurant. Sometimes several tables were occupied by people waiting for their turn to speak with him. Writing and translating went on also, and during the day people who wished to privately read chapters of Mr Gurdjieff's books came to our apartment. We lived one floor above Mr Gurdjieff in a house on Park Avenue South, and it was my duty to give them the text to read for a certain payment. In the evenings he invited people to his apartment for supper, which he himself prepared.

It was an extremely strenuous time for me because Mr Gurdjieff put more and more pressure on both Mr de Hartmann and me. Often I was on the brink of leaving everything and running away. Mr Gurdjieff reiterated that upon returning to Paris he would help us to arrange our life there, insisting that we ought to take a little house and have my parents live with us. This was bound to be difficult, because our lives were so different and my parents were then quite aged. They wished to live in a Russian house for old people, which was very good and where they had many acquaintances. (My younger sister was married by this time.) But Mr Gurdjieff insisted that we do as he proposed, saying that eventually I would be grateful to him. They lived with

* Published as Meetings with Remarkable Men, Harmondsworth, Arkana, 1985.

253

us for nine years. Mr Gurdjieff was right. I am grateful to this day . . .

On our return from New York, Mr Gurdjieff never again mentioned arranging our life in Paris. But when he made changes in the Prieuré, we had to move my parents temporarily to my cousin's in Paris; and then we looked for a house and found one in Courbevoie, on the outskirts of Neuilly. However, we ourselves continued to live at the Prieuré. Tension increased more and more. But we could not really believe Mr Gurdjieff actually wished us to go, as we had followed him for so long, in spite of every kind of hardship. Finally, he made conditions impossible, and one day in June, after a very strained and difficult conversation, we could do nothing but go. I was very unhappy and upset, and Mr de Hartmann, who was so much more sensitive and individualistic by nature, could not endure it and was on the verge of a nervous breakdown.

He could not even think of going back to the Prieuré once we had left, but his attitude towards Mr Gurdjieff and his teaching never changed. Once when someone said in his presence something unkind about Mr Gurdjieff, Mr de Hartmann shook him so violently that the man ran away, frightened. But my husband did not object when I continued to go to the Prieuré, though I could not go regularly, owing to the state of his health. Many of my duties had to be fulfilled by others.

We lived peacefully in our new house. Once someone knocked at our door and my mother called to me in French to tell my husband to go to the garden or the attic immediately. She had seen that Mr Gurdjieff was at the door. I went to meet him, and my mother was also very nice to him. We made coffee and I sat quietly with my mother and father. But quite suddenly Mr Gurdjieff said to them, 'Look, come back to the Prieuré. Leave this house; it will be much better for you.' My mother said, 'No, we are already settled here and everything is done for us. We are old and it is difficult for us to get into the life of the Prieuré.' Then, without changing his tone, Mr Gurdjieff said, 'Well, if you don't come in a week's time, a coffin will be in this room and your daughter will be in it.' My father got quite pale and I grasped his hand and told him not to pay any attention. But my father could not accept this kind of thing. My mother said, 'Mr Gurdjieff, why do you tell us such nonsense? We are not children!' And she laughed. Mr Gurdjieff began to laugh also and the conversation went on as before.

Later I told my father, 'Look, Mr Gurdjieff does this sort of thing to show you that one must not believe without understanding, and that is how he does it. He does it for me, to see if I will be afraid and send you back to the Prieuré. I know I will not do it and that you will not return there.' It did not bother me and it did not bother my mother.

During the autumn, however, I was able to go with Mr Gurdjieff to Berlin. This was another very trying time and I have very unhappy memories of this journey.

On our return from Berlin I went one evening to the Prieuré. Mr Gurdjieff asked me to do something that I felt I could not do. I went to my room. Sometime later Mr Gurdjieff came and told me that if I would not do what he asked, something bad would happen to my husband, who was at home at the time. We had no telephone, so I could not communicate with him. Neither could I go back to Courbevoie, as there were no late trains. In any case, I would only alarm him by returning unexpectedly. I was utterly in despair, frantically weighing the yes and no ... In the midst of this struggle I suddenly remembered how Mr Gurdjieff so often said that we must have faith only in 'something higher' in ourselves. I felt deep within me that if I could hold on to this and if I was afraid of nothing at all coming from outside – even from my teacher – nothing bad could happen. Perhaps my teacher was only testing me for the purpose of making me see something that I had forgotten. But in spite of this reasoning, in spite of the flash of understanding, I suffered terribly.

I went home on the first train in the morning and found my husband peacefully asleep in bed. Later, reading Milarepa, I found out that the Tibetan masters often made such difficulties for people so that they understood not to believe everything.

*

The following February Mr Gurdjieff again had to go to New York and some people accompanied him. He asked me to come on the evening before he was to leave, to arrange everything, and I certainly could not refuse him. He asked me to give him the key to his little chest of drawers that I always kept for him. He opened it and began to sort out papers, letters, passports and all kinds of objects, many of which he threw into the fireplace and burnt. I knew that there were passports among the papers, but I had not looked inside to know exactly what they were. I asked him why he was throwing the passports away, and he told me, 'You had the key. Didn't you ever look and see what was in the chest?' I told him, 'Certainly not!' He said, 'That was why I could give only you the key. Happily, you had not that awful quality of curiosity.'

I must say that in spite of all my sorrow and difficulties, I was very happy that Mr Gurdjieff never lost trust in me.

On the day of his departure for New York, I went to his flat at his request early in the morning for some last arrangements and had a wonderful talk with him, a talk that could occur only in exceptional moments. Then we went to the station and sat in a café. He told me that I was the only person who never had done what he demanded without wishing it myself. I certainly believed him then and was very happy. But, suddenly, he began to talk about how much he needed Mr de Hartmann and me in New York, that nobody would be able to help him in the same way and that I had to make it possible for my husband to rejoin him in a week's time. I replied that it was not possible, that my husband was not yet well at all. Perhaps he would wish me to go, I said, but I would not leave him alone . . .

The hour of departure approached and we walked slowly, in silence, along the platform to the train. I was very sad because Mr Gurdjieff was going away for so long, but more so because he could ask me to put pressure on my husband when he knew the state he was in.

I heard the first signal to board the train. Mr Gurdjieff mounted the steps of the dining-car. Fortunately, none of the people who

*were sailing with him was there. He stopped on the platform of
the car, I on the platform of the station, thinking of the numerous
trips I had taken with him . . .*

*Then, quite unexpectedly, Mr Gurdjieff said, 'Organize your
papers and come in a week's time with Thoma to the United
States. I need you both there.' I told him at once, 'Georgivanch,
I cannot. You know Thoma is not well.' Nevertheless, with a
cold, icy tone, Mr Gurdjieff repeated, 'Come in a week's time
or you will never see me again.' I told him, 'How can you ask
of me such a thing? You know I cannot do it.' He repeated
with the same tone of voice, 'Then you will never see me again.'
Although I had the feeling that a thunderbolt had struck me, a
voice in me said, and I repeated, 'Then . . . I will never see you
again.'*

*The train moved. Mr Gurdjieff stood motionless looking at me.
I looked at him without moving my eyes from his face. I knew
that it was for ever . . .*

*I stood there until the train disappeared from my sight. In my
thoughts I saw before me Prince Lubovedsky going away and
leaving Mr Gurdjieff alone. When he was dictating this chapter of*
Remarkable Men *to me I always wondered about this tragic
moment in his life and dreaded that it might happen to me. Then
slowly I went home, realizing that, having said what I had, all was
over. What else could I have done? If my teacher said that to me,
he must have known what he was doing and that I could not act
or answer differently.*

*Under pretext of a frightful headache I went to my room,
drew the curtains in order to stay in the dark and went to bed
. . . What I lived through cannot be described. But I did not
wish my husband to suffer, so I could not tell him anything . . .
It was four days before I felt strong enough to get up and
resume my life.*

For several years after we left the Prieuré, Mr de Hartmann continued to write music for films under a pseudonym to earn his
living. His pseudonym was Thomas Kross, Kross being the maiden

name of his mother. As soon as he had enough money from this activity, he was able to spend all his time on his own music.

In 1933, having sold the Prieuré, Mr Gurdjieff moved to Paris. Several times he sent someone to ask us to come back, but, like my husband, I had a very strong feeling that I could not and must not do it, no matter how much I wished. Nevertheless, neither my husband nor I changed our attitude towards Mr Gurdjieff. He always remained our teacher and we always continued to be faithful to his teaching.

Contact was never cut off, however. We continued to see Madame de Salzmann as often as possible, and kept in touch with the Ouspenskys. Several of Mr Gurdjieff's pupils came to have piano lessons with my husband. He also gave lessons in composition and orchestration to several distinguished musicians.

As he became better known, many of his new works – his first symphony, several concertos, song cycles and works for solo piano – were premièred by Les Concerts Lamoureux and other musical societies in Paris, Brussels and London, often with my husband at the piano. His new comédie-ballet, Babette, composed to the libretto of Henri Cain, was given its first performance by the Opéra de Nice.

About twenty years passed. We were living in Garches, very near Paris. One evening late in October of 1949, during a snowy night, Madame de Salzmann telephoned from the American Hospital in Paris, telling us that Mr Gurdjieff was seriously ill and had just been brought there. She said that she was letting us know in case we wished to come to the hospital and also because she would like us to be with her. How grateful we were to her!

My husband was in bed with an attack of heart palpitations, to which he was subject. On hearing the news, however, he jumped out of bed, told me to get the car, our old Panhard, and we went immediately to the hospital. We could not see Mr Gurdjieff because he was too weak. But nobody thought the end was so near. Late at night we went home, intending to go back early the next day, hoping to see him. But the next morning, at nine o'clock,

Madame de Salzmann telephoned us and said that, a quarter of an hour before, Mr Gurdjieff had died . . .

We went to the hospital. Mr Gurdjieff's body was lying in the little hospital chapel. His face had a wonderful expression of peace and beauty . . . For four days he lay in this chapel, because for religious reasons the burial could not take place sooner. Day and night the chapel was crowded with people.

The day before the burial the body was placed in a coffin and transported to the Russian church in the Rue Daru. Here a small group of people came to attend a short prayer. When the priest finished the ceremony and entered the altar sanctuary, he closed the curtains. At this moment the electric light went out. We thought that the priest had turned it off. The church was plunged into darkness, illuminated only by little candles burning before images. We stood in the dim light for about five minutes in deep concentration and peace.

Then Madame de Salzmann, my husband and I went to see the priest to inquire about the eulogy that he proposed to deliver at the burial ceremony. He said that he regretted that we had had to stay in the dark, because for some inexplicable reason the electric light had gone out just as he had closed the altar curtains.

Fearing that the priest would say something unsuitable, Mr de Hartmann gave him a eulogy that he had prepared for him. Being well acquainted with the regulations of the Russian Church, he wrote it in such a way that the last words pronounced by the priest in front of Mr Gurdjieff's coffin in the Russian church were words from The Struggle of the Magicians:

'God and all his angels, keep us from doing evil by helping us always and everywhere to remember our Selves.'

Chronology

The de Hartmann archives contain a surprising number of original documents, preserved despite the difficult travel conditions during their years with Gurdjieff. These include: Thomas's military postings, medical papers and release from the army; their Bolshevik passes for the mountain expedition; certificates of residence in different places in Russia; posters and programmes for concerts, operas and plays; passports with visa validations for many of their travels after Constantinople; occasional letters and journal entries; and, of course, a detailed record of dates for almost every piece of the Gurdjieff/de Hartmann music. All these dated items have made possible the compilation of a remarkably complete chronology of the Gurdjieff Work during those years.

New light on an old puzzle

No date for his own birth was written by Gurdjieff himself. The date remains uncertain. Many people have inferred a birth date from circumstantial evidence in his books, but the results are many, varied and unprovable.

The first edition of *All and Everything*, published after he died, gave the year of his birth as 1872 on the dust-jacket, but in later editions the date was changed to 1877 because his younger sister insisted upon it, apparently from a date that appeared on his passport. But 1877 as a birth date conflicts with almost every other piece of historical evidence. Gurdjieff would have had to be no older than eleven when he started out on his adult travels.

Olga de Hartmann was certain that Gurdjieff was considerably older, but she could never find the necessary evidence to prove an alternative to 1877. She had little faith in the reliability of passport dates, as her own was officially inscribed with a birth date of 1896, whereas her actual birth was in 1885.

The most concrete clue written by Gurdjieff, in *Meetings with Remarkable Men*, is that he was 'about seven years old' when a terrible cattle plague wiped out his father's numerous herds, along with almost all others in the Transcaucasian region.* But the history books of that era, giving dates for every battle, were silent about the cattle plague.

The only date attributed directly to Gurdjieff is from J. G. Bennett, in *Witness*: 'He told me later that he was born in 1866.'† But there were no independent data by which to confirm it.

More recently, we ourselves came upon a statement by Gurdjieff himself, transcribed from a meeting of one of his Paris groups on 16 December 1943, in which he said, 'I am 78 years old and I have had many disillusionments.' That would fix his birth date as 1866 if he was looking forward to his birthday the following January, or 1865 if he was thinking of his previous birthday. But, in the context, one cannot be sure that he was not simply wishing to make some special impression on his questioner. All the same, the coincidence is striking.

More recently still, Richard Smithies, in his far-reaching, un-published researches into Gurdjieff's background, made available to us information he had found in books by Frederick Burnaby and Henry Fanshawe Tozer.

Burnaby was an English army officer who had travelled in Transcaspia and Transcaucasia between 1875 and 1877. In 1875, in an area near the Caspian Sea, he noted that the nomad tribes

---

* G. I. Gurdjieff, *Meetings with Remarkable Men*, Harmondsworth, Arkana, 1985, p. 41.
† John Godolphin Bennett, *Witness: The Story of a Search*, London, Hodder & Stoughton, 1962, p. 64.

who migrated from place to place with their families, flocks and herds, 'had suffered a great deal of late years from the cattle pest . . . Vaccinating the animals had been tried as an experiment, but . . . with slight success.'*

The following year, riding through Asia Minor, he came across evidence of massive death and destruction of flocks and herds in that region. Whatever may have been the contribution of the cattle disease, it was augmented and compounded by a serious drought in 1873, followed by a catastrophic winter in which many people died and flocks and herds were ruined.†

Writing of the same event, H. F. Tozer gave figures: 'The loss of property was enormous, for about 100,000 head of cattle perished, and the number of sheep and goats was reduced 60 per cent.'‡

Summing up, Burnaby wrote: 'A few years ago the wealth of the Kurdish sheikhs was very considerable; many of them owned twenty, and even thirty thousand sheep, besides large droves of horses and numerous herds of cattle. The famine . . . was as disastrous for the Kurds as for the Turks. It has left them in a wretched state of poverty.'§

This catastrophe, which took place in 1873–4, is the only event to have come to light so far that remotely matches what Gurdjieff writes about his father's misfortune. That date, combined with Gurdjieff's written statement that he was 'about seven years old' when the plague struck, would also pinpoint Gurdjieff's birth very closely to 1866 or 1867.

With this supporting evidence, the editors have chosen, in the chronology of this book, to record Gurdjieff's birth year as *circa* 1866, a date that harmonizes well with just about all other circumstantial evidence.

---

* Fred Burnaby, *A Ride to Khiva*, London, Cassell Petter & Galpin, 1876/77; reprinted, with a new introduction by Eric Newby, London, Century Hutchinson, 1983, p. 136.
† Frederick Burnaby, *On Horseback Through Asia Minor*, London, 1898; reprinted Gloucester, Alan Sutton Publishing Ltd, 1985, pp. 66, 83.
‡ Henry Fanshawe Tozer, *Turkish Armenia and Eastern Asia Minor*, London, Longmans, Green, 1881, p. 90.
§ Burnaby, *On Horseback Through Asia Minor*, p. 85.

Day and date of the accident

In Thomas de Hartmann's manuscript no date or day of the week was mentioned for Gurdjieff's accident in July 1924. When publishing the first edition, Olga de Hartmann added 5 July, apparently from memory. That date has been much used by other writers ever since.

Study of de Hartmann's meticulously dated music diaries, however, showed that on 5 July, which in 1924 was on a Saturday, Gurdjieff was still at the Prieuré, working on the last piece of music before the accident. So 5 July could not be the correct date.

No other reliable date had been forthcoming. Contemporary newspapers that had reported the accident do not help, for it seems that none of these mentioned the day or the date specifically. J. G. Bennett wrote that it was on 6 July, but he was not at the Prieuré at the time and, 6 July being a Sunday, it doesn't fit with the facts for other reasons. There seemed no clear solution to the puzzle, until one day, searching for something else in the de Hartmann archives, we came upon a displaced file with a previously unseen document. It was in the very recognizable Russian handwriting of Olga de Hartmann on Institute letterhead paper. By its manner of expression it was obviously written within a few days of the accident itself. This document, as well as her rough draft for it, which accompanied it, both state clearly and unequivocally that the event took place on 8 July and that it was a Tuesday. It seems that forty years later when she was publishing the book, she had forgotten she still had the document or could not find it to verify the date.

'Old Style' and 'New Style' dates

Dates in old Russia were recorded according to the Julian ('Old Style') calendar, which is now nearly two weeks behind the Gregorian ('New Style') calendar used generally throughout the world. Dates in this chronology up to the end of 1918 are the official 'Old Style' dates. To bring them into accord with the modern calendar, add 12 days to dates before 1900, and 13 days to those

from 1900 on. From the beginning of 1919, dates were recorded
'New Style', as far as can be verified, and need no adjustment.

c. 1866? Birth of Georgi Ivanovich Gurdjieff (hereafter
abbreviated G), traditionally ascribed to 1 January.
Birthplace, in Turkey or Georgia, uncertain.

1885 28 *Aug*. Birth in St Petersburg of Olga Arkadievna de
Shumacher (hereafter abbreviated O).

21 *Sept*. Birth in Khoruzhevka, Ukraine, of Thomas
Alexandrovich de Hartmann (hereafter abbreviated T).

1894 At death of father, T placed in military academy, St
Petersburg.

1896 T accepted as pupil by Anton Arensky for music
composition and harmony, and by Anna Esipova-
Leschetizky for piano technique.

1903 T graduates from military academy as officer in the
Imperial Household Guards.

T receives diploma from St Petersburg Conservatory.

T's incidental music for the Dumas tragedy *Caligula*
performed at the Imperial Theatre.

1906 25 *Feb*. Death of Arensky.

T studies counterpoint with Sergei Taneiev.

12 *Nov*. Marriage of T and O.

1907 T's ballet *The Scarlet Flower* premièred by the Imperial
Opera; in repertory until 1913.

T appointed reserve officer by Tsar.

T offered conductorship of Imperial Orchestra, but
declines in order to continue composing.

1908–12 T and O live in Munich, while T studies conducting
with Felix Mottl. Both engage in the artistic,
theatrical and musical life of Munich.

O studies singing with Curelli in Naples, as advised by
Taneiev.

T composes much personal music, including *Danses
plastiques* for solo dancer Alexander Sacharoff,

performed in Munich at the Odeon in 1910.

Beginning of life-long friendship with Vasili Kandinsky. T collaborates with him on music for *The Yellow Sound* and contributes article 'On Anarchy in Music' for *Der Blaue Reiter*, a book on art, edited by Kandinsky and Franz Marc, published in 1912.

1912–14   T and O return to St Petersburg after death of T's mother.

O continues singing lessons at the Conservatory.

T completes song cycles begun in Munich; some of his piano pieces published by Jurgenson and Zimmerman.

1914   *1 Aug.* War declared on Russia by Germany. Reserve officers recalled to active duty. T and O stationed with Household Guards at Tsarskoye Selo.

O studies repertoire of operatic arias.

1915   *6 June* Death of Taneiev.

1916   *Dec.* T first meets G.

1917   *9 Feb.* T and O attend their first group meeting with G.

end Feb. T assigned to Austrian war front in Ukraine. O stays with sister-in-law in Kiev.

July G invites pupils to intensive work with him in Essentuki.

Aug. Mutiny of soldiers; T escapes with O to St Petersburg.

23 Aug. T reassigned, with period of leave, to Rostov-on-the-Don in order to hasten the manufacture of his model anti-aircraft invention.

28 Aug. T and O join G in Essentuki.

1 Sept. G moves to Tuapse. T and O follow.

9 Sept. Side trip to Rostov to validate T's military papers.

17 Sept. First expedition with G: Tuapse to Uch Dere. T's illness; hospitalized near Sochi.

end Sept. G moves to Olginka, near Tuapse. T and O left alone during convalescence.

15 Nov. Medical examination, showing T with heart trouble, provides three-month furlough for recovery.

T and O rejoin G, who directs them to Essentuki.

1918 *Jan.* G moves to Essentuki.

12 Feb. G sends letters inviting all pupils to work again in Essentuki.

18 Feb. T released from military service for medical reasons.

Mar. Intensive work of Essentuki Institute begins.

July Spreading revolution curtails work; G prepares to leave.

6 Aug. Start of second expedition, through Caucasus mountains to Black Sea: by train via Armavir to Maikop; then by horse and on foot through wilderness to Sochi.

Oct. G declares expedition finished. Pupils disperse. T and O stay with G in Sochi, making living from music lessons and concerts.

1919 *mid-Jan.* T and O accompany G by ship to Poti; thence by train to Tiflis.

T becomes Professor of Music at Tiflis Conservatory.

Easter Alexandre and Jeanne de Salzmann join G's Work.

c. late April Production of *Carmen*. O sings role of Micaela.

early May G sends O alone to Essentuki to recover carpets and other belongings.

26 May and 6 June T conducts concerts of Georgian music.

22 June G shares half of Jeanne de Salzmann's Dalcroze Institute demonstration to show his Sacred Dances, followed later by a second demonstration entirely of G's Sacred Dances and Gymnastics.

July G sends T and O to Armenia to lecture on, and give concerts of, music of Komitas Vardapet.

late July–Aug. T and O with G in Borzhom.

Sept. All return to Tiflis. Intensive work of Institute continues through autumn and winter.

1920 *Spring* Conditions worsening. Institute gradually dissolved.

May–June T commissioned by Moscow Art Theatre to compose music for performances of Knut Hamsun's *In the Grip of Life* and Rabindranath Tagore's *The King of the Dark Chamber*.

mid-June G tells T and O to prepare to leave for Constantinople.

c. 7 July T and O arrive with G in Constantinople via ship from Batum.

July–Dec. T and O re-establish a living through music lessons, voice and piano concerts, and conducting orchestral concerts.

31 Aug. O sings Violetta in *La Traviata*.

Sept. G opens his Institute for the Harmonious Development of Man, after arrival of Jeanne de Salzmann's women dancers and men from Ouspensky's lecture groups.

Autumn, winter and spring of 1921 Institute works intensively on Sacred Dances, G's ballet *The Struggle of the Magicians* and public lectures of his ideas. Public demonstration of G's Sacred Dances successfully repeated several times.

1921 *24 July* T meets Ali Rifat Bey, director of Mevlevi music, and hears him and his musicians play at concert of Turkish music.

July–Aug. Life in Constantinople deteriorating. Visas obtained for travel to Berlin.

13 Aug. T and O with G leave for Berlin by train, via Sofia, Belgrade, Budapest, arriving in Berlin about 23 August.

Autumn, winter and spring of 1922 Intensive work established on special Movements class, and pupils capable of teaching Movements.

1922 *8–30 Mar.* O accompanies G on trip to London, via Ostend, Dover; returning to Berlin via Calais, Paris, Jeumont.

14 July G and entourage arrive in Paris on train from Berlin.

July–Sept. Work continued temporarily at Dalcroze School, Rue de Vaugirard, in Paris.

1 Oct. G and pupils move into Château du Prieuré at Fontainebleau-Avon. O becomes secretary and general assistant to G.

Oct.–Dec. Study House building erected, ready for partial winter use. First version of Turkish bath also built.

1923 Interior construction and décor of Study House completed. Turkish bath rebuilt in its final form.

May G already planning public demonstrations of Movements in Paris in December. T for first time allowed to keep notes of music developed in collaboration with G. First entry: 30 May.

Summer T begins orchestrating music of Movements selected for forthcoming demonstrations.

13–25 Dec. Eight demonstrations performed at the Théâtre des Champs-Elysées in Paris.

1924 *5 Jan.* T and O with G and twenty-two pupils sail from Le Havre and travel to America. They give demonstrations in New York, Philadelphia, Boston and Chicago till early April.

13 Apr. T and O return to Prieuré with pupils. G remains in New York, works on writings.

early June G returns to Prieuré.

8 July G suffers near-fatal automobile accident.

26 Aug. G announces closure of the Institute. G continues his own work at the Prieuré, with a few pupils invited to stay.

5 *Nov.* O's parents and sister arrive from Russia, invited by G. Soon after, G's mother along with his brother, Dmitri, and family arrive to live at the Prieuré.

16 *Dec.* G dictates first pages of *Beelzebub* to O and continues during next several years.

1925   *June* Death of G's mother.

29 *July* G begins intensive period of composition, in collaboration with T, of the music now known as 'the Gurdjieff/de Hartmann music'.

1926   G's writing and music composition continue. He also begins frequent short trips with pupils to many destinations in France and nearby countries.

26 *June* Death of G's wife.

1927   1 *May* Last of the Gurdjieff/de Hartmann music completed.

Nov. G finishes first draft of *Beelzebub*, begins writing *Meetings with Remarkable Men*.

1928   T now generally working for G by day and for himself by night, composing music for films to earn money for himself and for the Prieuré.

1929   *mid-Jan.–mid-Apr.* G's second trip to New York, accompanied only by T and O. Purpose this time to promote *Beelzebub* and *Remarkable Men* by readings, and to acquaint people with the new music, played by T.

G advises T it is time he and O should live on their own. They take a house in Courbevoie, where O's parents can live with them.

June T leaves G, never to see him again, but insists O should continue to help G.

Oct. O accompanies G to Germany.

1930   *Feb.* O also decides to leave G. T and O remain deeply committed to G's work, and keep in touch with Jeanne de Salzmann.

1933   Prieuré sold, G moves to Paris.

1938 8 *June* O's father dies. T & O move to Garches and live there throughout World War II.

1939 3 *Apr.* O's mother dies.

1947 2 *Oct.* Death of P. D. Ouspensky. Madame Ouspensky urges his pupils to 'return to source': to G.

1949 29 *Oct.* Death of G. I. Gurdjieff. T and O close ranks with Jeanne de Salzmann, who takes primary responsibility for the continuation of G's Work.

1951 T and O move to New York to support groups there and work together with Madame Ouspensky and pupils at her farm in Mendham, New Jersey.

1950–56 T prints five volumes of a private edition of the Gurdjieff/de Hartmann music, produces six records of selections of the music, and works on writing his account of their experiences with G.

1956 26 *March* Death of Thomas de Hartmann. O now devotes her life to the G Work and to her husband's musical legacy.

1964 O publishes the first edition of *Our Life with Mr Gurdjieff* (Cooper Square).

1970 O publishes three more volumes of the Gurdjieff/de Hartmann music.

1979 12 *Sept.* Death of Olga de Hartmann.

Index

Russky, General Nikolai, 85

Sacharoff, Alexander, xxiii
Sacred Dances and Gymnastics
  ('Movements')
  in Essentuki, 19, 51–2, 131
  in Tiflis, 122–3, 131, 133, 139,
    141, 144
  in Constantinople, 155–7
  in Berlin, 163, 166
  in Paris, 168
  at the Prieuré, 170, 172, 184, 193,
    198–9, 203, 230–31
  exercises, 19–20, 51, 62, 122–3,
    131, 144, 155, 170, 205;
    'Obligatories', 51, 139, 170;
    'stop', 20, 51, 123, 207, 211
  see also demonstrations
St Petersburg, xviii, xxi–xxiv, xxvii–
    xxix, 4, 6–7, 9, 12–13, 15–16,
    34–5, 37, 40, 43–4, 47–8, 65, 74,
    98, 116, 124, 214
Salzmann, see de Salzmann
Sarpazan Horen, 136
Savitsky, Leonid ('Lonya'), 128, 152
Savitsky, Yelena ('Lenochka'), 19,
    21–2, 78, 128, 152
Scarlet Flower, The, xxii
Serbia, 4, 159, 161
Shandarovsky, P. V., 53, 62, 77–9,
    85–6, 91
Sirotinin, Dr, 225–6
Sochi, 4, 18, 22, 27, 30–32, 36, 89,
    109, 111, 113, 115–18, 214
Sofia, 161
Soghomon Soghomonian, see
    Komitas Vardapet
Sophia Ivanovna, see under
    Gurdjieff
Soutine, Chaim, 207
Stjernvall, Dr Leonid Robertovich,
    7–8, 11, 14, 19, 22, 34, 39–42,
    47, 59–60, 82, 86, 90–91, 102,
    113, 115, 117, 119, 138, 142,
    145, 156, 162–3, 177, 191, 208,
    215, 222, 224, 226, 235–6, 238
Stjernvall, Elizaveta Grigorevna, 19,

  22, 39, 82, 113, 117, 119, 236
Stjernvall, Nikolai Leonidovich, 236
Strauss, Richard, 215
Struggle of the Magicians, The, 123,
    141, 145–7, 153, 168, 178, 206,
    259
Study House, 170, 184–8, 194–5,
    199, 203–7, 230–31, 245, 249–50
Styka, Adam, 228

Tagore, Rabindranath, 148
Taneiev, Sergei Ivanovich, xxii,
    xxviii–xxix
Tanzlegendchen, 215
Tatars, 116
Tbilisi, 116; see also Tiflis
Tcherepnin, Alexandre
    Nikolayevich, 120
Tcherepnin, Nikolai Nikolayevich,
    119–20, 132, 206
Tertium Organum, 165
Thaïs, 115
Tiflis, 4, 18, 40, 103, 113, 116–21,
    125–6, 130, 134–6, 138, 142,
    148, 154, 158, 188
Tosca, 115
Traviata, La, xxix, 115, 153–4
Trebizond, 4, 18, 128
tricks, half-tricks and real
    phenomena, 159, 202–3, 213,
    215–17
Tsarskoye Selo, xxx, 4, 6, 9–10
Tuapse, 4, 18, 21–2, 30, 35–7, 47
Turadzhev, 27, 118
Turkey and Turks, 43, 134, 151,
    154, 157–8
Turkish bath, 110, 188–91

Uch Dere, 18, 27, 29, 47, 54
Ukraine, xxi, xxviii, 13, 49
'Universal Workshop', 219

van Gogh, Vincent, xxiii
Verevkina, Marianna, xxiii
Verlaine, Paul, xxiv
Vichy, 242
Violetta, xxix

ARKANA – NEW-AGE BOOKS FOR MIND, BODY AND SPIRIT

A selection of titles

With over 200 titles currently in print, Arkana is the leading name in quality new-age books for mind, body and spirit. Arkana encompasses the spirituality of both East and West, ancient and new, in fiction and non-fiction. A vast range of interests is covered, including Psychology and Transformation, Health, Science and Mysticism, Women's Spirituality and Astrology.

If you would like a catalogue of Arkana books, please write to:

Arkana Marketing Department
Penguin Books Ltd
27 Wright's Lane
London W8 5TZ

ARKANA – NEW-AGE BOOKS FOR MIND, BODY AND SPIRIT

A selection of titles

Weavers of Wisdom: Women Mystics of the Twentieth Century Anne Bancroft

Throughout history women have sought answers to eternal questions about existence and beyond – yet most gurus, philosophers and religious leaders have been men. Through exploring the teachings of fifteen women mystics – each with her own approach to what she calls 'the truth that goes beyond the ordinary' – Anne Bancroft gives a rare, cohesive and fascinating insight into the diversity of female approaches to mysticism.

Dynamics of the Unconscious: Seminars in Psychological Astrology Volume II Liz Greene and Howard Sasportas

The authors of *The Development of the Personality* team up again to show how the dynamics of depth psychology interact with your birth chart. They shed new light on the psychology and astrology of aggression and depression – the darker elements of the adult personality that we must confront if we are to grow to find the wisdom within.

The Myth of Eternal Return: Cosmos and History Mircea Eliade

'A luminous, profound, and extremely stimulating work . . . Eliade's thesis is that ancient man envisaged events not as constituting a linear, progressive history, but simply as so many creative repetitions of primordial archetypes . . . This is an essay which everyone interested in the history of religion and in the mentality of ancient man will have to read. It is difficult to speak too highly of it' – Theodore H. Gaster in *Review of Religion*

The Second Krishnamurti Reader Edited by Mary Lutyens

In this reader bringing together two of Krishnamurti's most popular works, *The Only Revolution* and *The Urgency of Change*, the spiritual teacher who rebelled against religion points to a new order arising when we have ceased to be envious and vicious. Krishnamurti says, simply: 'When you are not, love is.' 'Seeing,' he declares, 'is the greatest of all skills.' In these pages, gently, he helps us to open our hearts and eyes.

ARKANA – NEW-AGE BOOKS FOR MIND, BODY AND SPIRIT

A selection of titles

Head Off Stress: Beyond the Bottom Line D. E. Harding

Learning to head off stress takes no time at all and is impossible to forget – all it requires is that we dare take a fresh look at ourselves. This infallible and revolutionary guide from the author of *On Having No Head* – whose work C. S. Lewis described as 'highest genius' – shows how.

Shadows in the Cave Graham Dunstan Martin

We can all recognize our friends in a crowd, so why can't we describe in words what makes a particular face unique? The answer, says Graham Dunstan Martin, is that our minds are not just computers: drawing constantly on a fund of tacit knowledge, we always *know* more than we can ever *say*. Consciousness, in fact, is at the very heart of the universe, and – like the earth itself – we are all aspects of a single universal mind.

The Magus of Strovolos: The Extraordinary World of a Spiritual Healer Kyriacos C. Markides

This vivid account introduces us to the rich and intricate world of Daskalos, the Magus of Strovolos – a true healer who draws upon a seemingly limitless mixture of esoteric teachings, psychology, reincarnation, demonology, cosmology and mysticism, from both East and West.

'This is a really marvellous book . . . one of the most extraordinary accounts of a "magical" personality since Ouspensky's account of Gurdjieff' – Colin Wilson

Meetings With Remarkable Men G. I. Gurdjieff

All that we know of the early life of Gurdjieff – one of the great spiritual masters of this century – is contained within these colourful and profound tales of adventure. The men who influenced his formative years had no claim to fame in the conventional sense; what made them remarkable was the consuming desire they all shared to understand the deepest mysteries of life.

ARKANA – NEW-AGE BOOKS FOR MIND, BODY AND SPIRIT

A selection of titles

Working on Yourself Alone: Inner Dreambody Work
Arnold Mindell

Western psychotherapy and Eastern meditation are two contrasting ways of learning more about one's self. The first depends heavily on the powers of the therapist. *Process-oriented* meditation, however, can be used by the individual as a means of resolving conflicts and increasing awareness from within. Using meditation, dream work and yoga, this remarkable book offers techniques that you can develop on your own, allowing the growth of an individual method.

The Development of the Personality: Seminars in Psychological Astrology Volume I Liz Greene and Howard Sasportas

Taking as a starting point their groundbreaking work on the cross-fertilization between astrology and psychology, Liz Greene and Howard Sasportas show how depth psychology works with the natal chart to illuminate the experiences and problems all of us encounter throughout the development of our individual identity, from childhood onwards.

Homage to the Sun: The Wisdom of the Magus of Strovolos
Kyriacos C. Markides

Homage to the Sun continues the adventure into the mysterious and extraordinary world of the spiritual teacher and healer Daskalos, the 'Magus of Strovolos'. The logical foundations of Daskalos' world of other dimensions are revealed to us – invisible masters, past-life memories and guardian angels, all explained by the Magus with great lucidity and scientific precision.

The Eagle's Gift Carlos Castaneda

In the sixth book in his astounding journey into sorcery, Castaneda returns to Mexico. Entering once more a world of unknown terrors, hallucinatory visions and dazzling insights, he discovers that he is to replace the Yaqui Indian don Juan as leader of the apprentice sorcerers – and learns of the significance of the Eagle.

ARKANA – NEW-AGE BOOKS FOR MIND, BODY AND SPIRIT

A selection of titles

A History of Magic Richard Cavendish

'Richard Cavendish can claim to have discovered the very spirit of magic' – *The Times Literary Supplement*. Magic has long enjoyed spiritual and cultural affiliations – Christ was regarded by many as a magician, and Mozart dabbled – as well as its share of darkness. Richard Cavendish traces this underground stream running through Western civilization.

One Arrow, One Life: Zen, Archery and Daily Life
Kenneth Kushner

When he first read Eugen Herrigel's classic *Zen in the Art of Archery* at college, Kenneth Kushner dismissed it as 'vague mysticism'; ten years later, he followed in Herrigel's footsteps along the 'Way of the Bow'. *One Arrow, One Life* provides a frank description of his training; while his struggles to overcome pain and develop spiritually, and the *koans* (or riddles) of his masters, illustrate vividly the central concepts of Zen.

City Shadows Arnold Mindell

'The shadow destroys cultures if it is not valued and its meaning not understood.' The city shadows are the repressed and unrealized aspects of us all, lived openly by the 'mentally ill'. In this compassionate book Arnold Mindell, founder of process-oriented psychology, presents the professionals of the crisis-ridden mental health industry with a new and exciting challenge.

In Search of the Miraculous: Fragments of an Unknown Teaching P. D. Ouspensky

Ouspensky's renowned, vivid and characteristically honest account of his work with Gurdjieff from 1915–18.

'Undoubtedly a *tour de force*. To put entirely new and very complex cosmology and psychology into fewer than 400 pages, and to do this with a simplicity and vividness that makes the book accessible to any educated reader, is in itself something of an achievement' – *The Times Literary Supplement*

ARKANA – NEW-AGE BOOKS FOR MIND, BODY AND SPIRIT

A selection of titles

Herbal Medicine for Everyone Michael McIntyre

'The doctor treats but nature heals.' With an increasing consciousness of ecology and a move towards holistic treatment, the value of herbal medicine is now being fully recognized. Discussing the history and principles of herbal medicine and its application to a wide range of diseases and ailments, this illuminating book will prove a source of great wisdom.

The Tarot Alfred Douglas

The puzzle of the original meaning and purpose of the Tarot has never been fully resolved. An expert in occult symbolism, Alfred Douglas explores the traditions, myths and religions associated with the cards, investigates their historical, mystical and psychological importance, and shows how to use them for divination.

Views from the Real World G. I. Gurdjieff

Only through self-observation and self-exploration, Gurdjieff asserted, could man develop his consciousness. To this end he evolved exercises through which awareness could be heightened and enlightenment attained. *Views from the Real World* contains his talks and lectures on this theme as he travelled from city to city with his pupils. What emerges is his immensely human approach to self-improvement.

Shape Shifters: Shaman Women in Contemporary Society
Michele Jamal

Shape Shifters profiles 14 shaman women of today – women who, like the shamans of old, have passed through an initiatory crisis and emerged as spiritual leaders empowered to heal the pain of others.

'The shamanic women articulate what is intuitively felt by many "ordinary" women. I think this book has the potential to truly "change a life"' – Dr Jean Shinoda Bolen, author of *Goddesses in Everywoman*

ARKANA – NEW-AGE BOOKS FOR MIND, BODY AND SPIRIT

A selection of titles

On Having No Head: Zen and the Re-Discovery of the Obvious
D. E. Harding

'Reason and imagination and all mental chatter died down . . . I forgot my name, my humanness, my thingness, all that could be called me or mine. Past and future dropped away . . .'

Thus Douglas Harding describes his first experience of headlessness, or no self. This classic work truly conveys the experience that mystics of all ages have tried to put into words.

Self-Healing: My Life and Vision Meir Schneider

Born blind, pronounced incurable – yet at 17 Meir Schneider discovered self-healing techniques which within four years led him to gain a remarkable degree of vision. In the process he discovered an entirely new self-healing system, and an inspirational faith and enthusiasm that helped others heal themselves. While individual response to self-healing is unique, the healing power is inherent in all of us.

'This remarkable story is tonic for everyone who believes in the creative power of the human will' – Marilyn Ferguson.

The Way of the Craftsman: A Search for the Spiritual Essence of Craft Freemasonry W. Kirk MacNulty

This revolutionary book uncovers the Kabbalistic roots of Freemasonry, showing how Kabbalistic symbolism informs all of its central rituals. W. Kirk MacNulty, a Freemason for twenty-five years, reveals how the symbolic structure of the Craft is designed to lead the individual step by step to psychological self-knowledge, while at the same time recognising mankind's fundamental dependence on God.

Arkana Dictionary of Astrology Fred Gettings

Easily accessible yet sufficiently detailed to serve the needs of the practical astrologer, this fascinating reference book offers reliable definitions and clarifications of over 3000 astrological terms, from the post-medieval era to today's most recent developments.

ARKANA – NEW-AGE BOOKS FOR MIND, BODY AND SPIRIT

A selection of titles

The Ghost in the Machine Arthur Koestler

Koestler's classic work – which can be read alone or as the conclusion of his trilogy on the human mind – is concerned not with human creativity but with human pathology.

'He has seldom been as impressive, as scientifically far-ranging, as lively-minded or as alarming as on the present occasion' – John Raymond in the *Financial Times*

T'ai Chi Ch'uan and Meditation Da Liu

Today T'ai Chi Ch'uan is known primarily as a martial art – but it was originally developed as a complement to meditation. Both disciplines involve alignment of the self with the Tao, the ultimate reality of the universe. Da Liu shows how to combine T'ai Chi Ch'uan and meditation, balancing the physical and spiritual aspects to attain good health and harmony with the universe.

Return of the Goddess Edward C. Whitmont

Amidst social upheaval and the questioning of traditional gender roles, a new myth is arising: the myth of the ancient Goddess who once ruled earth and heaven before the advent of patriarchy and patriachal religion. Here one of the world's leading Jungian analysts argues that our society, long dominated by male concepts of power and aggression, is today experiencing a resurgence of the feminine.

The Strange Life of Ivan Osokin P. D. Ouspensky

If you had the chance to live your life again, what would you do with it? Ouspensky's novel, set in Moscow, on a country estate and in Paris, tells what happens to Ivan Ososkin when he is sent back twelve years to his stormy schooldays, early manhood and early loves. First published in 1947, the *Manchester Guardian* praised it as 'a brilliant fantasy . . . written to illustrate the theme that we do not live life but that life lives us'.